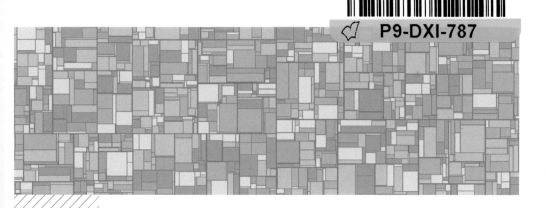

Mindful
WRITING

Fifth Edition

Brian Jackson

Brigham Young
University

hayden-mcneil
Macmillan Learning

P9-DXI-787

Macmillan Learning Curriculum Solutions
14903 Pilot Drive
Plymouth, MI 48170
www.macmillanlearning.com

JacksonB 1488-0 F19

Sustainability

Hayden-McNeil/Macmillan Learning Curriculum Solutions is proud to be a part of the larger sustainability initiative of Macmillan, our parent company. Macmillan has a goal to reduce its carbon emissions by 65% by 2020 from our 2010 baseline. Additionally, paper purchased must adhere to the Macmillan USA Paper Sourcing and Use Policy.

Hayden-McNeil partners with printers that use paper that is consistent with the environmental goals and values of Macmillan USA. This includes using paper certified by the Forest Stewardship Council (FSC), Sustainable Forestry Initiative (SFI), and/or the Programme for the Endorsement of Forest Certification (PEFC). We also offer paper with varying percentages of post-consumer waste as well as a 100% recycled stock. Additionally, Hayden-McNeil Custom Digital provides authors with the opportunity to convert print products to a digital format to use no paper at all. Visit http://sustainability.macmillan.com to learn more.

CONTENTS

PREFACE

Hi there, writing student! My name's Brian. I teach writing. And, heaven help me, I think about teaching writing all the time, even while I'm in the shower.

I've been teaching writing, and thinking about teaching writing, for eighteen years now, and I thought I'd sit down and explain what I know and what *we* know as a community of writing teachers. This book synthesizes some of what I think are the best practices for learning to write with power. I'm hoping you're reading this book because you want to write with *real power*—the kind that influences others.

In *Mindful Writing*, I want to persuade you of five principles:

- Successful writing is mindful writing.

- Successful writers are self-directed writers who plan, practice, revise, and reflect.

- Successful writers know how to think, write, read, and act rhetorically.

- Writing and rhetoric are subjects worth studying in their own right, like you'd study chemistry or psychology.

- What you'll learn in this book will help you take on any future writing task, both in your major courses and your career.

In short, I hope this book helps you grow as a writer.

I'd love to hear what you think about this book—how it's helped you, how it could be better. Drop me a note at mindfulwritingbyu@gmail.com.

Many thanks to Brett McInelly, Rebecca Clarke, Delys Snyder, Dawan Coombs, Grant Boswell, Dave Stock, Jon Balzotti, my 610 class (Brittany Bruner, Andrew Doub, Lauren Fine, Hayley Langton, Jean Little, Ian McArthur, Rachel Moberly, Chloe Moller, Jon Ostenson, Scott Porter, Marie-Reine Pugh, Camille Richey, Amanda Shrum, Heather Thomson), my 611R class that started this ball rolling (Elizabeth Brady, Brighton Capua, Brooke Downs, Christa Baxter Drake, Katie Fredrickson, Spencer Hyde, and Ali Porter), Julie Anne Helmandollar, and Julie Anne's writing class for reviewing parts of this book in progress. Thanks to the University Writing team (Jen, Erica, Kristen, and Alisha) and the BYU English Department for their support. Thanks to Jeff McCarthy, Lin Fantino, Ryan Young, and the Hayden-McNeil team. Thanks, also, to my wife Amy Jackson, who listened patiently to portions of this book as we drove around town. And thanks to Ben, Lydia, Louisa, and Charlotte, my dear kids, who make appearances in the text.

Ready? Let's go.

PART I

Foundations of Mindful Writing

YOU ARE A WRITER

You, my friend, are a writer.

You may not think of yourself that way. You may think of writers as tortured romantic souls who crank out thick novels, or maybe you think of professional bloggers or freelance journalists. In this book I want to convince you that *anyone writing anything for any reason is a writer.* Do you write text messages, emails, lecture notes, letters in the snow or sand, status updates, notes to friends, Post-it notes to yourself, or papers for classes? Then you are a writer. Wherever you are right now, even if people next to you will think you're a bit kooky, I want you to whisper, "*I am a writer.*"

That is the first Great Truth of Writing. Are you ready for the second Great Truth?

It's this: *Writers get better at writing by writing.*

It sounds obvious, but it isn't. Some people think writing is like learning to ride a bike: Once I figure it out, I can do it anywhere, any time, for all time. English professor Kristine Hansen tells us that our education system promotes this false assumption about writing when it lets us "get out of" college writing classes by taking courses in high school—as if writing were "a set of low-level skills" you master when you're young (Hansen 2).

Writing isn't like a polio vaccine—a one-and-done deal. It's *iterative*, meaning that it gets better with practice. When you write, your brain cells (called neurons) fire and wire together in what could be called literacy networks. The more you write, and especially the more you write specific types of texts (called genres), the more those neurons fire and wire together and the more proficient you become at that kind of writing.

Your first-year writing class, then, is outfitting you with a new brain—a writer's brain.

Which reminds me of basketball phenom LeBron James, who is also a writer: he tweets @KingJames.

As I write this (because, you know, I'm a writer too), Lebron James, forward for the Los Angeles Lakers basketball team, is one of the best basketball players to have ever played the game. He's an NBA champion three times over, a four-time MVP (most valuable player), and a perennial All Star. He was also Rookie of the Year. He averages around twenty-seven points per game. At the age of twenty-eight, he was the youngest player to have scored 20,000 points. Oh, and he's also a two-time Olympic gold medalist.

He has mastered the game at such a level that basketball geeks surely would rank him in the top three players of all time. In recognition of his mastery, the Laker franchise pays him thirty-five million dollars a year. I would be Captain Obvious if I said that LeBron James is an expert at basketball.

I'd also be testing your patience if I told you he got that way by *practicing*—which he still does, even at this elite level. We like to think that elite athletes or chess players or dancers or computer programmers are born with The Goods, and, yes, some people get a cheater's bump by genetics. But experts like LeBron build on their genetic foundation with lots of practice.

We know why LeBron is considered an expert: He scores more points per game than most players, and he can also pass, rebound, and guard opponents better than many other players. He takes his team to championships. He also has some qualities that are hard to put into words: He has *style*, he has *court presence*. His nickname is "King James," for goodness' sake. What, then, is the equivalent of "court presence" or "points per game" for a writer? What are the fundamentals that, like dribbling or rebounding or reading the defense, set apart the skilled writer from the novice?

And why should these questions matter to you? You may not think of yourself as a master-writer-in-training, a LeBron James of prose in the making. However, chances are that no matter what career path you choose, you will end up doing a great deal of writing. I know that's not happy news for some of you, but the world we live in runs on communication, and surely it runs better when communication is *good*. For much of your life, regardless of your profession, you'll write emails, proposals, reports, briefs, blog posts, instructions, newsletters, scripts, bids, descriptions, essays, letters, webpages, and maybe even books. Add to all this writing the writing you'll do when you're not at work—like texts or social media updates—and you start to understand how important writing is to all of us in our personal, professional, and public lives.

Writing is not something we do just in school. It is a vital means of influence, in all facets of life. The more you control it—in other words, the more writing skills you can take out of your toolbox—the more influence you'll have when the situation demands your words. At some point, you'll have to write your way into a job by sending a personal statement or cover letter. We connect with each other through writing, improving relationships and forging new ones. Through writing we collaborate, creating new knowledge and new perspectives. Critical conversations take place in writing, and so do essential instructions. When we read the writing of others, we improve our critical capacities as we learn how to analyze and evaluate. Writing changes attitudes and judgments, leading to higher forms of cooperation. Writing provokes, writing delights, writing moves and changes minds. Writing helps us learn and think. We learn what we really think when we write, and so do our readers. Writing is an extension of ourselves, the words and phrases composing avatars of influence. When we master writing, we master our universe.

And now you know that *writers get better at writing by writing.*

But there's a third Great Truth of Writing that adds to the second: *Writers get better when they're **mindful** about getting better.*

In *What the Best College Students Do*, Ken Bain explains that we are mindful when we "think about our own thinking" or when we're "consciously aware" of how we are learning and what we're hoping to get from what we learn (71, 73). Being consciously aware is tricky; we spend a significant amount of our lives on autopilot because mindfulness takes effort. One time when I was a graduate student at the University of Arizona, I was sitting through a long meeting about student services. As the meeting wore on, I started chatting, quietly I thought, with my good friend David. Halfway through the meeting, a man sitting in front of us turned around and said, through clenched teeth, "You have been talking the *entire meeting.*" That's all he said. Until that point, I'd been completely unaware of the consequences of my behavior. I was not mindful. I felt so stupid about my rudeness that I apologized to the guy after the meeting.

The Third Great Truth tells us that great writers get better by thinking about what they're doing—specifically, by mentally monitoring and controlling what they're doing. Great writers get better by:

1. **Planning**: by evaluating their writing skills, by making goals about what they need to write and how they'll get the writing done, by analyzing the task and situation.

2. **Practicing**: by learning effective principles and testing them out in writing through drafting, and by learning to give and take constructive feedback (also called *deliberate* practice).

3. **Revising**: by learning how to fail on first drafts, by analyzing feedback and making adjustments, by setting new goals, and by figuring out strategies for making writing better.

4. **Reflecting**: by assessing what they wrote, by explaining the decisions they made as they wrote, by thinking carefully about what they learned and what's left to learn, by constructing a writer's identity, and by anticipating when they'll use this kind of writing in the future.

We will come back to these four points in later chapters. For now, I want you to understand that these principles are based on significant research in neuroscience, learning theory, cognitive theory, and writing studies. This four-part model is based on the work of Susan Ambrose and her research team at Carnegie Mellon (Ambrose).

So writing improvement is mindful. If you're looking for a fancier way to say that, we can call it *metacognition*, or thinking about thinking. Metacognition is central to learning about thinking in order to monitor and control our powers to act. (National Research Council 12).

You improve as a writer when you plan, practice, revise, and reflect—mindfully.

Back to LeBron. The Lakers franchise is willing to pay LeBron James the big bucks because he has mastered several skill domains necessary for any MVP. He had to learn to dribble, rebound, pass, guard, shoot the long ball, go up against defenders under the basket, dish the ball to teammates when he's double-teamed, and make free throws. Even after being recognized as the NBA's MVP, he flew down to Houston to meet with Hakeem Olajuwan, a retired NBA hall-of-famer, to learn how to play more aggressive offense closer to the rim, a skill he considered a self-weakness. Now that's deliberate, mindful practice.

Like basketball, writing requires basic mechanical skills (like spelling or typing) that you need to master before you can improve. It also requires mastery of several major knowledge domains (see Figure 1). A "knowledge domain" is an area of expertise or know-how. The five domains in Figure 1 are based on years of research by writing specialists (i.e., writers who also happen to study writing for a living—bless their souls). I have adapted this list from Anne Beaufort's book *College Writing and Beyond* and John Bean's *Engaging Ideas*.

Notice how each of these domains grows out of the three Great Truths of Writing, represented in the center of the figure by the phrase, "Learning to Write and Get Better at It (mindfulness)."

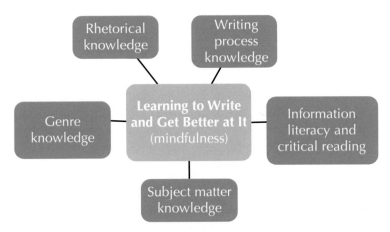

Figure 1. Domains of writing expertise, adapted from Anne Beaufort, *College Writing and Beyond* (2007).

Your instructor will help you understand what these domains mean and how you can improve your abilities in each of them. Here's a primer and a preview:

Rhetorical knowledge—When we write, we write for specific purposes at specific times in specific ways for specific audiences or readers. Writing, then, is *situated*, and effective writers have good judgment about what kind of writing is appropriate for each situation. Rhetoric is the study and practice of how people achieve various purposes through communication. When you write to get someone to feel, think, or do something, you're using rhetoric. Rhetorical thinking is vital to effective communication.

Writing process knowledge—Writing is not just a product but a *process* that involves various methods of planning, thinking, organizing, drafting, getting feedback, revising, replanning, and ultimately delivering it to audiences. Each writer has her own unique process; some processes work better than others.

Genre knowledge—Recurring situations in life require semi-formalized writing responses called genres. A genre is a particular kind of writing for a particular situation. Genres take their shape because readers expect certain moves in writing for certain situations (obituaries, for example, when someone passes away). Genres are rhetorical acts, not just textual conventions.

Information literacy and critical reading—Writing is closely associated with careful reading. Effective writers know how to find, analyze, evaluate, and use the ideas of other writers in their own writing. They read with purpose and mindfulness.

Subject matter knowledge—We're better writers when we write about things we know. Cognitive research tells us that the more "domain-specific expertise" we have (about, say, microbiology or Chinese history), the easier it is for our brains to produce writing (Kellogg 15). Good writers know what they're writing about.

Learning to write and get better at it (mindfulness)—Anyone who writes is a writer. Writers improve the more they write. Writers improve when they're mindful about improving.

I've written this book to help you improve your writing abilities in all of these domains. Subject matter knowledge is tricky in a writing class; you're going to have to major in something to get specific subject matter knowledge, though your instructor may assign a topic for your college writing class to write about. Research and reading, even if you cram it into a few short weeks, will make you a better writer on a given topic. Furthermore, I want to convince you to treat *writing and rhetoric* themselves as topics worthy of study, since they are, in fact, disciplines, with their own scholarly tradition going back 2500 years to ancient Greece. What you learn about writing and rhetoric will help you take on future writing tasks with confidence and skill.

Here's a breakdown of where and when we'll talk about the domains:

Writing Skills Domain	Chapter in This Book
Rhetorical knowledge	Chapters 2–11
Writing process knowledge	Chapters 4–7
Genre knowledge	Chapters 2 & 4
Information literacy and critical reading	Chapter 3
Learning to write (metacognition)	All chapters

Though this class will not make you a master writer in the few short weeks of a semester, it will start you on that path by giving you more hours of deliberate practice. By the end of the semester, you'll be a more effective writer than you are now. It will also give you the tools to *think of yourself* as a writer—one who is learning, deliberately and mindfully, how to be better.

You might find the Adventure of Writing Expertise intimidating. I understand the concern. But relax: You're just setting out. Learning to be a good writer is a lifelong process that will challenge you in every new rhetorical situation. I'm still learning how to write, after thirty-five years of doing it and eighteen years of teaching it. The reality is that the kinds of writing you do in first-year writing may not be the kind of writing you learn to do in your major. And when you start a career, you'll need to learn how to write all over again for various audiences in various genres for various situations in the workplace. But the concepts you'll learn in this course will stay with you. You'll master writing much quicker in each new situation if you remember the principles we talk about in this book.

A final word on learning to write. Writing—and I ain't tellin' you anything new here—is *hard*. It's a challenging task. Not only do you need mastery of basic mechanical skills like typing or spelling, you also need to hold in your mind simultaneously your purpose, your audience, and the text you are writing (Kellogg). Experts tell us that you need to clock around 10,000 hours of deliberate practice in something before you master it. Mastery takes years. In other words, don't plan on mastering powerful, persuasive writing in the few years you'll be in college, let alone the few weeks you have in a writing class. As I said, I've been writing and studying writing for a long time, and I still struggle to get my writing where I want it to be. Writing this book was agonizing good fun.

That said, I want to be your cheerleader here as you start your writing class. Though improving your writing will be hard work, it will be rewarding; it might even be fun. And the good news is that *anyone can improve as a writer*. In fact, let's call that the fourth Great Truth of Writing. Anyone, with focused practice and hard work, can improve as a writer. Good writing skills are not innate, like height. When some people tell me "I'm just not good at writing," it's as if they're saying, "I'm just not six feet tall, and I'll never be six feet tall." On the other side of that coin, I've also heard students say, "This class has nothing to teach me about writing because I'm already a good writer—my high school teacher told me so." Carol Dweck, psychologist at Columbia University, calls this kind of thinking the *fixed mindset*: When you believe that "your qualities are carved in stone," you're not as likely to improve (6). The antidote to the fixed mindset is the *growth mindset*: When you believe that "your basic qualities [like writing ability] are things you can cultivate through your efforts" (7).

No matter how good a writer you think you are, it's useful to think of yourself as a novice, with room to power up. Through a massive study of writing at Harvard University, Nancy Sommers discovered that "students who initially accept their status as novices and allow their passions to guide them make the greatest gains in writing development" (Sommers and Saltz 145). We learn from education research that many students think they're better at learning than they really are; and therefore, "we *underestimate* the amount of time and practice it takes to master a new skill" (Hattie and Yates 119). You can—and will—improve as a writer, regardless of your current ability, if you think of yourself as a novice, set some clear writing goals, seek feedback from your instructor and peers, and commit to the hard, rewarding work of writing. Every day.

I've heard it said before that writing is never really perfect, only due. As writers, we work toward perfection without ever actually reaching it. In some ways, writing mastery is like an *asymptote* in algebra. That's the line that a curve approaches but never touches. Daniel Pink, writer of the book *Drive*, explains that mastery is "a source of allure....The joy is in the pursuit more than the realization" (Pink 125).

I hope you will feel some of that joy as you improve your rhetorical powers through writing.

Works Cited

Ambrose, Susan A. *How Learning Works: Seven Research-Based Principles for Smart Teaching*. San Francisco: Jossey-Bass, 2010. Print.

Bain, Ken. *What the Best College Students Do*. Cambridge: Harvard UP, 2012. Print.

Beaufort, Anne. *College Writing and Beyond*. Logan: Utah State UP, 2007. Print.

Bean, John. *Engaging Ideas*. 2nd ed. San Francisco: Jossey-Bass, 2011. Print.

Dweck, Carol. *Mindset*. NY: Ballantine, 2006. Print.

Hansen, Kristine. "The Composition Marketplace: Shopping for Credit versus Learning to Write." *College Credit for Writing in High School*. Ed. Kristine Hansen and Christine R. Farris. Urbana, IL: NCTE, 2010. 1–39. Print.

Hattie, John and Gregory Yates. *Visible Learning and the Science of How We Learn*. London: Routledge, 2014. Print.

Kellogg, Ronald T. "Training Writing Skills: A Cognitive Developmental Perspective." *Journal of Writing Research* 1.1 (2008): 1–26. Print.

National Research Council. *How People Learn*. Exp. Ed. Washington, D.C.: National Academic P, 2000. Print.

Pink, Daniel. *Drive*. NY: Riverhead, 2009. Print.

Sommers, Nancy and Laura Saltz. "The Novice as Expert: Writing the Freshman Year." *College Composition and Communication* 56.1 (2004): 124–149. Print.

02

THINKING RHETORICALLY

This chapter is about rhetorical theory, which is another way of saying rhetorical *thinking*. By the end of this chapter, I want you to understand what it means to be a rhetorical thinker. Rhetorical thinkers know how to handle life.

Rhetorical thinking, you'll remember (or not—but here I am, reminding you), is one of our five domains of writing expertise. Learning to think rhetorically is one of the most important things you'll learn in college, so lean over the page, my friend, and let's do this.

Don't be intimidated by the word *theory*—or, for that matter, *rhetoric*. You're already crazy about theory. A theory is just a set of assumptions, ideas, or values that help us understand something or do something. When I tell my four-year-old daughter Charlotte to hum "Twinkle, Twinkle Little Star" two times while brushing her teeth, I'm expressing a theory about how much time a child should spend brushing her teeth. You probably have theories about text message etiquette, optimal study habits, why political discourse is so toxic, why we pay attention to celebrities like the Kardashians, why new Xbox games are incompatible with the old Xbox, what a third date means, or what life itself means. You're a theory machine.

Since humans are restless pattern-seekers, we use theories to help us deal with the constant stream of life. Think of a theory as a set of goggles you look through—goggles with tinted lenses that paint the world in a certain light. Theories help us explain, appreciate, analyze, classify, predict, interpret, and evaluate. But most importantly, theories help us *practice* life. Rhetorical theory can help you explain, appreciate, analyze, classify, predict, interpret, and evaluate writing experiences. In helping you understand this theory, I hope I give you equipment for better living.

It's important to note, too, that theories are kind of like propositions or arguments. Some are better (i.e., more supported by experience or evidence) than others. When we say *evolution* is a theory, we're not saying it is not true; we're saying that the theory of evolution is a set of assumptions, ideas, or values that help us understand natural selection and the origin of species. It's a well-established, convincing theory built from thousands of observations, experiments, and conclusions. I'm not saying that theory is the opposite of truth or fact. I'm saying that theory is an invitation to engage with a well-reasoned worldview.

Rhetorical theory is important because it can help you understand and respond well to *any* situation that requires you to communicate. In chapter 4 I'll explain how we can improve our writing by strengthening the central executive—that part of your working brain responsible for demanding tasks like writing. Rhetoric helps us do that by helping us think through the situations in which we write. Rhetorical thinking helps us approach communication with understanding, with purpose, with mindfulness.

So we need to do two things in this chapter: We need to define rhetoric and then set up a theory of rhetoric that will help you write more effectively whenever you need to write.

Rhetoric

Several years ago, a good friend of mine who was studying to be a chaplain in the Army received a letter from the United States military calling him to service in Iraq, where there was still a sizeable U.S. military presence. The timing was unfortunate: He was almost finished with his degree, and deployment would disrupt his progress to graduation and create a burden on his wife and two children. So my friend decided to write a letter asking that his tour of duty be deferred until he could finish his degree.

Imagine you're in his shoes for a moment. What are you going to write? (I'll tell you what happened to him in chapter 8.)

My guess is you've had such moments in your life—moments when your ability to write or speak might change everything for you. (Ever had to write a cover letter for a job or an essay for college admissions—or a declaration of love, or an email to angry family members?) *Rhetoric* is the study of such moments. It's also the study of the thousands of far less grand moments, like the time a few days ago when I drew a smiley-face on a text to my sister so she'd know I was joking.

Skilled writers understand that rhetoric is **the study and art of effective communication**, especially the kind of communication meant to influence others. Notice I said *both* the study *and* the art: Rhetoric refers to the study (i.e., the theories, research, or experiences) of effective communication, and its art (i.e., the way people actually use it through purposeful strategies). Communication can be writing, of course, but it can also be other symbolic behavior like body language, artistic composition, even architecture or gardening, if we think of gardening as the means someone uses to create attitude-influencing experiences for someone else. Rhetoric is the study and art of any effort by someone to use symbols (like language) to connect with another human being to influence their experience in some way.

The word *rhetoric* comes to us from the Greek word *rhetor*, for "speaker." A *rhetor* was someone who spoke to other assembled citizens in ancient Greece about problems they all shared. Some ancient philosophers—let's call them *rhetoricians*, people who study rhetoric—studied how people spoke and to what effect so the art could be taught as a general theory of communication. They wanted to make money of course—who doesn't?—but they also wanted to give potential speakers real power to promote shared values, to entertain and delight, to change the course of history with words. Aristotle (384–322 B.C.E.), one of the most important philosophers of all time, shares his thinking on this subject in a book titled *On Rhetoric*, in which he gives us a definition: "Let rhetoric be defined as an ability, in each particular case, to see the available means of persuasion" (Kennedy 37).

Aristotle used the word *persuasion*. What does that word mean to you? I've found it useful to think of rhetoric as the study of how attitudes are influenced by words—that's persuasion to me. Our attitudes are *judgments* about things. Judgments are products of experience: what we see, hear, and feel. Each day we're making and keeping judgments, and those judgments become attitudes. We use persuasion when we want to influence the attitudes of others.

Remember the guy I mentioned in the first chapter who sat in front of me during that meeting when I was rude? I'm sure he left the meeting feeling like I was an annoying jerk. He had a bad attitude about me, formed by his judgment of my behavior. But that's not the end of the story. When I saw him in the hall a week later, I went straight up to him and said, "I'm sorry I was so annoying during that meeting. I just wasn't thinking." He seemed surprised, and then *he* apologized to *me* for turning on me so sternly. Apparently we'd both been concerned about the attitude the other guy had for us, and we both apologized in order to improve that attitude and make a wrong situation right. Maybe subconsciously I thought that tweaking his attitude about me would help me achieve my goal for living harmoniously with others and not getting punched in the face. That's the goal of rhetoric: influencing attitudes through communication to achieve our goals.

This turns out to be tricky. Our attitudes, especially for things about which we care deeply, are hard to change. In *The Righteous Mind*, psychologist Jonathan Haidt explains that our moral judgments (about abortion, for example) are often formed by subconscious emotional responses we make rapidly and without much thought (40). Once these judgments form, they can become immune to change, even when good reasons to change are presented. If we have a strong intuition about something— say, that the federal government should redistribute wealth—anything that tells us differently creates what social psychologist Leon Festinger called "cognitive dissonance." Cognitive dissonance makes us uncomfortable because it makes us feel inconsistent inside; we don't want to be wrong or look stupid. That's just human nature. So we avoid considering evidence that runs contrary to our attitudes. (A college education, by the way, is supposed to help us get over the cognitive dissonance problem and actually embrace full-on frontal assaults to our attitudes through reason, rhetorical analysis, and reflection. Thanks, college!)

What powerful rhetoric can do is trigger a re-evaluation process in an audience; it can trigger "new intuitions" that help us see things "in a new light or from a new perspective" (Haidt 47). Rhetoric is most effective, writes Haidt, when laced with empathy—when a speaker can make an emotional connection with an audience through goodwill and love (Haidt 68—more on empathy in chapter nine). Of course there are many issues about which we do not care so deeply. When we moved into a house in Provo, Utah, a guy came around selling water softener. He told me that a water softener system would help keep our pipes from calcifying and would reduce soap scum in showers and washed dishes. And I said, OK: give me some of that soft water magic. That's how easy it was to sell me on a water softener. I didn't have a strong opinion (or any opinion) about it. *And* I thought his reasons were good reasons.

People who understand how rhetoric works (the theory) and can use it effectively (the art) are powerful people. They influence the attitudes of other people and change the course of history. By signing up for this writing course, you've accepted the challenge to become one of those people. This chapter is about how rhetoric works (the theory), and subsequent chapters will help you improve the way you use it (the art).

The Rhetorical Situation

Let's say Grandma dies. It's not too sad. She was old, she lived a good long life, and she died peacefully in her sleep. The funeral is coming up, and Aunt Sally asks you to speak at the funeral. *Of course they'd ask me*, you think. *I was Grandma's favorite.* And then you think, *What am I going to say on this important occasion?* You've entered a **rhetorical situation**. Rhetoric occurs in contexts in which various forces work together to create meaning for all those involved. Rhetorical situations are moments that invite us to communicate with others in a way that's appropriate or fitting for the moment.

(One time my dad was at a funeral in a church house. The casket was at the front, decorated with flowers. Suddenly everyone hears the rumbling of a motorcycle out in the parking lot. This gnarly biker guy comes into the church, walks down the aisle up to the casket, slams his fist down on the flower-decked lid, and shouts, "I'll see you in hell, buddy!" Maybe it wasn't fitting, but it was memorable.)

As the funeral approaches and you're jotting down a few ideas, you ask yourself some fundamental questions, questions that anyone hoping to influence others should ask when they find themselves in rhetorical situations. Questions like

- What *kind* of speech am I supposed to give? Like, am I supposed to just read her obituary, or offer a few memories from my experience playing poker with Grandma, or convey some kind of deep theological message about life and death?

- Or how about this question: Who's going to be at the funeral service? What do *they* want to hear, or expect to hear from my speech?

- What's my purpose in speaking? Do I want to entertain and comfort, or make everybody cry?

Effective communicators understand why these questions are so important for rhetorical situations. They know that these questions imply that in each situation there are *affordances*—things you can do, powers you can wield, freedoms you enjoy as communicator—and there are *constraints*—limitations, demands, expectations, no-no's. In this lesson, we'll go deeply into these questions and others you'll want to ask yourself when you take on a new writing task. You'll learn to remember these questions with a new acronym: GRAPE. It stands for genre, rhetor, audience, purpose, and exigence. Maybe it'll help you remember if you pretend that Grandma's favorite drink was GRAPE juice. Let's raise a glass for Grandma and learn the five essential parts of a rhetorical situation. (Dang, that's goofy. Sorry.)

Genre

Aunt Sally asked you to "speak" at Granny's funeral. What does that mean? Are you being asked to tell stories or read scripture? In some religions, there are set prayers and speeches one gives at a funeral; in other settings, the family gets drunk and tells embarrassing stories. The *form* in which you "speak" at a funeral is in large part conditioned by history and culture, by what is expected by the audience based on their experience with other speaky-things at funerals. That form is called **genre**.

The word *genre* refers to "recurring types of writing identifiable by distinctive features of structure, style, document design, approach to subject matter, or other markers" (Bean 46). Genres are not merely rigid forms of writing. They represent a social need. Professor Carolyn Miller defines genre as "typified rhetorical actions based in recurrent situations." Let's unpack this definition from back to front.

Recurrent situations: Culture is established through patterns of behavior and experience. Certain events, marked by urgent needs, keep happening, and those events invite communication of a certain kind.

Genres emerge from rhetorical situations that happen over and over in life. Someone has money; someone else wants it; the someone with money asks for a proposal arguing for the best way to spend that money. Someone dies; her loved ones gather to speak of her life and accomplishments. A dramatic political event occurs; someone writes to the newspaper arguing a perspective on that event—a perspective the writer hopes will help other citizens make better judgments. Someone finds a cute way to decorate a cake; that someone shares a how-to video on YouTube.

Rhetorical actions: Recurring events call for responses in writing and speaking and symbol-making. We take "rhetorical action" when we sit down at the keyboard and write. Through our writing, we're making certain moves that we hope will be fitting for what the situation demands (see "exigence," below). For example, people use funeral eulogies to praise the dead and encourage the living to emulate their good deeds. That kind of move does some good work in the world, work that the recurring situation invited. Genres are rhetorical actions meant to influence the world.

Typified: We organize the world in patterns, or types. Genres harden into recognizable forms because those forms serve our purposes. Emails have subject lines. Mystery novels have corpses. Websites include "About Us" links. Proposals have budgets and timelines. Wikipedia entries begin with a summative paragraph on the topic. Academic essays blend outside sources with the writer's own voice. Text messages are very brief, and good spelling isn't necessary. Some genres have fairly rigid formats (scientific journal articles); others breathe with creative life (personal essays). Genres represent fairly typical responses to everyday situations, and some genres are more rigid than others. The way you organize an essay, the style you use, the document and citation design, the kind of evidence you use to support a claim, or if you even make a claim at all—all are governed by the expectations of the genre.

There are a number of different writing genres, probably too many to name: memoirs, encyclopedia entries, lab reports, obituaries, posters, podcast scripts, blog posts, white papers, proposals, emails, complaint letters, etc. Each genre reflects the collective needs of society to do specific work in the world. Remember that genres are not strictly forms; they are rhetorical responses to real-world needs.

Rhetor

The second element in the rhetorical situation is the ***rhetor*** (pronounced like it rhymes with *better*)—the speaker or writer or creator of the message. In the case of our funeral example, the rhetor is *you*. You're the one with the power to decide what to say and how to say it. Your *ethos* (see chapter eight) will be on display. The words will come from your brain and through your body, not another's.

The rhetorical theorist Lloyd Bitzer thought the rhetor was significantly constrained by "the power of the situation" (11). For Bitzer, rhetors have to act within the bounds imposed by an exigence (it's coming!). Bitzer's critic Richard Vatz, on the contrary, believed that the situation's demands did not constrain the creativity of the rhetor and that meaning and urgency are in fact interpreted in large measure by the rhetor herself. When you are a rhetor, you analyze the situation and craft the message, but you're just one part of the rhetorical situation, as you may discover when you stand up to speak. Being a rhetor gives you rhetorical power, but it's power only to the degree to which the message is *kairotic* (i.e., a fitting, timely response to the situation) and the audience is open to the message.

The rhetor is the voice of the message—the perspective, the identity, the voice, the stance, the bias. In chapter nine, we'll talk more about how as rhetor you can wield convincing power by constructing a Self that your readers will recognize, and accept. There's this great moment early in the Broadway play *Hamilton* when Alexander Hamilton makes his grand debut in the late eighteenth-century intellectual scene by answering the question, "Who are you?" with, "I'm just like my country, I'm young, scrappy, and hungry, and I'm not throwing away my shot." He wastes no time establishing himself as a formidable voice, a rhetor worthy of attention.

Audience

The third element of the rhetorical situation—and perhaps the most important—is **audience**: that group of people who, according to Bitzer, "are capable of being influenced by discourse and of being mediators of change" (8). I say audience is the most important element because the audience holds what the rhetor wants to influence, the thing in which the entire rhetorical process culminates: the attitude, the judgment. One of the cardinal principles of rhetorical theory is *Know Thy Audience*. If you understand what motivates your audience, what makes them tick, what their interests and needs and attitudes are, why they need the genre you're working with, then you'll have rhetorical power as a rhetor. Audiences have power as well.

Speaking at a funeral is tricky. Sometimes people say things at funerals ("He's in a better place") that some people in the audience may not believe or may not find comforting. Tragic funerals (for children, for example, or a teen suicide) can be doubly complicated in this way. At Granny's funeral, you'll want to give your audience something good, something cleansing. Before you stand to speak, you'll want to think about the values, experiences, and needs of the people who will receive your words.

The idea of audience should be straightforward—and it seems so in moments when we speak. Someone speaks at a banquet, and the audience sits at round tables, their soiled cloth napkins crumpled next to empty plates, their heads nodding in agreement (or sleep). You talk to a friend at a party, and you look at her right in the face, and the audience smiles right back atcha. In such cases, the audience is clear. (The word *audience* comes down to us from the Latin word *audire*, to hear.)

When we write, the idea of audience gets a little warped. Let's say, hypothetically, that you're in Mrs. E.'s third-grade class and you write a note intended for (let's make up a name) Stephanie Martinez praising (let's say) her curly brown hair and asking for her eternal affections, and then, hypothetically of course, while the folded-up letter is being passed from student to student to Stephanie, who sits on the other side of the room so that the outside light gives her chestnut skin an ethereal and sumptuous glow, it is intercepted by Mrs. E. who, let's pretend, is old and cranky all the time because of a spastic colon, and she opens your epistle of love while walking back to her desk and she decides—we'll just pick a likely punishment—to make you write your name with a check mark next to it on the board.

Is Mrs. E. now the audience for the love note? Yes. Was she the intended audience? Certainly not. She was, in fact, the last audience the (ahem, purely fictional) writer imagined would read the letter. What does this complication do to our theory of audience?

There are two problems with the concept of audience. First, it's hard to anticipate the way people will respond to anything we say because they're *not us*. Other people have different brains, chemicals, histories. Jim Morrison of the rock band The Doors said it best when he sang, "People are strange." Inventing things to say takes guts and imagination; we assume other people will appreciate what we have to say because we assume they're like us in some fundamental way. Rhetoric invites us to accept as an article of faith that other people are, to some degree, predictable enough that we can use strategies of persuasion with confidence. But still: Rhetoric is a leap of faith we make with language; we hope that by some miracle we'll be not only understood but influential.

The second problem with audience is a problem related to the medium of writing. When we speak to someone, our eyes track their faces for responses. We look at their eyes, their lips, and their body. We can tell if they're interested or bored, or if we've offended or disgusted them or if they disagree with us, and we make little conversational adjustments to get back on track (Pinker 27). We are exceptionally good at reading faces; we've been doing it since we were babies.

But when we write, we don't have that kind of feedback loop. When we write, our recipients "are invisible and inscrutable," writes Harvard psychologist Steven Pinker, "and we have to get through to them without knowing much about them or seeing their reactions. At the time that we write, the reader exists only in our imaginations" (28). We have to guess how a reader might respond, and sometimes we might guess wrong. Sometimes we'll never know whether or not we guessed wrong. As we'll discuss in chapter 4, advanced writers can hold in their heads simultaneously their own ideas, the words they want to clothe those ideas in, and their "imagined reader's interpretation" of those ideas (Kellogg 5). That kind of rhetorical thinking takes time. And it takes—make me proud, beat me to it!—mindfulness.

So, when you write, you're challenged to hold in your mind an image of your readers, the kind of readers you hope will read you *and* read you the way you want to be read. Your text will reveal rhetorical decisions based on your assumptions about your audience—what you think about their attitudes, their desires, their judgments, and what you assume about your shared interests with them. The concept of *imagined audience* helps us accept the fact that sometimes we really don't know what an audience wants; in other words, that cardinal virtue we mentioned above (*Know Thy Audience*) is difficult to enact. We're trapped in our own bodies, with our own perspectives and prejudices. Who knows what will influence someone else's attitudes? When you write to apply for a job or for college admission or a scholarship, you're writing to people whose faces are blanks to you. And yet, you go ahead and make your best guess anyway.

Imagining audience, even audiences that we invoke or invent in our minds (see Lunsford and Ede; Ong), is a creative act, a "mark of cognitive maturity," as Irene Clark put it (Clark 111). Novice writers write "writer-based prose" (Flower)—that is, prose that represents the interests and needs of the writers themselves—because they can't represent in their minds or their texts the interests of the audience, or they choose not to (Kellogg). Writing is often boring because the writer isn't thinking about audience. The writer is like the one guy at the party, drink in hand, prattling on and on about all the insider fanboy trivia related to the new *Star Wars* movie, and he doesn't even notice that we've all slipped into a coma. Imagining audience—and writing *reader*-based prose—is not only an act of cognitive maturity; it's an act of goodwill. (And we'll talk more about goodwill in chapter nine.)

However, it's worth noting here that online and social media writing has changed the way we think of audience. Now more than ever in history, we get some sense of how audiences respond to our writing by comment threads, retweets, likes, stars, linkbacks (sometimes called pingbacks or trackbacks), text backs, and other connective love. But even then, we're still writing in the shadows. How representative of your full audience is a "like" or two? Have you ever sent a text message and then wondered if the recipient's kid, significant other, or mom is the one reading it?

Purpose

Fourth, the rhetor has a ***purpose***—what he or she intends to achieve by speaking or writing. You thought about purpose when you asked yourself what you wanted your audience to feel when you spoke at Granny's funeral. You can understand purpose by asking: How does the rhetor want to influence attitudes? What does he/she want the audience to feel, think, or do? What does he/she want to achieve? Why is he/she speaking/ writing/composing? I've noticed that students often mix up purpose and message. The main message of a text might be X, but purpose is what the rhetor wants the audience to feel, think, believe, or do about X. One way to discover a rhetor's purpose is to look carefully at the message and make assumptions about why the rhetor chose the strategies he/she did. Since we can't always ask writers what they intended to do, we have to reconstruct their purpose for them through rhetorical analysis.

Exigence

Usually rhetoric doesn't just happen. It's *called forth* by what Lloyd Bitzer calls ***exigence***, the final element in a rhetorical situation—though, confusingly, it happens first. (Notice that this term is *exigence*, with an "e" at the end, not *exigency* with a "y." Both mean essentially the same thing, but exigence is a rhetorical term, so let's geek out and go with it.) Bitzer defines an exigence as "an imperfection marked by urgency," which "strongly invites utterance" (Bitzer 5–6). Simply put, the exigence is the invitation to speak or write because speaking or writing might solve a problem. When Granny died and funeral arrangements were made, the family planned a service that included fitting messages for the living. Granny's death demanded it.

Exigences can be more or less demanding: If you receive a text from a friend accusing you of something you didn't do, you've received an exigence that demands a quick response. If a teacher asks the whole class, "What do you think about what we read for homework?", that's more of an invitational exigence, one that perhaps you can ignore and let some other poor soul respond to. There are millions of heated online comment threads we can, and should, ignore; sometimes, though, we see an exigence tailored for us and we write a comment.

The exigence is the invitation to speak, the wrinkle in the universe that calls for someone to say something, to make something with clever words, to patch up the problem with prose. In the Hero's Journey, the exigence calls the hero away from home and into danger. The exigence is the call to rhetoric.

Connected to the idea of exigence is **kairos**, another aspect of exigence that I think you should know about. *Chronos*, as you probably know, is a Greek word meaning "time" (think of the word chronology). *Kairos* is different: it's a Greek word meaning "the opportune or fitting moment" for action. *Kairos* is less about minutes and hours and days and so on; it's about opportunity, timing, and desire—it's more about "psychological time" (Hauser 40). You're in the woods alone with your Special Someone. The moon floats full and luminescent above you, the snow crunches beneath your feet, and your conversation is intimate and free. Do you reach out for his hand—for the first time? Any moron can see that the moment is kairotic. But maybe he's shy. Maybe he has a funky skin disease and would be mortified. What about a kiss? If it's a first date? At what point in the conversation do you lean in? What in your history together leads you to this moment? Timing is everything! The student of rhetoric understands how the right words at the right time can influence the right people.

Rhetorical situations have life cycles that we create with our words, our arguments, our actions. When Civil Rights activists were pushing for racial equality in the United States in the 1960s, many sympathetic Southern white citizens felt that black leaders like Martin Luther King needed to cool their political activism and wait for racist attitudes to change, which they thought they would—eventually. White citizens felt that the moment wasn't *kairotic* to push for equal rights for African Americans. They feared pushing civil rights through even peaceful protests would lead to civil unrest, even violence, which it did. King and his associates disagreed; in fact, in 1963 King wrote a book called *Why We Can't Wait* explaining why racial equality was an important *kairotic* rhetorical issue that, yes, could not wait—the opportune, fitting, appropriate rhetorical time, for King, was right then. *Kairos*, as you can see, is psychological rather than chronological in the sense that it is *debatable*: It is contested and determined by words rather than solar or atomic increments, or a cell phone.

You can make an issue timely when you write about it; you just have to be sure your rhetorical watch is set to everyone else's, or you have to invite your audience to set their rhetorical watches to yours. You're also responsible to acknowledge what has been said before. Think, for example, about how timing plays a role when you enter a conversation at a party by listening to what other people have said before you.

Rhetoric Goggles

Okay, you just leveled-up your game as a writer. We defined rhetoric as the study and art of effective communication. (You're studying it right now, so you can be more artful at it.) Effective communication, I suggested, is *persuasive*, which means that it influences someone's attitude and therefore behavior. Attitude is a *judgment* about something. Judgments are hard to change, but you're the kind of person to take on Mission Impossible.

Rhetorical thinking begins and ends in rhetorical situations, which have the GRAPE elements: genre, rhetor, audience, purpose, and exigence—all connected, all depending on each other to create meaning, all necessary for your success as a writer (i.e., a rhetor). By the end of this class, you should be able to rattle off these five parts of the rhetorical situation in your sleep. You now have a simple theory of communication that you can apply to any situation that calls on you to speak, write, create, act.

My goal for this chapter was to define rhetoric and introduce you to a theory of rhetoric that will help you communicate more effectively by influencing the attitudes of others. I hope I've given you *rhetoric goggles*: You put 'em on, and everywhere you look, you see purposeful communication from rhetors trying to influence an audience with a well-crafted, and timely, genre meant to achieve some kind of purpose.

I hope rhetorical theory will help you live better. When someone is trying to influence you, I hope you'll put on your Rhetoric Goggles so you can see the rhetorical situation more clearly.

I'd go even further to say that if you take only *one thing* with you from this book, I hope it would be a habit of rhetorical thinking. The next time an exigence creeps up on you and calls you to speak or write or create or compose or collaborate to make a text, I hope it'll be automatic for you to ask

- What kind of a genre am I being asked to create?

- Who am I as a rhetor?

- Who is my audience? What kind of audience are they?

- What is my purpose? What do I want my audience to feel, think, or do?

- What is the exigence, and what would be a fitting response?

Appendix: Blowing Up the Audience Concept

We're going to end this chapter by expanding on the notion of audience by addressing, briefly, nine kinds of audiences you may find in various rhetorical situations. Understanding these audiences will help you write to them, if the situation arises.

- **Discourse communities**—Various social groups have different ways to make knowledge and get stuff done. Discourse communities are composed of people with common interests, goals, vocabulary, and processes of inquiry (i.e., how they make knowledge through research, experiment, analysis, argument, etc.). When your college professors write articles, they're writing to specific discourse communities (like the American Psychological Association, or the Society for French Historical Studies). When you advance in your major, you'll be asked to write as a member of a discourse community oriented to a discipline (like exercise science). Fan clubs are discourse communities. Reddit is a discourse community. The labor movement, Baptists, the Society for the Prevention of Cruelty to Animals, poker fans and players, neuroscientists—all discourse communities. Effective rhetors will know when they need to write in the language and style of a particular discourse community.

- **Publics**—As I wrote this chapter, a twenty-nine-year-old woman named Brittany Maynard, who suffered from malignant brain tumors, ended her life by drinking a lethal mixture of water and sedatives. A doctor in Oregon had prescribed the medication legally as part of a death-with-dignity treatment for the terminally ill. Before Brittany died, media outlets lit up with arguments about whether or not ending your life should be a right of all those who suffer terminal illnesses. Brittany's case became an exigence that various citizens responded to with their own arguments, directed to each other in blog posts, op eds, TV interviews, and dinner table conversations. A *public* is this collection of citizens (sometimes called stakeholders) that emerge through rhetorical exchange about a particular problem or issue. Since publics are rhetorical (rather than merely political or geographical), they form, function, and disappear as important issues are discussed and then discarded.

- **Users**—This term comes to us from computer science and refers to people who will interact with the text you have made, especially when a genre has an interactive component (like a website), some kind of navigable dimension (like a table of contents), or instructions to perform some kind of action (like the manual for your car).

- **Incidental or secondary audiences**—Back to the Mrs. E. incident I totally invented earlier. Remember, she was not the intended audience; she intercepted ~~my~~ the love note intended for Stephanie Martinez, the primary audience. Sometimes people overhear things not intended for them. Boyfriends get dragged to so-called chick flicks. Atheists stumble into evangelical tent revivals. Children play violent video games rated M by the Entertainment Software Rating Board. One time a girlfriend of mine wrote me a mushy email and sent it to—her ex-boyfriend. (True story!)

We're going to call such audiences *incidental* or *secondary* audiences. Even though incidental audiences are not part of the original rhetorical situation, once they experience the text they form a *new* rhetorical situation, with a new exigence and *kairos*. If as a student you read Martin Luther King's "I Have a Dream" speech, you become a new audience, inviting King to influence your attitude from the grave. The concept of incidental audience is especially important for us as readers because it invites us to stand in judgment of the enduring rhetorical value of a text. Perhaps King's call for racial justice can be *kairotic* over and over each time racial strife draws us into debates about race.

- **Decision-makers**—Straightforwardly: those who have power to act to do something the *rhetor* wants done. Think proposals (for grants, or for marriage).

- **Universal audience**—Immediate audiences often share the prejudices of the rhetor, and, in turn, the rhetor will often play directly to their prejudices by making arguments that no one outside a particular in-group would accept. You see this happen on talk radio and political programs and websites. However, a rhetorician named Chaim Perelman argued that sometimes people craft their rhetoric for a *universal audience*, meaning an imagined audience made up of "competent and reasonable" people who care whether or not an argument is valid for any thinking person, not just a biased in-group (14). The idea of such an audience is useful for saying something like, "Well, such-and-such message would persuade other members of the National Rifle Association or the American Civil Liberties Union, but it wouldn't convince a universal audience of smart, unbiased people." The idea of the universal audience is a wish, really, for audiences of intelligent people who can listen carefully, weigh evidence, cast aside biases, and accept conclusions they might otherwise resist. Research papers are often written to a universal audience.

- **Evaluators**—are like teachers or peer tutors. Evaluators, though secondary audiences, help *rhetors* achieve their purposes. They help *rhetors* imagine how immediate or imagined audiences may respond to their genres. Your writing instructor, for example, will assign you a grade based on your rhetorical performance. I hope this is a relief to you, because some writing students tell me that they feel like grading is an arbitrary whim of the instructor, based on whatever the instructor "likes" or their glucose levels. But an evaluator-audience is supposed to dramatize what reading your work would be like for your intended audience. My sense is that they can do that more effectively if you tell them, in a reflection, who you're writing to and what you're trying to do.

- **Friends/followers/fans**—New media and social media make it possible for us to create networks of people who are guaranteed to have only one thing in common: You. When you post a status update on facebook, you're writing for an audience of (sometimes) hundreds of people with a variety of interests. It's hard to read this audience, for some people. (Ever unfriend someone because they post annoying or offensive things that do nothing for you as an audience?) And yet social media networks can lead to rhetorically rewarding exchanges motivated by interests that have nothing to do with school projects. And this is an audience that can flip the rhetorical situation by becoming rhetors and making *you* the audience.

- **Skeptics**—To sharpen your critical thinking as a *rhetor*, it's useful to think of your audience as people who may disagree with you or who aren't easily convinced by what you have to say. Their attitudes bend slightly away from you; you have to bend them back. How will you do that? Imagine your audience with a wry smile, their eyebrows pointing down in skepticism, an expression that seems to say, "I doubt it, but convince me!" Or: Maybe you imagine your audience being completely unmoved, but you're willing to at least chip away at their bias by presenting the best possible case for the opposition.

All this talk about audience is meant to get you thinking about your own rhetorical situations, both in school and out of school. You already know this, but it's challenging to think about rhetorical situation when you write for teachers. When you get an assignment to write something, you feel you've been placed in an artificial situation in which your purpose is to get an A on the paper, and the genre is a "research paper," and your audience—everyone knows—is the teacher who will grade the paper. It turns out that most writing assignments in secondary school and college are informative (as in, present some data about this or that) and written to "teacher-as-examiner" (Melzer 28). But even with these limitations, you can use your rhetorical knowledge and hold in your mind a vision of your audience, beyond your instructor, that works for your purposes. Every time you write, write to *engage* someone else in ideas and arguments that matter, even if your understanding of that "someone else" is a little fuzzy. Remember that audience is a rhetorical invention: We cast a spell with our words, and they appear.

Works Cited

Bean, John C. *Engaging Ideas*. 2nd ed. San Francisco: Jossey-Bass, 2011. Print.

Bitzer, Lloyd F. "The Rhetorical Situation." *Philosophy and Rhetoric* 1 (1968): 1–14. Print.

Clark, Irene L. *Concepts in Composition*. NY: Routledge, 2012. Print.

Ede, Lisa and Andrea Lunsford. "Audience Addressed / Audience Invoked: The Role of Audience in Composition Theory and Pedagogy." *CCC* 35.2 (1984): 155–171. Print.

Flower, Linda. "Writer-Based Prose: A Cognitive Basis for Problems in Writing." *College English* 41.1 (1979): 19–37. Print.

Haidt, Jonathan. *The Righteous Mind*. NY: Pantheon, 2012. Print.

Hauser, Gerard. *Introduction to Rhetorical Theory*. 2nd ed. Prospect Heights, IL: Waveland, 2002. Print.

Melzer, Dan. *Assignments Across the Curriculum*. Logan: Utah State UP, 2014. Print.

Ong, Walter. "The Audience is Always a Fiction." *PMLA* 90.1 (1975): 9–21. Print.

Perelman, Chaim. *The Realm of Rhetoric*. Notre Dame UP, 1982. Print.

Pinker, Steven. *The Sense of Style*. NY: Viking, 2014. Print.

Vatz, Richard. "The Myth of the Rhetorical Situation." *Philosophy and Rhetoric* 6.3 (1973): 154–161. Print.

READING MINDFULLY

HALT! Before you fling your eyeballs on this chapter, I want you to:

1. decide whether or not you're ready to give this chapter your undivided attention (are you sitting somewhere comfortable? is your cell phone off? do you have enough time—say, an hour—to commit to it? are you ready to focus?); if so, then

2. look up from the book right now and predict what this chapter is about (i.e., what it will cover, what it won't, what it will argue, etc.);

3. ask yourself, "What do I know about reading, or what have I been taught about reading strategies before?";

4. preview the chapter by flipping through it quickly, looking for key terms or concepts (in headings, or in **bold**), reading the conclusion (spoilers!); and, finally,

5. decide what you hope to get out of this chapter (like, "I hope to learn X" or "I hope that by reading this chapter I learn to do Y because Z").

Okay. Fair warning: While you read this chapter, I'm going to interrupt you from time to time and ask you to do stuff. (But since **HALT!** makes me sound more like a police officer or border guard than a teacher, I'll just say **PAUSE**.) What I'll ask you to do will help you become a more effective and efficient reader, and there's research to prove it.

It's occurred to you by this point that *Mindful Writing* is a textbook and not, as you'd hoped, a treasure map or fanfiction for your favorite anime. I'll make it up to you by sharing something that will make your college life easier—strategies for reading. I'll share three:

Reading mindfully

Reading rhetorically

Reading to research

Reading mindfully is the central idea here. When we read mindfully, we read (just like we write) attuned to how we are reading, why, and how we could read better. You'll want to read mindfully throughout college, but there are two important moments when you'll use mindful reading to accomplish specific rhetorical tasks: reading rhetorically and reading to research.

Reading Mindfully

Consider the following reading situations:

1. One time while on an outing to Jackson Hole, Wyoming, with a youth group, the back-right tire of my truck exploded while we drove on an old dirt road. I'd only had the used truck for a few months, so I wasn't familiar with the mechanics of how to get the spare tire off the underchassis. I tried a few things, and failed. So I opened the glove box and found the owner's manual and flipped to the index where I found several topics under "Tire." I flipped to the "Tire" section, read the instructions, and fixed the tire.

2. In fifth grade, I went to my local library and checked out horror writer Stephen King's book *Christine*, the tale of a demonic Plymouth Fury that terrorizes a small town. It was my first "adult" book—before that, it was all *Encyclopedia Brown* and *Choose Your Own Adventure* and *Dragonlance*. *Christine* was scary, and mature; it terrified and excited me. I read it all the way through in just a few days and could barely sleep afterward.

3. A few weeks ago, while in Denver International Airport, I powered up my smartphone and opened my news app and flipped through a few headlines. Then I thumbed through my Twitter feed.

4. Many years ago, as a young student on a study abroad program in Jerusalem, I received a kind, hand-written letter from a fellow student that I kinda liked. I read the letter carefully and then hand-wrote her back a letter, complimenting her on several traits I admired in her. To my surprise, she wrote me back, and this time I had to read *very carefully* because it seemed to me she was telling me she loved me, without saying it directly. I then had to decide the best way to respond: *Should I dial this back a little, or pick up my pen and go Romeo on the situation?* (We're married now.)

5. Several years ago I was writing an article about neuroscience and rhetoric. I know very little about neuroscience, which should have made me think twice about writing the article in the first place. In

our university library, I found a book titled *Affective Neuroscience* by American psychologist Jaak Panksepp. I might as well have been reading the book upside down for all I got from it, but I did note how Panksepp defined emotions in the context of brain chemistry. I quoted his definition in my paper, comparing it to definitions from other experts like Joseph LeDoux and Edmund Rolls and a few scholars whose articles I'd found on Academic Search Premiere online. I then added my own definition.

Now **PAUSE**. Before going further, answer these questions: What do you think I'm going to say about these anecdotes? Do you agree with what you think I'm going to say? What anecdotes could you tell me about your own reading experiences?

This process is called "priming" or "generating" by psychologists who study how we learn. By asking you to puzzle out a problem before hearing the solution, I'm hoping the principle will be "better learned and more durably remembered," in the words of one research team (Brown, Roediger, McDaniel 86).

Reading Is Not Reading Is Not Reading

We think of reading as a simple decoding process, but reading is a complicated cultural act that changes depending on the situation we're in. Think about my five reading anecdotes. When I got a flat tire, I didn't read the entire manual; that would have been a waste of time. When I got the letter from my friend and future wife, I didn't just scan it like you would an online news article; I savored the sentences. If we read the same way for every situation, we're doing it wrong.

Remember what we said in chapter one about metacognition—that out-of-body awareness of how we're thinking and learning and writing? The same mindfulness should be applied to reading. If we approach reading mindfully, we'll get more out of it. We'll read with purpose. When I buy a used book and find that nearly every sentence in the first chapter—and first chapter only—has been highlighted, I think, "The past owner did not read this text mindfully." Reading is not reading is not reading. One exigence requires one reading approach, another another.

Yes, I just used the word *exigence*. That key term should trigger thoughts about **the rhetorical situation**, which we discussed in the last chapter. Like writing, reading takes place in rhetorical situations in which genre, rhetor, audience, purpose, and exigence can be identified. Only now, as reader, you're not only interested in the writer/rhetor's exigence, kairos, purpose, genre, and audiences. You're also interested in your own purpose and experience as audience.

Writing is a social act. Texts appear because someone wants to influence someone else in some way. Reading, too, is a social act; as audience you complete a circuit and connect with another person. When you read, you should read *rhetorically*, meaning that you should read with a mindful awareness of

- who writers are (rhetors),

- why they wrote *when* they did (exigence and kairos),

- what they hope readers will feel or think or do (their purpose),

- what rhetorical strategies they use when they write (genre + ACES),

- and how they have constructed an experience for a specific kind of reader (audience).

Now, I have to admit something I hope some of you are thinking at this point. When the tire on the truck popped and I pulled out the ol' driver's manual, I didn't take the time to ask myself, "Who are the writers of this lovely instruction manual and what do they hope I feel when I read this?" I didn't give two hoots who wrote the manual. I couldn't have cared less when the writers wrote it or their emotional appeals, and I sure didn't care about whether the writers varied their sentences or used rhetorical schemes. However, I was quite grateful to see that the manual was laid out in the genre of manuals, with a thorough index and a "troubleshooting" section for hapless people like me who know little about the cars they drive. In that moment, out there in the sagebrush of Wyoming, I had one purpose for reading: Find out how to fix a flat tire before we're all eaten by bears. That manual, crammed in the glove box with insurance papers and Jiffy Lube receipts, was written for such moments.

Mindful reading means knowing when to turn on the full force of your analytical skills and when to just sit back and enjoy a text for the joy of texts. In this chapter, I hope to help you calibrate your reading mind.

Literacy, Literacies, and Reading in College

Often we have too narrow a view of reading as this decoding process; literacy, for some people, is the act of decoding words, an "individual cognitive tool" (Street 437) you either have (i.e., you are literate) or you don't (illiterate). Literacy is far more than that. British linguist Brian Street talks about literacy as a plural, as *literacies*—all the "social practices" and "cultural concerns and interests" that go into reading and writing (430). A literacy is a social practice that reflects culture. Such literacies begin in families, in the way relatives (like parents and siblings and other kin) value and use language at home. Other institutions (neighborhoods, schools, governments, economies) impose various reading and writing values or practices that we learn to use (or resist) as we grow up. Linguist James Paul Gee reminds us that we learn to think, write, and read as members of communities who think, write, and read in certain ways, with certain values and purposes.

Think for a moment about your earliest memories of reading and the environment of reading you grew up in.

PAUSE. Go ahead—think about it! Think about specific books or images, situations in which you read or learned to read, people who taught you to read, people who encouraged you to read, people who discouraged it, your early attitudes and practices and struggles.

Perhaps you had family members read picture books to you. When we were little kids, my brother Kevin would stay up way past our bedtimes, huddled under the covers with a flashlight, reading books that he'd then cram in the space between his bed and the wall. Perhaps you saw older brothers and sisters reading comic books, or fantasy novels on an e-reading device. Perhaps you never saw a parent read for pleasure, or maybe Dad didn't read anything but *The Economist* magazine. Perhaps you have a learning disability that made reading a struggle when you were a child. Perhaps you read every Harry Potter book multiple times. Perhaps most reading for you feels like staring at the sun: forcing yourself to concentrate when you want nothing more than to stop.

You learned to read—and all the cultural values, benefits, and challenges that come from reading—from people that Deborah Brandt calls "sponsors of literacy," which are "agents, local or distant, concrete or abstract, who enable, support, teach, model, as well as recruit, regulate, suppress, or withhold literacy" (25). Parents are sponsors of literacy; so are schools, libraries, houses of worship and religious leaders, SparkNotes (don't deny it!), video games, app designers, prize-granting institutions (like Pulitzer or Newberry), various technologies (including print books), or companies like General Mills (I read a lot of cereal boxes growing up). Standardized tests function as sponsors of literacy, a fact lamented by educator Kelly Gallagher who accuses schools of "readicide," or "the systematic killing of the love of reading" (2). Our reading attitudes and practices come from the "patterns of sponsorship" we're exposed to in our literate lives (Brandt 26).

For the last couple of decades, the most important enabler of new reading practices has been the screen, our ever-present text-delivery device(s). With high-speed connections, we can download entire books to our devices in five seconds. We can open up our phones and scroll through social media updates and news feeds while waiting in line for a movie (especially if we want to ignore the humans standing next to us). Digital texts are cheaper to distribute than print texts, and they're cheaper to buy—and more portable, storable, searchable, sendable, and interactive-able. When we read online, we read sideways, jumping from place to place, forming associations and foraging for what's important to us; and when we read on our phones, we *scroll*. There's no doubt that digital sponsors of literacy have ignited a new reading culture.

Colleges are sponsors of literacy on a grand scale; on a smaller scale, so are your textbooks and teachers and assignments and student newspaper and registration website and class management software and syllabuses and even those spots on campus where people post stuff they want to sell or parties they want you to come to. Some of the most important reading you'll do in college is the unassigned reading you do for your own pleasure or enlargement. Of course you'll have plenty of assigned reading to do, too, as your new sponsors of literacy (a.k.a. your professors) invite you into texts they hope will help you achieve class objectives.

College reading can be a struggle for students. In his book *Engaging Ideas*, writing scholar John Bean lists all the ways reading can be a real challenge for college students:

- our testing culture rewards surface reading rather than deep reading

- students balk at the time commitment to read texts carefully

- professors often lecture over readings in class, making reading unnecessary

- students don't adjust their reading strategies for different situations

- new genres might be unfamiliar, and therefore confusing

- disciplinary terms, concepts, or rhetorical strategies are new and daunting

- students can't see themselves as audiences for difficult texts—audiences with the right to talk back/with professional authors. (Bean 162–6)

It may sound odd at first to say that college students need to learn how to read, but it's true. Like writing, reading is an iterative skill strengthened by mindful, deliberate practice. It may be a challenge for you to learn new study strategies, but you can do it! We're here to help.

PAUSE. Look up from the book and summarize, in your own words, what you've learned so far in this last section on literacy, literacies, and reading in college. Use specific key terms from the chapter.

OR, If you're feeling really ambitious, try this: Get out a piece of paper and draw three columns. (You could use a table in a Word doc, too.) Label the first column "my summary," the second column "my uses," and a third column "my questions." In the first column, write a brief summary of this last section, with key terms and ideas. In the second column, explain in writing how you might use this material in this class or other classes you're taking, or in your personal life. In the last column, write down 2–3 questions you have about what you've read.

Strategies for Reading Mindfully

Real learning and growth come from mindfulness. Rhetorical thinking and acting require mindfulness. If we think about how we're approaching our learning, we act with greater purpose and skill. Our powers of rhetorical influence grow. Below I describe several strategies for reading as a mindful, self-directed learner.

Plan

When you get a reading assignment, and after you've taken a brief look at the text, ask yourself the following questions:

1. Why am I reading this? What does my instructor want me to get from it? What do *I* want to get from it?

2. What is the specific assignment here? Am I being asked to *remember the content* of this text, or will I be asked to *respond to this text* in class discussion or in writing? (Your purpose will influence the reading strategy you take—and this one, between content and conversation, is essential to understand.)

3. Who wrote the text? Why? What are the credentials of the author? What kind of audience is intended?

4. What genre is this text? What is the purpose of the genre? What discourse community is served by it? Why do people write texts like these?

5. What do I already know about this topic and its key terms and moves? How is this text like texts I've read before? What background knowledge from my previous learning or experience do I bring to this text?

6. How will I monitor myself as I read? How have I limited distractions? How will I monitor myself to make sure I understand what I'm reading and why I'm reading it? Who will I talk to in order to understand the text better?

Preread

More often than not, you don't want to pick up a text and start reading cold, right from the top of the first page. You'll want to do some prereading; Kelly Gallagher calls it "first-draft reading" (*Deep Reading* 51). You want to know a little bit about who the writer is and what she's up to. You'll want to know the writer's background and rhetorical perspective (cultural context, history, potential biases); websites have sponsors and creators—who are they? You may want to do a little background research on the topic of the text (Wikipedia, baby!). Flip through the text itself, studying its genre and layout. Take a tour of the table of contents—or, if you're reading online, the navigation system of links and tabs and headings—and make some predictions about what you'll get from it. Before diving in, read the intro and conclusion (unless you don't want to spoil the reading experience; you wouldn't want to preread a novel with a surprise ending). Check out the chapter or section headings, and look at the way the pages are designed or data displayed. As mentioned above, ask yourself, "What does this writer want me to feel, think, or do? What kind of judgment am I being asked to make?"

Brake for the Unknown

If you stumble onto a term or concept you don't understand, slam on the brakes. Crack open a dictionary (apps work fine) or search for the term online. If the word, term, or concept is particularly important, you may want to circle it or draw a box around it, if possible, or maybe write the definition in the margin, like I did here in my copy of Reza Aslan's book *No god but God*, a history of Islam, when I stumbled onto the word *henotheism* (notice I boxed the abbreviation "def" in the margin):

> This remarkable proclamation, with its obvious resemblance to the Muslim profession of faith—"There is no god but God"—may reveal the earliest traces in pre-Islamic Arabia of what the German philologist Max Müller termed *henotheism:* the belief in a single High God, without necessarily rejecting the existence of other, subordinate gods. The earliest evidence of henotheism in Arabia can be traced back to a tribe called the Amir, who lived near modern-day Yemen in the second century B.C.E., and who worshipped a High God they called *dhu-Samawi*, "The Lord of the Heavens." While the details of the Amirs' religion have been lost to history, most scholars are convinced that by the sixth century C.E., henotheism had become the standard belief of the vast majority of sedentary Arabs, who not only accepted Allah as their High God, but insisted that he was the same god as Yahweh, the god of the Jews.

allah = yahweh

I'm convinced that one of the biggest buzzkills for reading is a lack of background knowledge about a topic. If we don't know much about mortgage-backed securities or the oxidation process of metals, then reading about that stuff is going to drives us crazy. But if we learn more about the topic we're reading about, we will enjoy the text more and remember it longer.

Make Marginal Notes

Taking notes in/on texts is popular. You can take notes right on the text—digital texts have all kinds of cool options for note-taking—or in a separate notebook if you plan to sell your texts. The tactile experience of writing while we read reinforces what we're reading, and it gives us an archive of our reading experience that we can review later.

John Bean says that some teachers forbid underlining or highlighting. It does seem too easy to underline or highlight a text to death, turning a once pristine page into what looks like a glowing nuclear accident. Bean suggests that when we feel the urge to highlight, we should instead write in the margin *why* we feel like highlighting that part. "Use the margins," he writes, "to summarize the text, ask questions, give assent, protest vehemently" (Bean 177). I really like this advice. Highlighting is useless if later we can't remember why we highlighted. So I try to use the margins of my texts to write questions, draw smiley faces when I find jokes and frowny faces when something depresses me, write exclamation marks when I'm shocked and awed, jot down or define key terms, or "star" key points and main arguments that summarize the text.

Skip

Yes, I'm giving you permission to skip stuff from time to time. You *have* to—and, hey, you *want* to. One of the most liberating moments of my life came when Professor Boswell, a rhetoric scholar in a graduate program, told my class that if we weren't understanding the texts we were reading, we were reading too *slowly*. The advice seemed contradictory, but it worked for me. I was so caught up in the minutiae of the scholarly articles I was reading that I couldn't see the Big Picture. Often, a text's Big Picture can be discovered in thirty seconds. Think about articles in academic journals. A scientist might open up a 15-page scholarly article on particle physics and read the abstract and conclusion and skip the rest. When I'm working on a project, I'll go to the library and stack up a dozen books and search for the main argument in the introduction and then discard it. If you feel like a text you're reading is tedious, it might be that you've figured out what the writer is trying to say and now you're just forcing yourself to read stuff you already know. (But beware of illusions of knowledge! More on that in a moment.)

I find I can skip more readily if I'm reading mindfully enough to know what each section or paragraph is doing ("Okay, here's the author's set-up, and here is the main point—got it!, and here the author is responding to critics—I don't care about that, so I'll skip ahead to here, where the author explains the whole research project, and now I'm bogged down in research methodology, so I'm skipping to the evidence, but now there are too many examples so skipping ahead..."). Sometimes topic sentences tip me off that I don't need to read further. I'm all for deep and slow reading when the situation requires it, but there are reading moments when you'll save time and comprehend more if you skip mindfully. Varying your reading speed is another example of "varied practice," which is more "cognitively challenging" and therefore more likely to lead to retention (Brown, Roediger III, McDaniel 51).

Draw Pictures

Sometimes we retain what we read more deeply and carefully if we can make a visual representation of the text we're reading (Duke and Pearson 219). Consider drawing a text map or flow chart or timeline to capture what you've read. Use conceptual principles like contrast, development, or hierarchy in the visuals you draw. The rise of infographics has opened up incredible rhetorical possibilities for visualization. Such drawings are often called *concept maps*.

Summarize

Learning to summarize is essential. It's a survival skill; you can't read everything, and you can't remember everything about the texts you read. A summary captures the main point/argument/conclusion/message/theme of a text in as few words as possible. It's an art of synthesis, focus, and also neglect. When you summarize, you use language like, "The author argues that _____" or "This author presents evidence that _____ is the case" or "This author agrees with OR denies that OR synthesizes the research on OR supports the common opinion that OR takes issue with OR asks the question _____."

Summary is tough to do, in part because earlier sponsors of literacy train students to read in preparation for quizzes, not for holistic comprehension. One Harvard study from the 1960s found that out of 1500 first-year students, only *fifteen* (that's 1% of the class) could summarize the main point of a thirty-page history chapter, even though they all scored well on a multiple-choice test (Harvard Report). Psychologist William Perry concluded that when students are assigned to read, they often slip into "obedient purposelessness" by reading without knowing why they're reading or what, in a macro-sense, they're reading. Another problem: Students often search texts for what Rebecca Moore Howard calls "killer quotes" instead of conclusions or overarching themes because they need to quote stuff in research papers. She and her colleagues discovered that only 6% of citations in student research papers reflected summary; everything else was some form of quoting (Jamieson, Howard, and Serviss).

Summary breaks this habit. When you summarize, you search a text for the main point. When I ask students to write annotated bibliographies, I'll often ask them to write the main conclusion of a text, the methodology used to come to that conclusion (experiment? survey? interviews? observations? analysis? the Pensieve at Hogwarts?), and the implications (so what?). I also ask students to tell me what they want to use the text for (i.e., if they're working on writing with sources).

When I'm reading a book I own, I'll often try to "nutshell" the argument of a particular chapter on its first page, like I do here in Jane Mayer's book *The Dark Side*:

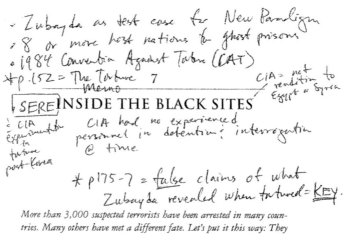

> More than 3,000 suspected terrorists have been arrested in many countries. Many others have met a different fate. Let's put it this way: They are no longer a problem to the United States and our friends and allies.
>
> —President George W. Bush,
> State of the Union Address, January 28, 2003

You'll notice I put a star next to "p175–7 = false claims..." because I wanted to remind myself of *New Yorker* journalist Jane Mayer's startling claim that many post-9/11 tortured terrorist suspects did not reveal anything of value to U.S. national security personnel. I thought that point was the major "take home" of the chapter.

A particularly powerful method of summary is to look up from a text when completed, put away your notes, and talk through the main point of the text you're reading. This hard cognitive work is called *retrieval* or *self-quizzing*, and psychological research tells us it's far more effective than rereading the text (Brown, Roediger III, McDaniel).

Self-Monitor

We know from research that good readers are "*active* readers" who "constantly *evaluate*" their reading process and goals and "read *selectively*, continually making decisions about their reading—what to read carefully, what to read quickly, what not to read, what to reread" (Duke and Pearson 205). I don't know if this happens to you, but I often find myself rereading a paragraph because I've completely spaced out or, yes, dozed off. If you catch yourself dozing or spacing, stop reading. Stand up, take a walk, get a drink. Remind yourself why you're reading in the first place. Quiz yourself. Ask what the reading is preparing you to do (test? class discussion? living life more fully?).

Write Your Reading

We talked about taking notes in the text. It's also immensely helpful to take notes *about* the text—to write what you read, to put it in your own words (especially if you can do it "with your eyes closed," i.e., by not looking back at the text). I like Kelly Gallagher's idea to use "sentence starters" when we write our reading. He suggests we begin a written response with the following phrases:

I don't understand…

I noticed…

I wonder…

I was reminded of…

I'm surprised that…

I'd like to know…

I realized…

If I were…

The central issue(s) is (are)…

One consequence of _____ could be…

If _____, then…

I'm not sure…

Although it seems…. (Gallagher *Deeper Reading* 70)

You might want to try a "graphic organizer" or "T-chart" to organize your ideas as you write. A T-chart is a two- or three-column record of your reading experience (you draw the "T" on paper for the columns). As

Gallagher points out, T-charts encourage deeper reading by inviting you to read once for comprehension (what a text says) and once for analysis (what a text does).

Here are a few T-charts:

what does it say?	what does it mean?	what does it matter?

(from Kelly Gallagher *Deeper Reading*)

my summary	my uses	my questions

what do I expect the writer to say (before reading)?	what did the writer say (after reading)?	what does the writer want me to feel, think, or do?

main idea/point/argument	evidence/reasons/support

what does it say?	how does it say it?	what are the consequences or implications?

rhetorical strategy	example from text	effect on audience

Reading Rhetorically

I hope you can see now how you can read mindfully for any college course, for any text, any time. However, often you are asked to be a certain kind of reader for a specialized writing task. One of those instances may be when you are assigned to read one text very closely and carefully.

Do you ever wonder, as you click on "I Agree" after *not* reading a long Terms and Conditions of Use, what exactly you're agreeing to? Neither do I. I hope we're not in some kind of legal jeopardy.

Sometimes we need to read something closely, either to understand it as fully as possible or to appreciate its rhetorical mastery in a new light. You likely did some close reading in high school on a literary text. One reading method you might be asked to try is *rhetorical analysis*, which is the close reading of a rhetorical text to classify and evaluate the various strategies a rhetor uses to influence an audience's judgment.

Recently my university had the privilege of hearing a speech from Bryan Stevenson, executive director of the Equal Justice Initiative, a nonprofit group working to reverse wrongful convictions, mass incarceration, and racial injustice in the United States. In his book *Just Mercy*, Stevenson shares some stunning statistics about mass incarceration: "from 300,000 people in the early 1970s to 2.3 million people today,"; "one in every fifteen people born in the United States in 2001 is expected to go to jail or prison"; "we've sent a quarter million kids to adult jails and prisons to serve long prison terms, some under the age of twelve," and so on (Stevenson 15). These statistics can be powerful. They provide the facts that support his argument that there has been injustice in our legal system.

But readers of *Just Mercy* cannot fail to notice the other rhetorical strategies Stevenson uses which could be considered even more powerful than those statistics. Stevenson tells lots of stories about individuals caught in the criminal justice system. We know their names; we hear their words and see their tragic lives up close. In humble language, he tells of his own experiences working as an attorney—for free—on behalf of these individuals. He describes crime almost in the language of a legal thriller. He paints in vivid detail the lives of women, children, and the disabled who are victimized, imprisoned, abused. He appeals to Judeo-Christian values, which for some people are synonymous with American values. It's a virtuoso rhetorical performance and one worthy of our attention.

When we do rhetorical analysis, we slow down and look carefully at what makes a text like *Just Mercy* work for its audience and purpose. Then we write up our reading so that we might influence others' opinion on the text in question. In fact, rhetorical analysis is an act of *writing* just as much as it is an act of reading. By doing rhetorical analysis, we hope to educate our own audience on how rhetoric works in this particular case.

Start with the Situation

When we do rhetorical analysis, we start not by diving into the specifics of the text but by zooming out to the context. Each text has its own rhetorical situation. For example, remember that in the last chapter we talked about genre as a sociological phenomenon. Texts take unique shapes because certain societies, cultures, communities, or groups have wanted the text to be like that. Remember that we call semi-formalized rhetorical action *genre.* You start rhetorical analysis by classifying the text as a genre, with a particular kind of rhetor, audience (or community), purpose, and exigence.

Let's say you're writing an analysis of fortune cookie messages. Why not? That's a genre. You gather as many examples of the genre as you can find, and you look at the attributes of the genre we've discussed so far. You'll notice in the following that sometimes I have to separate the *imagined* rhetor/audience and the *actual* rhetor/audience. This is a good critical practice, since communication requires us to co-construct our understanding of reality. When we write, we create the ideal audience that we invite our real readers to become.

> *rhetor:* The rhetor of a fortune is anonymous. None of the examples I looked at had an author's name attached to it. However, the rhetor implied in a fortune is supposed to be a wise person. Many of the fortunes are not just fortunes—i.e., predictions about future good or ill for the audience—but aphorisms or pithy, wise sayings, like proverbs. The dispenser of a proverb is a wise person who knows a truth about the world and wants to share it. In the fortunes I reviewed, I saw examples dispensing wisdom on friendship, gambling, memory, love, beauty, action, the happy life, even rhetoric ("Fine words butter no parsnips"). We don't know by what authority the rhetor gives this wisdom. The imagined rhetor is the wise Asian sage, but we have to keep in mind that the *actual* rhetor, the one who put the words on the slip of paper, is likely an employee at a cookie-making company. Genres reveal the character of the writer.

audience: How about the *audience* of a fortune cookie message? The imagined audience is a person willing to take advice from strangers, someone humble enough to learn and cherish wisdom. When you think of fortunes, you often think of predictions fit specifically for the recipient, and some of the fortunes I analyzed fit that category: "A fresh start will put you on your way," "A beautiful, smart, and loving person will be coming into your life," "All will go well with your new project," or "A golden egg of opportunity falls into your lap this month." I like this last example because it gives a specific time (this month) for the fortune to land. The actual audience is mostly people who, after finishing a meal of Chinese food, get a little stale cookie with a piece of paper in it. If people are eating in groups, they'll likely share their fortunes with each other for a three-minute laugh. No one I know takes a fortune seriously nor ponders its advice long after tossing it back on the table with all the dirty dishes. Related to this, in brief, is the *exigence*, which is that we just ate Chinese food and the server has brought us fortune cookies with the check. There's not much more to say about that, other than to speculate that the server brings fortune cookies with the check to "sweeten" the tip.

purpose: What is a fortune writer's *purpose*? What does he/she (and why by default do I think of fortune rhetors as male? Is that sexist?) want me to feel, think, or do when I open up a cookie? He wants me to feel anticipation of good fortune or warm gratification at receiving wise words. Proverbs invite philosophical introspection, or at least that's the genre game we play. Some of the fortunes I looked at prompted more than just casual thinking: "A short pencil is usually better than a long memory," "Better ask twice than lose yourself once," "Fear and desire—two sides of the same coin," "Man is born to live and not prepared to live." Most of the fortunes I read were earnest and in fact wise; they said uncontroversial things that had the ring of truth to them. Am I supposed to just read them and go on my way or incorporate them into my life forever? Many of the fortunes are written as commands rather than koans, so the rhetorical purpose for the audience is action: "Take the high road," "Distance yourself from the vain," "Carve your name on your heart and not marble." (That last one is kind of stupid.) In sum, it seems the purpose of the fortune is three-fold: (1) prepare for good or bad future events, (2) ponder on the meaning of a truth-saying, or (3) take action in your life. All three of these purposes suggest that the rhetor, as life coach, has good intentions.

Once you feel like you understand the rhetorical situation of the text, you can evaluate the text to determine whether or not as a genre it serves the purpose of the genre for its intended audience. If I get a fortune cookie message that says, "Buy more Chinese food," I might feel like my genre expectations had been ruined by a crummy commercial. It is useful to analyze whether the text you're reading abides by its genre conventions, deviates from them in a way that might be acceptable, or deviates in an ineffective way.

Look Carefully at Strategies

After you've analyzed the situation, you can look carefully at the text itself to see what strategies the rhetor uses for his or her purposes. You can start, first, by simply summarizing what the writer is trying to say. What's the message here? That's the *what* of the text, and it will more often than not reveal the writer's purpose (i.e., what he/she wants the audience to feel, think, or do). But rhetorical analysis is never satisfied with the what; rhetorical analysis is about the *how*. What specific persuasive strategies did the writer use to influence our judgment? And how do they work together for the writer's purpose?

There are so many different rhetorical strategies you can look at. In *Just Mercy*, as I explained, activist Bryan Stevenson uses research evidence to support his arguments. He also uses personal narrative, emotionally-effective stories, and other devices. In *Mindful Writing*, we'll use the acronym ACES to describe four popular rhetorical strategies related to argument, character, emotion, and style.

You want to look at strategies that support the overall purpose of the text. Cherry-picking one word here or there is a weak way to do analysis. Find strategies in the text that seem essential to the writer. Once you find that strategy, start thinking about what effect that strategy is supposed to have on the audience *and/or* whether that strategy + effect serves the writer's purpose.

In sum, reading rhetorically (by writing rhetorical analysis) may take on the following steps:

1. Find a text that interests you as a rhetorical artifact.

2. Study the rhetorical situation (GRAPE) of the text, showing specifically how the rhetor uses the genre to achieve specific purposes for audiences, both real and as imagined.

3. Search for rhetorical strategies: argument, character, emotion, and style. Use the vocab you learn in *Mindful Writing* in chapters 8–12. Select 2–3 strategies you believe are important for the text as a whole. Find specific key terms or quotes from the text showing those strategies in action.

4. Describe how the rhetor uses those strategies to achieve the rhetorical purpose.

5. Evaluate whether that strategy is effective, considering the purpose. (This step could be optional.)

As you go through this process, you will discover new rhetorical strategies that you may want to use in your own writing by imitating their moves. Think of the texts you analyze as *mentor* texts to help you understand how rhetoric works.

Reading to Research

The last reading strategy we'll talk about relates to reading to answer questions, like when you're writing with sources for a research project. Like rhetorical reading, this kind of reading is specifically related to a writing task we often call a *research* task.

I have a child (more than one, actually) who was diagnosed with Attention-Deficit/Hyperactivity Disorder while in elementary school. When my wife and I received the news, we knew zilch about ADHD beyond the common understanding you pick up from the news. We had so many questions: What do we do now? What's going on in our kid's brain? How widespread is ADHD? Should we medicate, or not? What effects will the medication have? What kind of life strategies do we need to teach? How does diet or exercise or screen time influence ADHD?

We bought a few books. We read a few articles, a few web pages. We talked to a specialist or two, and a few other parents of children with ADHD. At first our searching was vague; we just wanted to get all the info we could. As we read, we developed more focused questions. We learned key terms. Our reading became more targeted; we read more quickly, looking for what we needed and ignoring the rest. For example, in exploring the relationship between ADHD and diet, we discovered that some sources recommend fish oil supplements, since omega-3 fatty acids can improve cognitive performance. Or at least, that's what WebMD said. However, an article in the *Journal of Pediatric Neurology* shared data from several large-scale studies showing that omega-3 had limited or no substantial effect on school kids with ADHD. Consequently, we threw those big fat fish oil pills in the trash.

I want you to notice a few things about this experience: First, we were curious about something that was meaningful to us personally. Now, I know you can't always write from your own interests. Throughout your lives, you will be assigned to write about stuff you couldn't care less about. That's the nature of being a writer. However, you can find a way to be curious about any number of things—even topics you consider boring at first—if you can find ways to connect those topics to what you already know (or don't know) and who you are.

Second, we didn't start our exploration with answers; we started with *questions*, genuine questions we didn't have the answers to. Lots of questions. Questions in a great big list. We didn't even know which questions were more important to us than others. Third, we gathered information and just read up and down and around in it, looking not so much for answers to all our questions but for some way to *refine* what we needed to know. We could have wasted half our lives on this step, since reading up and down and around in texts can be engrossing, even when it's aimless. As we read, we discovered that there was a *conversation* going on about ADHD involving many participant-rhetors giving information and expressing opinions. By reading their words, we were listening in on their conversation.

Fourth, as we read more, our vision became clearer, our scope more narrow. We found out what to pay attention to and what to ignore. Our aimless, but curious, searching revealed key terms and ideas and specific issues we wanted explore more deeply. We found out that there were some sources that were more credible than others. We learned which voices had authority (like Edward Hallowell) because other sources referred to their work and/or because they had credentials (e.g., PhDs) and had performed research that had been published. We learned that so much of what we find online when we google something, especially if it concerns health, is commercial garbage.

Finally, what we discovered changed the way we lived. We made adjustments to help our child flourish as much as possible considering the challenges ADHD posed. In other words, our inquiry—our focused exploration—had *consequences* in the real world.

As writers, more often than not our writing takes its meaning from other texts that already exist. As a college student, and then as an employee, you will be asked to read and respond to other texts, to fuse your writing with someone else's. When we read in preparation to write with other sources, we must read the way we should always read—mindfully, with our focus on purpose. Below I suggest a few strategies to consider if you are reading to explore, to inquire, to write with sources.

Ask questions: Any true inquiry begins with questions. If you've been assigned a research project, don't begin with strong opinions that you hope to support. That's boring. Start with genuine questions you don't know the answer to. Avoid yes/no questions. Try out the *topoi* exercise I suggest in chapter five to help you ask specific questions that will help you narrow your project.

Listen to the conversation: If you already have a topic and a question, go online and just read up and down and all around on the topic. Don't plan to use the sources you find just yet. Read for key terms, ideas, concepts, people, and lines of exploration that interest you. Look for diverse opinions—what are people disagreeing about? Search your library database for books on your topic. Yes, books! Walk on over to the library and pull a few books from the shelf and read around in them. Take notes. Find an encyclopedia or two; Wikipedia is a great read-up-and-down source to start with. Pretend like you've been assigned to write the Wikipedia page on your topic. What would you need to read to do that?

Use genres: The texts you read will take the form of genres, as we've said like a billion times in this book. Genres take on certain semi-formal shapes. As you read for research, pay attention to these shapes and use them to your advantage. Specifically, find out how to read quickly for conclusions or findings. Read the abstract or table of contents. Peruse the index. Read the executive summary and move on.

Research the research: When you find a source online that seems promising, get out of the text for a moment and google the author or sponsoring institution to find out more about them. You may find that the source has a particular commercial or political bias that may skew the information they give you (see chapter 9). You may find that the source has significant credibility because the writers have performed research in their specialized field. Look for the methods the writers used to come to their conclusions. In academic writing, *methods* are discipline-specific ways of asking questions and finding answers. Comparison studies, surveys, experiments, interviews, and archival research are all methods specialists use to create knowledge that other specialists consider legitimate.

Look at the publishing source: Is the text a website choked with advertisements, or an academic journal or publication that vets manuscripts carefully? If you find a text about your topic in a popular online news source (like the *Wall Street Journal* or *The Daily Beast*), is it based on interviews with credible sources or eyewitness accounts? Or is it just opinion? What data is presented to support the position it takes? Have other sources used the text as an authority, giving it social credibility? When was the research published? Is it new and therefore more compelling than sources 5–10 years old or more?

Read disciplinary texts: Texts work in *contexts*, in rhetorical situations that meet the needs of discourse communities who use specific rhetorical practices to get work done in the world. If I am reading a text written *by* a disciplinary specialist (like a psychologist or botanist or art historian) *to* other disciplinary specialists (in a peer-reviewed academic journal, for example), I've found a specific reading strategy quite useful. The linguist John Swales has studied the academic article as a genre, and he's discovered that experts across disciplines use a common pattern to "create a research space" (CARS) for themselves (Swales). More often than not, you can find the CARS moves in the first few pages of a text, even in the abstract paragraph. Here's how I would summarize the three rhetorical moves Swales sees in disciplinary texts:

> Move 1: *Why is this topic important?* In move 1, the scholar might explain, "Here's what we know about this topic AND/OR here's why it's important right now (*kairos*) AND/OR here's what previous research or texts have said about it." The writer might share previous research, effectively summarizing the conversation you want to listen to.
>
> Move 2: *What's the problem?* In move 2, the writer justifies his/her text by showing, like a good storyteller, the trouble: "Here are the questions that remain AND/OR here's what hasn't yet been done AND/OR here's why or how previous texts have been wrong or mistaken AND/OR here's why we should keep talking

about this topic." This is the move that makes the writer's own writing important because it solves a problem.

Move 3: *How do I intend to solve or explore this problem?* Move 3 is the gravy: "Here's the reason why I'm writing AND/OR here's my main point or argument AND/OR here's what I hope to add and what I hope it does for us AND/OR here's how I'm going to lay out the argument."

This model has been immensely important to me as a scholar because it helps me track the *conversation* we're having about a topic. When I write with sources, I enter these conversations myself, creating my own research space with these three moves. In short, you can read disciplinary texts more effectively if you think about how the writer uses these three moves to enter and contribute to a conversation. Conversations, in public life as well as disciplines, proceed when people make assertions or arguments and other people agree or disagree (in varying degrees), or change the subject (Graff).

Read to engage: When you read sources to write with sources, you prepare to enter a conversation by making certain rhetorical moves. You want to position yourself in relation to what has been said before—for, against, with, or on a totally different track, etc. Joseph Harris points out that this conversation metaphor is a little problematic because we're almost never writing directly to the people we're reading in our research. (I'm not going to pick a fight with the folks who wrote the ADHD article in *Journal of Pediatric Neurology.*) Rather, you "recirculate" the writing of others by (a) using them as "examples of a point you want to make," (b) presenting their authority as support for your argument, specifically by stating that authority in your own writing (*example:* "According to David Mandelbaum, Professor of Neurology and Pediatrics at Brown University, ADHD is a..."), (c) borrowing "terms or ideas" from their work, (d) putting "your own spin on the terms or concepts" they present" (Harris 39).

Sometimes you want to recirculate someone else's perspective by putting it in play with other perspectives. In that case, you would write something like, "Like Source X, Source Y argues that..." or "Source X, Source Y, and Source Z support the position that...," or "Unlike Source X, Source Y argues that..." or "Source Y takes issue with (or contradicts/corrects/offers a different perspective from) Source X for the following reasons...."

And sometimes, as you read texts, you discover that you yourself are ready to take a stand with or against a text. In their book *They Say/I Say,* writers Gerald Graff and Cathy Birkenstein give us dozens of templates for how to

- disagree without being disagreeable ("While I understand X's point, I...")

- disagreeing with reasons ("X's point of view is questionable because...")

- agreeing with a difference ("X's theory about _____ is useful because it sheds light on _____")

- agreeing and disagreeing simultaneously ("Although I disagree with X, I conclude that _____")

- making concessions while standing your ground ("Although I agree with X that _____, research shows that _____") (Graff and Birkinstein 309–327)

As you read, you become in some ways a stage director, organizing the main pieces of the play in complex relations with each other. The energy comes from the tensions and interplay of these sources as you put them on the rhetorical stage.

PAUSE. Now that you've finished this chapter, let's do some "retrieval practice." In *Make it Stick*, psychologists Henry Roediger and Mark McDaniel (and their collaborator, novelist Peter Brown) explain that retrieval, or "self-quizzing," is so much more effective than underlining, highlighting, or rereading (201–2). "Repeated recall," they argue, "appears to help memory consolidate into a cohesive representation in the brain and to strengthen and multiply the neural routes by which the knowledge can later be retrieved" (28–9). Retrieval practice takes *effort*, and effort aids memory.

So, as we finish this chapter, answer the following questions (without looking back at the text): What new terms did I learn from this chapter? How did these concepts validate or challenge what I already knew? How did this chapter connect with what I've learned previously in this book and elsewhere? What will I do differently as a reader now that I've read this chapter?

03

Works Cited

Ambrose, Susan A. et al. *How Learning Works: Seven Research-Based Principles for Smart Teaching*. San Francisco: Jossey-Bass, 2010. Print.

Bean, John. *Engaging Ideas*. 2nd ed. San Francisco: Jossey-Bass, 2011. Print.

Brandt, Deborah. *Literacy and Learning*. San Francisco: Jossey-Bass, 2009. Print.

Brown, Peter C., Henry L. Roediger III, and Mark A. McDaniel. *Make it Stick: The Science of Successful Learning*. Cambridge: Belknap, 2014. Print.

Duke, Nell K. and David Pearson. "Effective Practices for Developing Reading Comprehension." *What Research Has to Say About Reading Instruction*. 3rd ed. Eds. Alan Fostrup and S. Jay Samuels. International Reading Association, 2002. 205–242. Print.

Gallagher, Kelly. *Deeper Reading*. Portland, ME: Stenhouse, 2004. Print.

— — —. *Readicide*. Portland, ME: Stenhouse, 2007. Print.

Graff, Gerald. *Clueless in Academe*. New Haven: Yale UP, 2003. Print.

Graff, Gerald and Cathy Birkenstein. *They Say/I Say*. 4th ed. NY: Norton, 2018.

Harris, Joseph. *Rewriting*. Logan: Utah State UP, 2006.

Harvard Report on Reading. Cited in "Active Reading: Comprehension and Rate." Dartmouth Academic Study Skills Center. n.d. Web. 10 April 2015.

Jamieson, Sandra, Rebecca Moore Howard, and Tricia C. Serviss. The Citation Project. n.d. Web. 10 April 2015.

Street, Brian. "The New Literacy Studies." *Literacy: A Critical Sourcebook*. Ed. Ellen Cushman et al. Boston: Bedford/St. Martin's, 2001. 430–442. Print.

Swales, John. *Genre Analysis: English in Academic and Research Settings*. Cambridge, 1990. Print.

Urist, Jacoba. "What the Marshmallow Test Really Teaches About Self Control." *Atlantic*. 24 Sept 2014. Web. 10 Apr 2015.

PART 2

The Mindful Writing Process

04

PLAN

A writer in the act is a thinker on full-time cognitive overload.
—Linda Flower and John Hayes

In this chapter, I want to help you understand how to think about the writing process in a sophisticated way so you can use it to your advantage as a writer.

You sit down at a computer, you think stuff, and suddenly your fingers tap the keys and words appear on the page in front of you. Quite a magic trick. How the heck does that happen?

I don't know. Frankly, I'm as baffled as maybe you are at the mysteries of how our brains produce language. I know that writing is *not* like speaking; if you were raised in a house with other people, you did not need to be taught how to speak (if you were raised by wolves, however…). Language is an "instinct," says Steven Pinker, the famous Harvard psychologist, and we "know how to talk in more or less the sense that spiders know how to spin webs" (5). Children just somehow start talking, and they put their subjects before their verbs and verbs before objects and they pluralize nouns, when they need to, and they past-tensify actions with brilliant internal logic, even when making what we perhaps mistakenly call errors ("I *holded* the doll").

Writing, however, is not an instinct—not by a long shot. Pinker tells us, further, that "Children must be taught to read and write in laborious lessons" (186). A toddler's first instinct when given a book is to eat it. I'm sure you have early memories, as I do, of large colorful letters on blocks and toys and posters and games and books, all suggesting to our three-year-old brains that these squiggles not only sound something but *mean* something when they stand around in groups. Words appear gradually as we synthesize sound, shape, and meaning. We struggle to read out loud with a parent, and then, like magic, we're reading chapter books like *Magic Tree House* on our own. And at the same time, we're struggling to write our own words, on paper with green lines like little roads running across them—first letters, then words, then sentences, then paragraphs, then stories. Being a writer is a miraculous and inspiring thing.

It's also incredibly taxing on our brains. For little children, the first big hurdle, after grasping the letter-sound relationship, is mastering the mechanics of producing letters. Writing, we must remember, is a mechanical skill, and children struggle to get their ideas on paper when they haven't quite mastered the physical process of writing (called *transcription* in the research; see McCutchen). To get a sense of what it's like to struggle to write when transcription is a problem, sit down at a keyboard and cross your arms at the wrist and type with your hands in reverse order. Children under the age of 10 or children with literacy or motor disabilities feel that way all the time when asked to write. We become more fluent writers when we master how to make words appear. You've likely seen this in your own life as you've mastered thumb-texting on a cell phone. Writers get better by writing.

Transcription (i.e., creating words with tools) is just one of several tasks that cognitive scientists tell us our brains must handle when writing. There are other processes going on at once (like monitoring what you've written), and there's one manager that oversees the entire process. It's important for you to know this as a writer, so stay with me.

Cognitive scientists call this overseer the *central executive*. (A cognitive scientist studies how we think; cognition is the action of thinking, understanding, or perceiving.) Let's use an analogy to describe the role of this cognitive function. Imagine you are invited into the control booth for a major television event like the Super Bowl or the Grammy Awards. The booth is full of computer banks where people with headsets press buttons and turn dials and monitor flashing lights. You notice that one person in the booth, sitting higher than everyone else at the back of the room, is telling everyone else what to do. If you're observing a football game directed by Bob Fishman, legendary director for CBS Sports, you see him scanning 100 TV monitors, each showing a different angle on the football game; he's looking for the next live shot, and then the next one, and the next one. ("Ready camera three. Take three!") In a thirty-second interval, Bob Fishman—called "Fish" by his broadcasting team—might shift live shots every three seconds (Bowden). For three straight hours.

Your central executive does that for your brain when you write. Generally speaking, the "Fish" of your mind has three major tasks: *planning* to write, *producing* the writing, and *reviewing* or *revising* what's been written. Each of these tasks requires knowledge, skills, and habits that all help the central executive do its job. For example, deep in long-term memory—that's the place that stores information you may need some time in the future—you have a bank of possible words to use, some grammatical understanding, knowledge about your topic or audience, strategies for writing that worked in the past, and a cache of potential "text structures" we call genres (McCutchen, Teske, and Bankston 460). These tasks are also influenced by your own disposition as a learner emotionally engaged (or not) in the creative work of writing. The central executive draws from these resources to make your writing work (see Kellogg 2–3).

If the central executive gets stressed, well, it's harder to write. We already talked about what happens if you struggle physically to write or type words. There are other ways to burden your central executive. If you know absolutely squat about your topic, then the central executive is going to stress out trying to get the writing done. If you don't set goals or plan your writing effectively, if you're writing in an unfamiliar genre, if you can't predict how a reader might respond, if you don't have a tried-and-true writing process, if you're not interested at all in what you're writing about, if you try to write something while your cell phone pings with incoming text messages—you make writing harder for yourself because your central executive is getting slammed with other tasks.

And of course in the background of all these issues is the *why* of writing, and the *to whom*—what's called the "task environment" of writing (Hayes "New Directions"). We talked about the task environment in chapter two when we talked about the rhetorical situation.

While I do want you to understand the cognitive challenges related to writing, in this chapter I'm more interested in helping you learn to use *writing plans and processes* as a way to aid your central executive while you write. At this point, I hope you have some sense of why it's important to develop a writing process so that planning, producing, and revising your work will be rewarding for you, even as it challenges you. I told you all this stuff about writing and cognition because I want you to be a mindful writer; remember from chapter one, you're a writer who thinks about how to improve as a writer. It's going to take time and practice, of course, but that's why you took this class. (Nice move!)

A Model for Writing Tasks

Before we go further, I want you to take a moment and think about how you've produced writing in the past. What is your standard writing process? ("Standard" is a misleading word, I guess, because we go through different processes for different situations and purposes.) If someone made a gripping Netflix Original Series about your writing process, what would we see you (the hero!) doing as you get the writing done? Where would you be writing? And how? What would you do first, second, third? And which celebrity would you want playing the role of distracting love interest?

Based on what I used to do in high school when assigned a writing task, I know what my television drama would look like:

> Scene, home office. Camera zooms in on our hero, slouching in a chair in front of an eight-inch green-screen Compaq-brand computer the day before the paper is due. He rubs his temples. He hasn't given Thought One to this paper that needs to appear magically in the next few hours. He cracks his knuckles. He says, "Okay, let's do this!" He plays a few rounds of *Bushido: The Way of the Warrior*, just to get warmed up. Then, he writes. Fast-cutting montage of our hero typing each sentence, putting one word in front of the other, checking each phrase and clause for glaring errors, until the small screen is filled with words in 14-point font. A close-up of our hero-writer, sweat on his brow, a look of satisfaction as he takes fifteen seconds to look over what he's written, making sure his commas are where he thinks they should be. He adds a comma in one sentence because he's been told to add commas where you take breaths. Camera pulls back as hero prints out paper on a dot matrix printer and then slides the finished product into a plastic sleeve that reeks of clueless desperation. A hard-rock power jam from the 80s plays as he crams his paper into his backpack, a smug look of triumph crossing his face.

What can I say? It got the job done—sort of. Okay, not really.

Does my writing process sound familiar to you? Of course not, because you care more about your work than I did. Or maybe some of it does resonate. Maybe you, too, have cranked out a paper in an energy-drink-induced sleepless fury the night before it was due. Extensive research on the writing processes of novice writers has revealed that the way I used to write papers is by no means uncommon. We know from research that novice writers "show little concern for conceptual planning," "fail to plan adequately for their readers," and focus mostly on "surface features" like punctuation when revising (McCutchen, Teske, Bankston 454–5). Skilled writers spend much more time than novices planning their writing, setting goals, finding the right genre, thinking about their audience, and working to discover the meaning of what they want to say (Torrance). Like novices, they revise for surface-level issues (gotta get your commas to behave!), but they also revise "holistically," meaning that they take in what they've written "as a *whole*" to make sure they've got it right (Sommers 386). The skilled writer sees the whole project as a *whole*, from beginning to end, and there's power in that.

We want you to have this kind of power when you write. So, I want to teach you a new process for managing writing tasks. Think of this process as your own hero's journey through a creative struggle, from the moment you're assigned to write (the "call" to writing) to the moment you see the results of what you wrote and—like Bilbo Baggins after returning to the Shire from his encounter with the dragon Smaug—start writing the memoir of your quest.

The following chart represents your quest through the writing task:

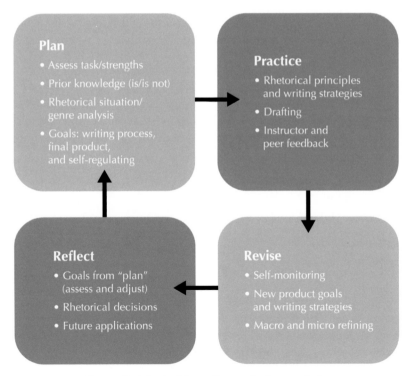

Figure 2. Adapted from Susan Ambrose et al.,
How Learning Works (2010), p. 193.

You'll recognize these four steps from chapter one when we talked about mindfulness in writing. In *How Learning Works*, professor Susan Ambrose and her research team explain that the most effective students go through a metacognitive process of "self-directed learning" when confronted with an intellectual challenge, like a writing assignment (Ambrose et al. 193). I've adapted this process for writing tasks from this remarkable research. Study this chart carefully. Tattoo it onto your brain. It's one of the things you learn in this class that should go with you to future writing challenges.

In this textbook, we'll cover each of the four steps of the writing process. In this chapter, we'll talk about *planning*, something that novice writers don't do enough of.

Plan

Every writer will adopt a different strategy for writing—a different writing process that best suits his or her particular needs and talents. I was taught a fairly linear prewriting-writing-revising method, but in practice you may do all these things over and over during a complicated writing task.

This is a crucial point: There is no *single* writing process that suits everyone. You'll have to figure out what's best for you as you write your way, mindfully, to glory. And yet there is a more or less better way to think about how to manage writing tasks from the start. Skilled writers, for example, take considerably more time planning their writing than developing writers.

In the *planning* stage, a writer

1. assesses the task and

2. sets goals.

What do we mean by these activities?

A few years ago, my wife asked me to build a shed-like shelter in the backyard so we could store the lawn mower, a rusty wheelbarrow, and other implements of torture. I'd never built such a thing, so I did what I always do when assigned to do something outside my comfort zone: I stared blankly at the problem. I went out to the potential construction site, on the left side of the house next to the fence, and I stared at the site and tried to imagine what a structure like that might look like. At first I imagined building a full-scale shed with walls and sliding doors, and then when I realized how long that might take me, considering my sub-par acumen with power tools, I imagined a wall-less structure with four wooden posts and a pitched roof. I'd built similar structures when I was a carpenter's apprentice after high school. Maybe I could do that. And if I couldn't, I could ask my friends to come help me with the hard stuff. I decided I'd spend the next whole Saturday working on it, and then every night for a couple of hours after dinner. I needed to be done before it snowed.

I had a hard time at first imagining how the posts would go into the ground and how the roof would go into the posts. So I took my phone around the neighborhood and took pictures of other sheds and lean-tos, paying particular attention to the way the roofs were constructed. I also watched videos on YouTube for how to make lean-to-like shelters. (Are there such videos? Only 171,000 of them.) At work, when I should have been thinking of other things, I daydreamed about what materials I'd use, how much it would all cost, how it all might come together, whether my neighbors would sue me because it blocked their view of the Wasatch mountains. I'd borrow my friend Cam's cement mixer. My neighbor Paul, who built something like this in his backyard, could talk me through the first steps. I'd see if Billy would work with me on the shingles for the roof—he owed me because I helped him paint his house. My wife, of course, would let me know as I drew up some plans whether I was on the right track.

By the time I went out in the yard with a post-hole shovel and all the lumber, I had given the project considerable thought. I had a global sense—a "big picture" sense—of what I was going to do, even if the specific *how* wasn't quite set in mind.

You already know where I'm going with this, so let's go there. Starting a writing project is like what I've just described. An event in your life triggers a *writing task*—a teacher or a future employer will give you a writing assignment, and before you start writing you'll plan your approach. Not always, of course. You don't plan, necessarily, to write a text message or a Post-it note to roommates to stop stealing your milk. But what I'm about to describe is an ideal process for important writing tasks—the kind that get you good grades or scholarships or promotions.

Assess the Task

Here are a few steps you might take while you assess the task (and we'll talk more about these steps in chapter five):

1. **Read the assignment carefully**, making sure you understand what's being asked of you. Before building, I talked over with my wife what she wanted me to do. For writing assignments, you make sure you understand what your instructor wants you to do. Ask yourself: Do I get this assignment? Do I understand what key terms (like "critical thinking") mean? Check due dates. When am I asked to submit outlines, bibliographies, or previous drafts? What is the purpose or outcome? How will I be assessed?

2. **Assess the rhetorical situation.** Who is the audience for this assignment? What do I know about them? What do they want from me? What discourse community do they belong to? What is my role as writer? What do I want my audience to feel, think, or do as a result of reading my stuff? What strategies will I use to achieve those goals? My shelter would serve my immediate family's purposes, but it would also be seen by neighbors and visitors. What would they think of me when they saw it?

3. **Analyze the genre in which you're supposed to write** (see chapter two). Shelters serve various purposes for various people in various situations. Before I built the shelter, I looked at how other people built their shelters to achieve similar or at least related purposes. Genres, according to Carolyn Miller, are "typified rhetorical actions based in recurrent situations" (159). A genre isn't necessarily a convention or a form we follow; it's a rhetorical act we do because the situation (i.e., audience and purpose) calls for it. When someone dies, a relative usually writes an obituary. An obituary is a genre. It's a rhetorical act that follows a familiar pattern and uses semi-typical strategies (like providing life details) that are appropriate for the moment. Rarely do you see an obituary describing the immoral or criminal activity of the deceased—which is unfortunate, because obituaries would be a lot more entertaining if they included that stuff. But that would be *inappropriate*, in a rhetorical sense. Genres take certain shapes because we need them to do certain things for us.

   When you write, you write genres (letters to the editor, proposals, lab reports, grant proposals, analyses, personal statements, etc.), and some of them are more clearly defined than others. For example, at some point you probably wrote a "research paper." What are the genre conventions of a research paper? It depends on who you ask. If you ask scientists, they'll say that a research paper has a section, usually titled "methods," describing how the scientist set up the experiment. Historians will tell you that research papers must have copious footnotes or endnotes listing primary sources the writer consulted for historical analysis. If you'd asked me when I was a junior in high school, I would have told you, "It's this thing you write when you look up some stuff in the Kearns (my hometown) library and write down a few cool quotes and then vomit it all up in a paper with a works cited page and an awesome plastic sleeve." Regardless of the occasional fuzziness surrounding genres, it's important to your success that you write a genre appropriate to the situation. How do you get it right?

Scholars of genre have described a useful method for analyzing the genre most suited to your writing situation (Devitt, Reiff, and Bawarshi). First, you get your hands on samples of the genre. You collect examples from as many different sources as you can, including examples written by professionals and previous students of the course you're taking. (Maybe your instructor has copies of previous student work you can borrow.) Second, you identify the rhetorical situation for which that genre would be suitable. You ask yourself: Where does this genre show up? Whose purpose does it serve? Who writes these genres and who reads them and why? Third, you analyze the patterns (called rhetorical strategies; you'll learn about them in Part III) you see in the genre, asking yourself questions like: How is this genre structured? What rhetorical strategies do the writers use? What kind of style or argument or document design or language do I detect across examples?

Analyzing genre in this way will help you understand what's typical in the rhetorical situation you find yourself in before you write a single word.

4. **Review how your prior knowledge or experience might apply.** We know from research that what we already know can either "help or hinder" what we're trying to do now (Ambrose et al. 13). Before I started the shelter, I kind of knew what I knew how to do and what I didn't know how to do. My prior experience helped me understand my limitations and strengths. Before you start a writing task,

you should think about what you know about the topic you're supposed to write about and whether you've written that kind of genre or something similar to it before. (How is this rhetorical analysis like the literary analysis I wrote in high school? How is it *not* like that?) Sometimes prior knowledge can hurt us in new writing tasks. I've had college writing students who had mastered the five-paragraph essay in high school and could not write themselves out of it in my writing class. I'd get five beastly paragraphs stretched out to eight pages, and I'd think, "Gee, their prior knowledge isn't helping them!" You should also think about what prior writing processes have helped you or hurt you before.

5. **Assess your ability to perform the task.** You may also want to spend a few moments thinking about your own abilities as a writer. How confident are you with this kind of assignment? In some ways, it doesn't matter whether or not you think you're a "good writer" in some generic sense: How do I feel about *this* assignment? We know from research that self-perceptions will influence whether student writers work hard, "persevere" when the going gets tough, and bounce back after failure (Pajares and Valiante 159). Remind yourself: I can do this if I work hard each day and get good feedback. *Writers get better at writing by writing.*

6. **Decide what you want to get out of the assignment.** Ask yourself: What's in it for me? What do I want to learn from this writing task? What will writing this genre help me do in the future? How will I make personal connections to this writing task so that I won't be bored or discouraged? As with all the other steps for assessing the task, you should write down answers to these questions to refer to as you work.

Set Goals

The second part of planning after assessing the task is *setting goals*.

I know. The phrase "setting goals" might evoke mixed feelings. You might be thinking about those times when someone—likely a well-meaning adult with power over you—made you set goals you had no intention to keep. January is a busy month for membership gyms because of fleeting New Year's resolutions.

But think about it this way: Most of our actions are goal-oriented. When I stand up from my desk to walk down the hall to get a drink of water,

I've set a goal for myself. It's an easy goal to achieve, as long as I don't go into cardiac arrest in the 100 yards it takes to get to the drinking fountain. Most action is goal-oriented: We want something, we try to get it. What we're talking about, though, is more purposeful, more (yes!) mindful.

For our purposes here, I suggest two kinds of goals you'll want to set for yourself as a writer at the outset of a writing task:

1. **Specific product goals.** Once you've analyzed the genre you're supposed to write, you'll know better what you need to do as a writer. A "product goal" is a statement explaining to yourself what you want your writing to look like when it's done. And genre helps direct these goals. For example, if I'm writing an opinion editorial on a political topic, one of my product goals might be to end my op ed by calling on Congress to act on some piece of legislation—a futile call, surely, but one that satisfies my desire to tell powerful people what to do. Sometimes the assignment you've been given has explicit goals written for you (like "support your thesis with evidence from peer-reviewed scholarship"). Sometimes you'll make your own (like "I'll use transitional language to help the reader go from one part of my argument to the next" or "I'm going to throw a pop culture reference in my intro to attract interest and set the tone"). The point is to make specific product goals that are not too broad ("I will develop my argument effectively") or too restricting ("I will write three sentences after every topic sentence—one to provide an example, one to…").

   Summarizing research on effective writers, English professor Debbie Dean tells us that "product goals are most effective either before drafting or during revision" (57). Debbie implies here that sometimes your specific product goals, like carry-on luggage, will shift midflight. That's okay! The point is that you're paying attention to those goals, letting them serve as your guide as you crank out the good stuff. Your instructor might include an assignment sheet or rubric that will help you make product goals.

2. **Self-regulating goals.** Sometimes we're our own worst enemies. Wanna get up earlier than you normally do? You'll have to convince yourself, and your self wants to sleep. Gonna get that paper written long before it's due? Shoot, they're playing ultimate frisbee out there on the lawn, and it's such a beautiful day…. Writing is hard, and we do all kinds of things to avoid it. Sometimes when I'm staring at a blank screen, I'll find myself either cleaning my desk with obsessive

compulsion or playing the video game Pac-man online. (I just played it now!) Skilled writers have strategies to "regulate" themselves to get their work done. They trust the better angels of their nature, but they also believe those angels need a nudge now and then. Think of self-regulating writing goals like the alarm clock that shreds dollar bills if you don't get up and turn it off. (Yes, there is such a product.)

When you get a writing assignment, you may feel overwhelmed by the task. ("I've never written one of those before…How many pages?…I don't even know where to start!") You'll see a looming deadline and wonder how you will possibly manage to have something ready by then. Self-regulating goals keep the panic at bay by helping you manage the writing task. Don't stew—*do*. Experts on this subject divide potential regulating strategies into different categories (Graham and Harris). Here are a few you might find useful:

a. **Environmental**—Decide where and when you're going to write, and stick to a schedule. Block out time each day to write or even just to think about your writing project. Write every day, and then when you get stuck, you can quit without freaking out that the paper's due tomorrow; you'll let your work percolate subconsciously while you do other things (see Carey's chapter "Quitting Before You're Ahead"). Surprisingly, there is some evidence that varying *where* we write might actually help us make useful mental connections; consider that as you plan (Carey 61).

When you sit down to write, turn off your cell phone. Multitasking is a delusion strongly contradicted by cognitive science ("Multitasking: Switching Costs"). You're either writing your paper or text messaging your friends—you can't do both, at least not at the same time. Even listening to music while writing, especially music with lyrics, can throw you off your writing groove because of your "selective attention" (Hattie and Yates 191). Just trust Uncle Brian on this one: You'll get more writing done if you're not shifting attention from your words to your phone or an irrelevant webpage, unless, of course, you're using your phone to write, read, or research something related to your task. Set goals for how you'll control your environment for the most effective writing.

b. **Personal**—Set a goal to check your own progress—this is called "self-monitoring." After each day or writing period, reflect on how well you're doing and decide what you need to do next. Set deadlines for yourself, but adjust them if they don't work for you. The most popular self-monitoring strategy: reward yourself. For example, tell yourself "As soon as I write 500 words, I'll check sports scores on ESPN," or "If I write for one hour today, I will go buy myself a mango pineapple smoothie."

c. **Social**—Just as I talked about the shelter project with friends and neighbors, talk about your writing project with other people. Talking about your work out loud can be a powerful writing tool. Your instructor will likely assign you to work with peers to review each other's writing. Set a goal to have more people than your peer group review your work. Take your writing to a tutor (in the Writing Center, for example) or a trusted roommate. Listen carefully to your readers, even though you should always think of yourself as the owner of your own work.

I've spent all this time on the planning stage for two reasons: (1) skilled writers spend more time planning than novice writers, so you should develop a planning approach that works for you, and (2) learning how to plan effectively will help you tackle future writing tasks in school and beyond. Your instructor might ask you to set down these plans in writing so he or she can help you make the most of them.

Like all good plans, you'll make adjustments and revisions as you start writing and get feedback. I can't tell you how many times I've tried to write portions of this textbook only to have my plans crash-land in a field of failure. You'll get this. Much of the planning process will become intuitive for you, with practice.

Works Cited

Ambrose, Susan A. et al. *How Learning Works: Seven Research-Based Principles for Smart Teaching*. San Francisco: Jossey-Bass, 2010. Print.

Bowden, Mark. "The Hardest Job in Football." *The Atlantic*. Jan/Feb 2009. Web. 8 May 2015. Print.

Carey, Benedict. *How We Learn*. NY: Random House, 2014. Print.

Dean, Deborah. *What Works in Writing Instruction*. Urbana, IL: NCTE, 2010. Print.

Devitt, Amy, Mary Jo Reiff, and Anis Bawarshi. *Scenes of Writing: Strategies for Composing with Genres*. NY: Pearson, 2004. Print.

Graham, Steve and Karen R. Harris. "The Role of Self-Regulation and Transcription Skills in Writing and Writing Development." *Educational Psychologist* 35.1 (2000): 3–12. Print.

Hattie, John and Gregory Yates. *Visible Learning and the Science of How We Learn*. London: Routledge, 2014. Print.

Hayes, John R. "New Directions in Writing Theory." *Handbook of Writing Research*. Ed. Charles A. MacArthur, Steve Graham, and Jill Fitzgerald. NY: Guilford, 2006. 28–40. Print.

Kellogg, Ronald T. "Training Writing Skills: A Cognitive Developmental Perspective." *Journal of Writing Research* 1.1 (2008): 1–26. Print.

McCutchen, Deborah. "Cognitive Factors in the Development of Children's Writing." *Handbook of Writing Research*. Ed. Charles A. MacArthur, Steven Graham, and Jill Fitzgerald. NY: Guilford P, 2006. 115–130. Print.

McCutchen, Deborah, Paul Teske, and Catherine Bankston. "Writing and Cognition: Implications of the Cognitive Architecture for Learning to Write and Writing to Learn." *Handbook of Research on Writing*. Ed. Charles Bazerman. NY: Lawrence Erlbaum, 2008. 452–470. Print.

Miller, Carolyn R. "Genre as Social Action." *Quarterly Journal of Speech* 70 (1984): 151–167. Print.

"Multitasking: Switching Costs." American Psychological Association. 20 March 2006. Web. 4 Nov 2014. Print.

Pajares, Frank and Gio Valiante. "Self-Efficacy Beliefs and Motivation in Writing Development." *Handbook of Writing Research*. Ed. Charles A. MacArthur, Steven Graham, and Jill Fitzgerald. NY: Guilford P, 2006. 158–170. Print.

Pinker, Steven. *The Language Instinct*. NY: HarperPerennial, 1994. Print.

Sommers, Nancy. "Revision Strategies of Student Writers and Experienced Adult Writers." *CCC* 31.4 (1980): 378–388. Print.

Torrance, Mark. "Is Writing Expertise Like Other Kinds of Expertise?" *Theories, Models, and Methodology in Writing Research*. Eds. Gert Rijlaarsdam, Huub van den Bergh, and Michel Couzijn. Amsterdam: Amsterdam UP, 1996. 3–9. Print.

05
PRACTICE

The second stage of the writing quest is *practice*. When we talk about practice, we're talking about how you'll use writing strategies—methods for getting the writing done once you've assessed the task and set goals.

When we talk about practice, we're talking about the time period after planning when

> you start thinking about what to write

to the moment when

> you receive feedback on a full draft of your writing from someone (a teacher, a peer, anonymous commenters on your blog, the worker guy at 7-11, your mom).

I've said before that writing processes vary from person to person and project to project, so in some ways this time frame I've laid out is arbitrary. However, I really like the idea of practice as preparation time for, and a separate activity from, performance. When it comes to writing, performance is when you publish your work or turn it in for a grade. Before then, you take time to practice. Even though practice is meant to improve performance, in practice you permit yourself to take risks, look stupid, write awkward and silly things, make tentative claims, test ideas, and fall on your face—all for the glory of writing!

You already know some of the buzzwords we use when we talk about getting the writing done: brainstorming, clustering, outlining, freewriting, drafting, reading, talking to people, writing paragraphs, reading drafts out loud. You also have various rhetorical principles to guide writing, like thinking of your audience, supporting your claim with good reasons, making effective appeals, writing an appropriate genre, organizing your writing effectively, and writing with an effective style. Your instructor will give you time to practice these writing strategies, so I won't go over them in detail here. Writing strategies are very much genre-specific, meaning that the way you come up with something to say is influenced by the kind of thing (genre) you're writing. So in this chapter I'll share a few general strategies that will help you generate different genres.

Before we get to the strategies, two brief complications: These strategies may not help you unless you know what you want to write about—i.e., you've landed on a topic, a specific question, or a problem you want to explore. Your instructor will help you think through how to come up with a topic; the assignment will guide you, but so should your own interests. We know that students who are passionate about their topics, even if their instructor assigned them, have more motivation as writers, and they write better. At any rate, let's proceed with these practice strategies under the assumption that you've settled on at least a provisional topic to write about.

The second complication is that writing research has shown that effective writers don't necessarily use these strategies in a linear way (i.e., "first I do this...then I do that..."). In grade school, you may have learned a model that looks like this:

prewriting ——⟶ drafting ——⟶ revising

While this model is helpful for starting out, it doesn't quite describe what happens when you're on a writing quest. You may find that your writing process is *recursive*, meaning that sometimes you start revising before you get a draft done or sometimes you'll brainstorm even after completing an entire draft because you hit a dead end. The mindful writer studies her own process to see what works best. (I say "her," but I mean "his," too. I usually pluralize my subjects to avoid sexist problems, but sometimes I want to express a single writer, and then, just because we've used *his* for so long, I use *her* to even things out. What do *you* do to solve this rhetorical problem?)

The three stages of practice we'll talk about in this chapter are invention, drafting, and feedback.

Invention

The philosopher Aristotle believed that studying rhetoric meant studying rhetorical *invention*—or finding, as he put it, "the available means of persuasion." Invention is the process we use to come up with stuff to write. (Invention is kind of a big deal in rhetorical studies.) As you already know, coming up with something to write is particularly hard when you have no idea what you're going to write about. For this section, I'm going to assume that you've settled on a question or problem related to a topic you've been assigned in your class. Of course, invention can also help you land on a problem or question, too; it can also help you narrow your topic to make your writing project more manageable.

What methods of invention have you used in the past? How have they worked for you?

I like to think of invention methods as either *structured* or *unstructured*. When you use structured invention, you attack your topic with specific kinds of questions or categories of thought that writers have used for ages. Unstructured invention taps into more intuitive, organic, and surprising stores for creativity. Both are useful.

Structured Methods of Invention

Using a *structured* method can be helpful if you don't know how to start. For example, students of rhetoric in ancient Greece and Rome used a system called *topoi* to invent arguments. The word topoi is the plural form of the Greek word *topos*, which means place. Topoi are starting places for discovering things to say—places you can go to come up with arguments. The Greeks invented these starting places, I think, because they noticed that there are certain patterns we follow when trying to figure out the world, certain categories of thought we find useful over and over, in different settings. For example, one topos is *definition*—how a word or key term or principle has been defined.

It's useful to think of topoi in terms of the questions they provoke. You've probably heard of the journalist's Who-What-When-Where-Why questions; topoi are like that. The following table lists useful topoi and the questions they provoke to help you come up with something to say related to your writing task.

Topos	Related Questions
definition, category, or essence	What is this thing? How is it defined? How is it classified (with other things)? How does this thing work? What is its purpose?
division	How can this topic be divided? What are its parts? How do the parts relate? Which parts are most important?
comparison	What is this thing like? What is it *not* like? What analogies or metaphors could be used to compare this to other things?
cause or consequence	What happens because of this thing? What are the consequences of it? Who or what is influenced by it?
antecedent or origin	Where did this thing come from? Who started it? What is its history? What is it a consequence of?
authority	Who speaks about this? Who are the experts or stakeholders? Who knows the most about this? Who cares about this?
value	Who values this thing? Is it good or bad? How is this thing evaluated? What laws, morals, or practices are influenced by this? What's the consensus on it? The disagreements?
space	Where is this thing? What is its reach, scope? Where is it concentrated? How far does it go?
possibility	What's possible related to this thing? How much can it change? Who has power to change it? What's difficult or impossible about this?

Once you have a potential writing topic, you can blitz it with these questions to see what comes up. Let's say you're writing a research paper about illegal immigration in the United States. You're not sure what to argue, which is a wise and critically sound place to start, but you have your topoi on hand to help you think through the subject systematically. You could make a table like the one above and write questions or issues related to immigration in the right-hand column, like this:

Topos	Related Questions/Issues
definition, category, or essence	What is immigration? What makes immigration *illegal*? What is the scope of the issue? What is it like to cross the Mexican-American border into the U.S.?
division	Various people immigrate for various reasons, from various places *to* various places in the U.S. What do these differences tell us about immigration? What organizations in the U.S. have an interest in this issue (border patrol, local businesses, human rights activists, etc.)?
comparison	How important is immigration compared to other political issues? We could compare various groups or nationalities who immigrate and what becomes of them.
cause or consequence	What are the consequences of illegal immigration? Who benefits? Who gets hurt? What would happen if immigration stopped?
antecedent or origin	What's the history of immigration in the U.S.? Where does the immigrant's journey begin? We could look at how attitudes or policies about immigration have changed across time.
authority	Who knows the most about this topic? Who are the experts, and who are the "experiencers" (those who experience immigration and its consequences)? Which think tanks or organizations understand this issue most clearly?
value	What are the ethical issues related to illegal immigration? Are illegal immigrants criminals or valuable contributors to culture and economy? What laws govern immigration? We should think, too, about how or why we value this topic.
space	Where does immigration take place? Where do immigrants come from? I'd be interested to know where illegal immigrants end up living and working.
possibility	What can or can't be done about illegal immigration? How do we make changes in the system? Who should change it?

Another structured method of invention is *writing an outline*. No, it ain't sexy. I remember being compelled to write outlines for papers in high school: writing the Roman numerals, tabbing over the subcategories, creating a roadmap I was sure to junk once I started writing. But here's the crazy thing: There's research evidence suggesting that outlining can help you map out the relationship between possible ideas you want to represent in your writing, especially when you haven't thought much about the topic you want to write about (Hayes "New Directions"; Kellogg). They can help you plan out your writing and make product goals. They help you separate your writing task into parts and organize those parts into helpful hierarchies.

At their simplest, outlines can help you think through your main point and all the support you hope to gather, like the following outline for a generic essay:

I. Cool intro
II. My first point
    A. Support for this point (evidence, arguments, details)
    B. More support for this point (etc.)
III. My second point
    A. Support for this point
    B. Etc. etc.!
IV. An amazing conclusion that ties it together and blows the minds of my readers

Since you're the boss of your writing, you can change your outline to suit your needs as you write. A good outline, though, can give you a path through the thicket before you start out. It sets up a working blueprint for your thinking. Outlines, though, should be *genre specific*, meaning that the kind of writing you're doing will dictate the kind of outline you'll write. Science writers often follow a specific outline with the acronym IMRD: introduction, methods, results, discussion. Sometimes simple outlines are helpful only if you're writing an academic essay. If you're writing a resume or creating a digital document, you'll have to think differently about how to arrange your argument.

One final structured method is *clustering*. My guess is you've already been taught how to do this, but just in case you haven't:

> To cluster, just write a word you're interested in at the center of a
> piece of paper. (You'll need to go Old School for this one: pencil and

paper, not computer.) It can be a topic or a question related to your topic—like immigration. Draw a circle around that word or phrase. Then think of related topics or words that have some kind of connection to that center word. Write those words and draw lines like wagon-wheel spokes connecting the ideas. Then, do the same for the words you've just created around the original word, getting more specific the further you go from the key word.

I said go pencil and paper on clustering, but I can also imagine some pretty cool clustering happening digitally on a word processor or design program. I've used presentation slides to invent arguments before.

Unstructured Methods of Invention

So much for the structured invention strategies. If you're more interested in freewheeling, hippie-dippie, space-case, unlock-your-consciousness kind of invention strategies, you might want to try more unstructured strategies, like the following:

Inquiry—Ask questions. If you have a vague sense of a topic, jump on Google and read till your eyeballs fall out. Consult Wikipedia. Do the unthinkable: Go to the library and find a book and read it. Find key terms or authorities from an informal search. Talk to experts about your topic. Gather data from experimentation, surveys, or interviews. Form a hypothesis about your topic, like "I think X influences Y, but I'm not sure" or "I think X is the case, but I'm not sure" or "I think X would be a solution to Y, but I'm not sure." It's so important to begin a writing task with *questions* and not answers; don't do research merely to support your preconceptions.

Freewriting—Just start writing. As fast as you can, as much as you can. Don't think at all about what you're writing; if you can't think of something to say, write "I'm not sure what to say here so I'll keep writing until something comes…" Take American author Jack Kerouac's kooky, almost incoherent advice and just write "'without consciousness' in semitrance… allowing subconscious to admit in own uninhibited interesting necessary…language what conscious art would censor, and write excitedly, swiftly, with writing-or-typing-cramps" (58). You may discover that there are sentences and ideas that just emerge, almost out of nowhere, from your stream of consciousness. Tap into the inner writing genius hiding behind all that fear of making a mistake in writing.

Some writers also use a strategy called *looping* with freewriting. They'll take a kernel of an idea or sentence out of the freewrite and start freewriting about *that*, just to see where it goes.

Journaling—Keep a journal in a notebook, document, or even blog about your quest to finish the writing task. Write whatever you want—questions, concerns, goals, responses, quotes, issues, prewrites, doodles. When I'm journaling, I'll often make "to do" lists with little boxes to check when I get stuff done (like "look up the study on sleep and test performance mentioned in the *New York Times* science section").

Talking to people—Talk about your topic with everyone you know. Tell your roommates, friends, neighbors, hair stylist, and family members what you want to write about. Annoy people about your plans while on the basketball court or in the hot tub. Talk through your concerns. Use Facebook or some other social media to play around with possible directions and ideas. When you think you have a possible argument (called a *thesis* by some), tweet it out there; my colleague Gideon Burton calls this a "tweethis," which sounds like a word a kid would say after his two front teeth fell out.

Drawing—Doodle while you think about your project. Draw a picture, or some kind of chart or graphic that represents some faint shadow of an idea. Draw shapes to represent various approaches or concepts. Express relationships in abstract symbols and diagrams. Nancy Duarte, design guru, encourages us to represent abstract concepts in diagrams that suggest flow, structure, relationships, hierarchies, or processes (45).

Drafting

Invention can be fun, but at some point you have to sit down and open a word processor (like Google Drive or Microsoft Word) and start writing complete sentences. The second stage of practice, then, is drafting. Some students approach drafting as if they're carving into stone the epitaph of a cultural hero. For some developing writers, drafting is a painful, almost letter-at-a-time process. Writing words should not be like passing kidney stones, but it can feel like that if we're too fixated on getting things right from the start. Remember: You're *practicing* at this point. Drafting is essentially thinking in words and sentences and paragraphs. Though it's essential that you keep in mind your audience as you write, Peter Elbow (a wonderful writer about writing) tells us that during drafting time, it makes sense to write with our eyes closed to our audience, so to speak, so that we are uninhibited, so that we can explore and express before we communicate and connect.

You may encounter writer's block during the drafting process. That's natural, even for professional writers. We get writer's block because we have "inflexible plans" for the writing (Rose); we get it because we're tired, or frustrated, or sorta played out for the day. If you're writing every day, writer's block shouldn't be too big of a problem—if you've set reasonable self-regulating goals, then you'll benefit from the writing habit. But quitting is often the best thing you could do for the writing (remember the *percolating* principle from the last chapter). You can always go back to the invention stage or talk over your problem with someone or even talk through the problem out loud to yourself and record it. A word to the wise: "binge writing" has been shown to cause writer's block and even "dysphoria," which means "general dissatisfaction" (Kellogg and Whiteford 257). You don't want dissatisfaction—that's five syllables of sadness.

I'm assuming your instructor will be your guide for approaching the drafting of your paper, but consider these principles:

1. **Keep your audience in mind.** Yes, I know that a moment ago I echoed Peter Elbow's advice about writing with our eyes closed—i.e., writing with our gut and to heck with audience. But keeping an audience in mind can guide your thoughts as you draft, even if your mental concept of audience is vague. (For example, you imagine you're writing to smart people who enjoy a witty pop culture reference but who are skeptical about your main point.) As you think about what would delight or convince that audience, writing flows from that act of empathy. More on this principle in chapter six.

2. **Keep your genre in mind**. If you've studied several examples of the genre you're being asked to write, then you know your options for shaping the writing. How you design your document, organize paragraphs and/or various figures or images, use transitions, make rhetorical moves in your intro or conclusion—all will depend on the kind of document you're producing.

   I can't stress enough this point about genre. If I were writing a standard handbook, I'd tell you specifically, right here and now, how to write an effective introduction, thesis, body paragraph, or conclusion. But different genres call for different shapes of intros, different types of theses, different approaches for conclusions, etc. I hope I'm not shaking your faith in a well-ordered universe by telling you that some genres don't even have a thesis. I want this advice on drafting to be portable for all kinds of writing. If you have absorbed the mindful approach, you'll be mindful of your particular genre as you write.

3. **Divide the big task into smaller tasks**. Straightforwardly: Maybe you begin by writing a thesis or an intro. Then you take each section at a time, until you've written a working conclusion. As you draft, think of the writing task as a series of steps you need to take on the way to a complete draft. You might even want to think of yourself as a *paragraph* drafter. Paragraphs function as unique, hopefully coherent segments of information that break up the reading experience and sequence ideas for your reader. The most popular handbooks suggest different types of paragraphs (like description, compare/contrast, cause and effect, example, and so on). It may help you to think of the drafting process at the level of the paragraph.

4. **Think of drafting as *drafting*.** If you're stuck on the idea that your first draft has to be your best, then it'll be hard for you to want to change anything about that draft. Just convince yourself that you're writing to *discover* what you want to say, not to finalize what to say. Think of your draft as "drafty"; prepare to change what you've written as you come to understand your purpose better. Writer Anne Lamott famously wrote that we're entitled to *really bad* first drafts—though she used more colorful, interesting language to describe this entitlement.

5. **Ignore, as much as you can, sentence-level issues. At least at first**. Novice writers fixate on whether each sentence they write is error-free. There will be plenty of time to work out style and error once you're satisfied with the main point you want to make and the evidence you'll use to make that point. You won't be able to do this very well because your central executive will chime in with monitoring feedback, like an annoying backseat driver. So do your best to write as freely as you can. Shush the backseat driver.

6. **Write every day**. I know I've already said it, but let me say it again. If you write every day, even if it's for just 15 minutes, you'll have more material, more ideas, more text to work with. When you start writing the next day, your brain will have been working, subconsciously, on your writing problem, and you'll pick right up where you left off.

You could set a goal to write for a certain amount of time a day; my friend Joey sets word count goals for himself: 1000 words a day, or something like that.

Your goal in the drafting stage is to finish a draft of your writing complete enough to show someone so you can get feedback on how well you're accomplishing your rhetorical goals.

Feedback

In the third stage of practice, you prepare to receive feedback. Without feedback, we're dead in the water as writers. My eighth-grade English teacher was a gifted gusher. She thought everything we wrote sang with poetic power. I remember writing a rap—yes, a *rap*—about Edgar Allen Poe's "The Tell-Tale Heart," in which I rhymed heart with…well, with something only a thirteen-year old boy would think of. With tears welling up in her eyes, my teacher praised my rap as a masterpiece. But vague praise, no matter how tearful, gets you only so far, or, actually, not far at all. And vague criticism is even worse. A lone C+ at the bottom of an otherwise blank paper doesn't tell you much as a writer except that you've earned a C+, which, depending on the kind of expectations you have, can be either devastating or exhilarating. We need task-specific, timely feedback on our writing during the practice stage so we can make the kind of changes that matter. If you're not getting that, you're not learning how to write.

Once you have a full draft, you're ready for someone to take a look at the whole thing to give you feedback on your rhetorical goals so far. (Again, you'll likely want feedback all the way through the project, even from the planning stage.)

We're lucky to have other people who are willing to give us feedback. Peers and teachers and tutors can help us think about what it's like to read our work. They *dramatize* the audience experience for us and offer us direction for revision. But only if we help them help us.

Sometimes when people find out I teach writing, they will ask me to look at something they've written. "Tell me what you think," they'll say. That could mean, like, a hundred different things. "What do I think about… what?" I'll ask. "The topic? The intro? The way the writing is organized? The cunning double-spacing? The use of the word 'plethora' on page three?" Much of the time, they're just looking for a proofreader, because they assume that's what writing teachers were invented for. What I'm wanting as an inspector is some kind of direction. And your reviewers will want some, too.

Here are a few principles to consider as you prepare to give a teacher or peer a draft to review. Nancy Sommers encourages us to write a "Dear Reader" letter to engage our reviewers in a dialogue about our work (Sommers 12).

1. **Tell them what you're trying to accomplish.** Give them answers to questions like: Why am I writing? Who is my audience, as I imagine them? What am I trying to do, and why?

2. **Give them a brief self-assessment of your draft.** Tell them what you think you're doing well ("I feel like my organization is clear and my transitions are effective...") and where you're most unsatisfied with the draft as it stands ("...but my conclusion is weak—I don't suggest any meaningful implications and my wrap-up seems too obvious, too boring"). This exercise will help you learn whether your assessment of your own work agrees with your readers' assessment of it.

3. **Give them specific tasks as readers.** Give the reviewer some directives, like "Please look at page three where I try to do X" or "Please feel free to cross out any material that you think is redundant," or ask questions like, "How does my organization work for you?" or "Where are you the most confused or bored?" or "Have I sufficiently persuaded my audience of X—why or why not?" or "What's your favorite part of my paper?" Notice how these questions avoid simple yes/no answers. You can also tell them what *not* to pay attention to (e.g., "Ignore the way I've cited the sources; I'm still working on my APA formatting").

When you receive feedback, you'll be tempted to defend your writing decisions if you disagree with the reviewers. It's natural to be defensive about our darling sentences, but it's not really helpful. You don't need to confront your reviewers; it burns goodwill if you look like you can't take criticism of your work. Thank them for their insights, and consider their feedback seriously. We suffer from *myside bias*, which is a condition in which we think we're right about most things because, hey, we're awesome. Just take all the feedback into consideration, knowing that ultimately you are the owner of your own writing and you'll have to depend on your intuition and understanding to get your writing as good as it can be.

One last note on getting feedback: I suggest that you consider planning separate review periods for *rhetorical* issues (relating to audience, purpose, argument, genre, organization—overall effectiveness) and *surface-level* issues (like grammar, usage, punctuation, diction, spelling, mechanics, or document design). Proofreading an unconvincing paper is like painting a car with no engine or wheels. I encourage you to tell your first reviewer(s) to ignore surface-level issues as they read, since you'll likely revise your sentences in the next stage, based on their feedback. Consider asking for feedback in two stages: for macro issues (like genre, argument, support, organization) and then separately for micro issues (like grammar, punctuation, or word choice). Of course sentence-level issues build into the overall effectiveness of the paper; in practice, it's hard to separate the two, and if you have too many errors, your reviewer will have a difficult time providing macro feedback because of all those speed bumps.

As a peer reviewer of other writers' writing, you'll want to follow whatever protocol your instructor gives you. If you don't receive specific instructions for peer review, consider doing some of the following:

1. **Be positive.** Give the writer praise for the things you think he/she did well, and give him/her *specific* praise (with page numbers) describing the strengths you see in the paper.

2. **Use shared criteria.** If your instructor gave you a rubric, use its language to describe what you see in the paper. Use key terms (like argument, organization, evidence).

3. **Be specific.** Avoid vague "good job" or "it could be improved" kind of talk. Be specific about the paper's strengths and weaknesses.

4. **Stay focused on the macro.** It's easy as a reviewer to get caught up in *micro* (sentence-level) issues, like mistakes. Ignore them, assuming that the writer will proofread before publishing. Focus on the rhetorical situation: the genre, audience, and purpose. Is the purpose clear? Is the genre appropriate for the situation? What is the overall feel of the paper?

5. **Ask questions.** Sometimes the best feedback is a good question written in the margins: "Why is this here?" or "Where is the evidence of what you've just said?"

6. **Respond as a reader.** Trust your instincts. You can tell things about the paper based on your own experience reading it. Where did you disengage, get lost or confused, raise an eyebrow in skepticism? Are you convinced by the argument? Did the writer do something powerful with language? Tell them.

Practice: Feeling the Flow

In the practice stage of the writing process, we put our plans into action. We set out to achieve the goals we made for ourselves. My hope is that once you're knee-deep in the drafting process, you'll feel an emotional connection to your work, even if you weren't that excited about it at the start. You'll see the words fill the page and feel a sense of accomplishment, even as you know you'll end up scrapping half of those words. Psychologists talk about how when we're in the "flow" of an activity like writing that's challenging, governed by clear goals, and rich with useful feedback on our performance, we're in an "optimal experience"—the kind that makes time melt away, the kind that brings us joy (Csikszentmihalyi 71). At times, you'll feel this flow as a writer, especially when you write each day, with no other distractions.

Works Cited

Csikszentmihalyi, Mihaly. *Flow: The Psychology of Optimal Experience.* NY: Harper Perennial, 1990. Print.

Duarte, Nancy. *Slide:ology.* Beijing: O'Reilly, 2008. Print.

Elbow, Peter. "Closing My Eyes as I Speak: An Argument for Ignoring Audience." *College English* 49.1 (1987): 50–69. Print.

Hayes, John R. "New Directions in Writing Theory." *Handbook of Writing Research.* Ed. Charles A. MacArthur, Steve Graham, and Jill Fitzgerald. NY: Guilford, 2006. 28–40. Print.

Kellogg, Ronald T. "Training Writing Skills: A Cognitive Developmental Perspective." *Journal of Writing Research* 1.1 (2008): 1–26. Print.

Kellogg, Ronald T. and Alison P. Whiteford. "Training Advanced Writing Skills: The Case for Deliberate Practice." *Educational Psychologist* 44.4 (2009): 250–266. Print.

Kerouac, Jack. "Essentials of Spontaneous Prose." *The Portable Beat Reader.* Ed. Ann Charters. 57–8. Print.

Lamott, Anne. *Bird by Bird.* NY: Anchor, 1995. Print.

Rose, Mike. "Rigid Rules, Inflexible Plans, and the Stifling of Language: A Cognitive Analysis of Writer's Block." *College Composition and Communication* 31.4 (1980): 389–401. Print.

Sommers, Nancy. *Responding to Student Writers.* Boston: Bedford/St. Martin's, 2013. Print.

The third dimension for handling writing tasks (after planning and practice) is *revision*. And it's *painful*.

Well, not necessarily. It's just that because writing is a challenging cognitive task—your central executive working overtime to coordinate planning, finding ideas, forming sentences, monitoring what you've written—we feel like our sweat has been in vain if we have to change what we've put on the page. We become attached to what we've written—so much so that revising feels like we're "murdering our darlings," as nineteenth-century author Arthur Quiller-Couch put it. And yet if we want to improve, we have to be willing to take the wrecking ball to our writing in the service of success. Revision takes courage. Annie Dillard—a writer like you—thinks of writing like a hammer tapping at the walls of a house you're trying to build:

> Some of the walls are bearing walls; they have to stay, or everything will fall down. Other walls can go with impunity; you can hear the difference. Unfortunately, it is often a bearing wall that has to go. It cannot be helped. There is only one solution, which appalls you, but there it is. Knock it out. Duck. (4)

Revision is reseeing. It's also rewriting in the sense that you get a do-over before you publish your work or turn it in or give it to your boss or post it on the Web. As a mindful writer, you'll need effective *task schemata* for revising. A *schema* is a plan or theory about something; *schemata* is the plural. Developing writers have limited task schemata when it comes to revision. After they've written a draft, they focus mostly on "surface features" rather than concepts, making limited changes to "spelling, punctuation, and word choice" (McCutchen, Teske, and Bankston 455). In one study, young adult writers spent most of their revision time proofreading and actually missing many existing errors in the process (Perl). In another study, students understood revision mostly as "a rewording activity" that left the overall shape and meaning of the writing intact (Sommers 381).

Revision, though, should mean more than merely proofreading your paper with a thesaurus in your hand. Skilled writers tend to think beyond the surface: They want to know whether they've been effective rhetorically. Revision is the process by which we evaluate the full force of our writing, top to bottom, as it influences a particular audience. And in that process, sometimes you have to take a sledgehammer to your own work. As Annie Dillard said, "Knock it out. Duck."

Because the writing process is recursive, you'll be revising the second you put a single word on a page, and even before that. You'll brainstorm an idea on scratch paper, and then maybe crumple up that idea and toss it over your shoulder. You'll write a few sentences and then think, "That sounds absolutely idiotic" and erase them. You'll see errors appear in a sentence you're writing, and instead of finishing the sentence you'll stop typing and reach for the mouse and go back and make corrections. You can't help it. While you want to shut off that annoying mental editor in the drafting stage, you also want to remain mindful enough to make adjustments and improvements as you write. When I'm drafting, I'll usually read (sometimes out loud) what I wrote the day before, making changes as I go.

However, in the last chapter I encouraged you to draft as quickly as you can in the practice stage without worrying much about missteps. Let yourself get into a writing groove before your central executive gets too picky, or some of your best ideas might disappear before landing on the page, like a spring snowflake that never makes it to the pavement. In the early stages, let your ideas flow out of you without interruption.

In this chapter, I'm talking about the kinds of changes you make once you've received feedback from instructors, peers, and others.

Approaching Revision

Revision is a second chance—and a third, fourth, fifth—to do your best, most engaging work. Revision, remember, is not really for you; it's for your audience of readers who are ready to engage with your ideas. An audience-centered writer will spend more time revising than a novice writer who may think of revision as nothing more than proofreading. An effective approach to revision will include the following:

1. **Read (or listen to) feedback carefully and respectfully**. Make sure you understand what your reviewers want you to do, and then decide what to pay attention to and what to ignore. Not all the advice you receive will work for your project. Give it all a fair hearing, though—especially the feedback you receive from your instructor. Ignoring instructor feedback tells your teacher, "I know better than

you." Maybe you do, but that's a bold statement to make, and it might damage your *ethos*. (More about *ethos* in chapter nine.) If you receive feedback face to face, repeat the feedback to make sure you understand it, and then jot down notes (preferably on the draft) to remind yourself what needs to change. Some instructors tell writers to say nothing while peer reviewers provide oral feedback; just listen and take notes. Keep yourself open to feedback, always.

2. **Make a *revision plan*.** Now that you've planned and practiced and received feedback, you may find your plans need to change. Your revision plan may include revised product and self-regulating goals based on the feedback you receive. Your instructor might even ask you to write a revision plan and share it.

Revision Strategies

You'll want to respond to the feedback you got from peers and instructors. As you develop a revision routine that works for you, consider the following possible strategies:

1. Use the "**track changes**" option in your word processor, so you can keep track of the revisions you make and review them when you're done.

2. Ask yourself the "**big picture" questions** first: How effectively have I achieved my purpose or answered the needs of the assignment? Is my purpose or main point clear to my audience? Have I used the genre effectively, considering the rhetorical situation and purpose? How will an audience experience my writing as a journey through an idea? Do I sound like a reasonable person—the kind of person who has authority, intelligence, balance, and goodwill? How do I keep my readers emotionally engaged with my work? How have I used my introduction to captivate and excite my audience? How does my conclusion answer the question, "So what?" Have I used enough evidence to support my main point? Your answers to these questions will guide revision decisions, from top to bottom.

3. Once you've settled on the big picture, look at **paragraphs**: Do they flow together well enough? Do they each develop one main point expressed in a topic sentence? Do they have internal coherence (in other words, do the first and final sentences connect, showing some kind of development)? Do the sentences lead into each other? Could

any of the longer paragraphs be broken apart and developed more effectively? Are they arranged in a way that makes sense, or could I rearrange them? I've found it helpful from time to time to print out what I'm writing and cut up my paper into paragraphs so I can look at them separately; you could also give the separated paragraphs to a friend and ask him or her to put the whole essay together using the first sentence of each paragraph as guides. (I notice many of my students draft with the double-spacing enabled from the beginning, maybe so they can feel like they're filling the page faster. I like to keep everything single-spaced so I can read the paragraphs more effectively as single units.)

4. **Add new material**, if necessary, **or cut.** You may sense that some of your writing is underdeveloped. Maybe you have a particularly weak paragraph or an argument that could use some support. Maybe you need more examples to make your case. Perhaps adding an image or table would be appropriate for the genre you're writing in. On the other hand, maybe you sense that you're boring your audience with too many details. Your sentences might be too long or too choked with clauses. You may find that some of what you've previously written seems irrelevant. Highlight, delete. Duck.

5. Review **sentences for style**. Read each sentence out loud to see how the words play in the open air. Use principles from chapters ten and eleven on style to help you refine your sentences. And, of course, remember that your style will be influenced by your audience and purpose. Ask yourself: Do my sentences come in a variety of lengths? Do I write mostly in active voice, with clear subjects and verbs? Do I avoid starting too many sentences with the same grammatical constructions? Is there an interesting person behind those words—in other words, can my readers *hear* a human voice? Have I been, at times, *bold*? Are my key terms defined well enough?

6. Once you're satisfied with the way your sentences sound, then you can move into **editing and proofreading.** Read each sentence carefully, with a handbook at your elbow in case a rule is unclear. Have someone else look at it, too (like a Writing Center tutor or a trusted friend). Check to see if you've followed the conventions and document design principles your instructor wants you to follow for the assignment. If you didn't receive document design requirements, then make some design decisions that will make your work distinct. At this

point, you're doing the down-in-the-grass detail work because you want to project the best, most convincing self you can in the writing.

If writing is like problem-solving, then the best problem-solvers will try new strategies in their writing if they learn that what they tried first didn't work well. Bad writers—and I include here writers who think they're so amazing they don't need to change anything—will stick with what they're doing, even if it's not working (Ambrose et al. 199). I'm inviting you here to be flexible enough in your writing process to develop some good task schemata for revision—the kind that knock down walls and kill darlings, if necessary.

We've now covered three of the four steps for handling writing tasks—plan, practice, revise. The fourth step—reflect—we'll talk about in the next chapter.

Appendix to Chapter Six: A Revision Checklist

The following checklist will help you gauge how willing you've been to revise your work to make it better. We know that revision is genre-based—you revise, as you write, in a particular situation for a particular reading audience. However, most of the following statements could be used for any writing project you do. Don't feel bad if you can't check off all these statements for every paper; you may decide to *scaffold* your revision, as we suggested in this chapter, by looking first at rhetorical situation and then, in the home stretch, flow and style and other editing matters.

Review

I have used an effective writing process that includes goal-setting.

I have been willing to cut, rewrite, and rework my writing so I can *re-see*.

I have saved editing and proofreading till the end (as much as I can).

I have read my writing out loud.

I have revised the sentences that don't sound good to my ear.

I have proofread it—closely, in hard copy if necessary.

I have asked peers, the Writing Center, and my instructor for feedback.

I have incorporated their feedback through multiple drafts.

I have consulted a handbook or reliable online source to understand conventions.

I have done my best—or, the best I could do within the time constraints.

Rhetorical Situation

I have written in the genre appropriate for the rhetorical situation.

I have studied a variety of examples of the genre.

I considered my audience carefully—their needs, their values, their time.

My purpose is clear.

I have used the conventions my instructor expects.

I establish my credibility by showing I understand the topic (i.e., I've done my research).

I establish my goodwill with my audience.

I treat rhetorical adversaries fairly.

I present alternative opinions with fidelity.

I have shown balance by anticipating and respecting alternative viewpoints.

I considered the assumptions I'm making.

I have provided sufficient credible evidence to support my point.

I make emotional appeals fitting for the situation.

I have tried to give readers a good reading experience.

Flow

In my introduction, I capture my readers' attention.

My introduction is relevant, specific, and compelling.

When appropriate, I forecast the organization of the rest of the paper.

I transition between paragraphs using signals/transitional words.

My paragraphs develop single ideas.

My paragraphs roll out in a sequence that makes sense.

I use cohesive strategies (like transitional phrases) to connect sentences together.

My conclusion does not merely reiterate the introduction.

My conclusion ties together the writing and gives readers something to think about.

I have checked for topics/ideas that don't apply to my main thesis and taken them out.

I have checked my paper for balance. I don't spend too much time on trivial information.

My tone is consistent.

Style

I used an editing/proofreading process *only after* I wrote a rough draft.

My sentence types vary—I use openers, interruptors, and closers.

My sentence lengths vary.

I've considered carefully my word choice.

I've cut back all the dead wood, the wordiness.

I use concrete words.

I use powerful words for imagery or compelling connotations.

I avoid sexist or demeaning language.

I avoid cliches.

I use "to be" verbs sparingly and purposefully.

I write in active voice most of the time, with clear subjects and verbs.

My sentence fragments are intentional.

I've read my paper out loud and revised for rhythm, flow, voice, and mood.

I use metaphors to argue, delight.

I use rhetorical schemes (like balance or repetition).

I use commas purposefully (as in, I understand where to put them).

I use other punctuation appropriately, and for variety and emphasis.

Formatting

I have given my writing a *catchy* and *descriptive* title that will draw in readers.

I have proofread my paper! Get off my case now!

My paper is in the documentation style (like MLA or Turabian) the genre demands.

My sources are cited appropriately (for the documentation style).

If I cite sources, I have a works cited page in the proper format.

I summarize sources in my own language.

I use block quotes sparingly, if at all, and I contextualize them.

My sources are cited ethically (to distinguish my writing from the writing of others).

I have consciously selected a font and format to maximize my rhetorical effect.

06

Works Cited

Ambrose, Susan A. et al. *How Learning Works: Seven Research-Based Principles for Smart Teaching*. San Francisco: Jossey-Bass, 2010. Print.

Dillard, Annie. *The Writing Life*. NY: Harper Perenniel, 1989. Print.

McCutchen, Deborah, Paul Teske, and Catherine Bankston. "Writing and Cognition: Implications of the Cognitive Architecture for Learning to Write and Writing to Learn." *Handbook of Research on Writing*. Ed. Charles Bazerman. NY: Lawrence Erlbaum, 2008. 452–470. Print.

Perl, Sondra. "The Composing Processes of Unskilled College Writers." *Research in the Teaching of English* 13.4 (1979): 317–336. Print.

Sommers, Nancy. "Revision Strategies of Student Writers and Experienced Adult Writers." *CCC* 31.4 (1980): 378–388. Print.

The Stories We Tell Ourselves

When I was in sixth grade, tragedy struck. No, I'm not talking about the one time I defended Tawni Bell's honor and got the tar beaten out of me by Ben Eason. I'm talking about math.

I was never not good at math. That's my double-negative way of saying that I did OK in math but never thought of myself as a "Math Person." But in sixth grade, I started falling behind. Long division and percentages did me in. Mr. Meldrum would toss a worksheet on my desk, and I'd stare at it, my gut sinking to the floor with the weight of woe. My friend Jeremy, who sat next to me, would race through his worksheet with dizzying speed, while I sat there, frozen, my pencil hovering over the numbers, wondering why my brain had stopped working.

Mr. Meldrum noticed my slide and sent me down the hall to Ms. Dawn's fifth-grade class for math. I'd been demoted. When that happened, I injected a little poison into my brain by telling myself, *I'm not good at math.*

It amazes me how utterly convincing that sentence was. It rang so true to me at the time that it took on the power of an identity: Brian Jackson—*not* a Math Person! It did not occur to me to tell myself alternative statements that might have been equally convincing, like *Looks like you'll need to work a little harder,* or *I'm not getting percentages—maybe Jeremy can explain the concept to me,* or *Math is hard for me, but I like trying hard things.*

In other words, I had no metacognitive tools to help me work through my math difficulties. I told myself one thing, believed it, and never questioned the validity of it until many years later, well after high school, when I took an exam—the Graduate Record Examination (GRE)—that included math problems.

The first time I took the GRE, I scored somewhere close to the 25th percentile on the math portion. (That means 75% of test-takers scored higher than me.) My low score didn't surprise me—after all, I was not a Math Person—and since my graduate program in English didn't care how well I did on the math part, I didn't either. However, two years later when I took it again for a new graduate program, I decided to study the math stuff out of pure vanity; I didn't want a low score again, even if the schools I applied to ignored the scores. I studied the math, and when I scored in the 65th percentile (not great, but mathematically above average), I had a new thought jump into my brain, revising the old thought I had in sixth grade, the toxic thought that told me I wasn't good at math: *I can do math if I study.*

It wasn't until later that I discovered the cognitive science behind my struggle with math. It turns out that none of us sees the world as objectively as we think. Rather, we see it through *interpretation*, through the way we perceive events and make sense of them to ourselves. University of Virginia psychologist Timothy Wilson explains this process with the word *narrative*: We tell ourselves stories about ourselves, our abilities, our relationships, our world. These stories become "*core narratives*" that influence our behavior, helping us overcome adversity and find happiness in the challenges of life (Wilson 9). Our core narratives can hurt us, too.

As I've said before, improving your writing is a challenge. It takes motor control, substantial cognitive effort, and our best creativity to connect with people and influence their attitudes, judgment, and behavior. Our ability to take control of the available means of persuasion is influenced by the way we understand ourselves as writers. Our core narratives influence our writing identities, and those identities influence our writing performance.

Luckily, our core narratives can be *revised*, just like a college essay. Dr. Wilson calls this process "*story-editing*," which he describes as "a set of techniques designed to redirect people's narratives about themselves and the social world in a way that leads to lasting changes in behavior" (11). Story-editing happens through reflective writing. In fact—and I was amazed when I read about this—scientific studies prove that reflective writing helps sufferers of post-traumatic stress disorder, personal tragedy, anxiety, depression, racial prejudice, failure in school, struggling marriages, unhealthy pessimism, low self-esteem, and criminal tendencies (see Bolton; Kost-Smith et al.; Pennebaker; Wilson). Writing is, indeed, a powerful source for good in the world.

This chapter is meant to help you shape a core narrative about your identity as a writer. Remember that *reflection* is the fourth stage of our model for taking on writing tasks (see chapter two). Reflection is the process by which we think about what we're doing, why we're doing it, and how we're doing; reflective writing is the process by which we put those thoughts in writing in a personal, informal style (Yancey 6).

Reflective writing is the ultimate act of *mindfulness*. When we write about our goals, processes, successes, and failures, we "open a conversation" with ourselves, as Ken Bain writes in *What the Best College Students Do*. We learn about the "power of our own paradigms"—the mental frames of reference that shape our experience (Bain 67, 71). We can sort of jump outside our bodies and view our own rhetorical situations with a higher degree of awareness.

Reflective writing strengthens your *self-efficacy* as a writer. Reflection builds confidence; confidence strengthens our writing. Self-efficacy is the term writing experts use to describe how we think about our abilities as writers—our competencies, our weaknesses, our willingness to try hard things, our goals, our sense that the writing we do has value (Bandura). The higher the self-efficacy, the higher the writing proficiency. Writing students with high self-efficacy work harder, persist when the going gets tough, and bounce back more quickly when they fail (Pajares and Valiante). They're also more eager to write and rewrite. Reflective writing helps you assess situations, set goals (both product and self-regulating), and practice with the confidence that you'll succeed as a writer if you write consistently and seek help. Reflective writing helps you balance between the confidence you need to write well and the humility you need to learn new skills. (Yes, *overconfidence* is a debilitating core narrative. I've taught many students who think of first-year writing as a remedial class they don't need. Low grades convince them that they do.)

Finally, reflective writing helps you take control of your own learning, becoming a *self-directed learner*. When I started struggling with math in sixth grade, I let the system wash me down the hall to an easier math class. I had no sense that I could take charge of my own fate, that I could, in fact, become a Math Person if I wanted to. Self-directed learners control their own learning (Ambrose 188–216). Self-direction is the engine of our four-part writing task model (plan, practice, revise, reflect). As Timothy Wilson writes, "it helps to view ourselves as strong protagonists who set our own goals and make progress toward them" (51). We become that personal hero through reflective writing.

The Art of Reflection

So: How do we do it? Your instructor will have some guidelines. I have a few suggestions, too. I've found it helpful to think of reflective writing like Kathi Yancey does in *Reflection in the Writing Classroom*: the art of *projecting* on future tasks and *reviewing* what has been accomplished already. I want you to think of reflection not simply as an afterthought to the writing process—a 200-word busywork thing you dash off after finishing your final draft—but as integral to the entire process. You want reflective writing to catch you in the act of thinking, like you'd catch a bird in flight with a really good camera.

Below you'll find questions you might answer with reflective writing to project and review. You'll recognize some of these questions from chapter two on writing plans and processes.

Projecting

1. **Assignment questions**: What does my instructor want me to do? What key words from the assignment sheet do I need to understand to be successful? What due dates do I need to be aware of? What technology will I be required to use as I write? What kind of reading will I need to get done? How will my writing be evaluated?

2. **Rhetorical situation**: Who is my audience? How *specific* is my audience, based on the writing prompt? What do I know about the values, needs, or attitudes of my audience? What is the exigence and *kairos* for writing? What is my purpose for writing? What rhetorical strategies will be most effective in this situation?

3. **Genre**: What is the genre I'm being asked to write? Is it a specific genre familiar to a specific discourse community? How will I collect and analyze examples of this genre? What moves do I need to make? What do readers of this genre expect? How do audiences, readers, or communities use this kind of writing? Which conventions must I follow? What kind of style is appropriate? How much freedom do I have to innovate? How do I need to format or arrange my writing for this genre? What purpose does this genre serve for the audience for which it's intended?

4. **Prior experience**: What kind of writer am I? How is this writing like writing I've done in the past? What can I use from previous writing experiences to help me with this one? How is it *not* like previous writing tasks? How much do I already know about this topic? How familiar am I with this genre? How has my writing process in the past helped or hurt my success?

5. **Ability**: How confident do I feel about tackling *this specific* writing task? What do I need to do to get more confident? What are my

strengths or weaknesses as a writer? Who can help me along the way? If I'm already confident in my abilities, what will I do to prepare to receive feedback that might tell me I've got more to learn?

6. **Personal value**: What do I want to get out of this assignment? What will this writing teach me how to do that will be valuable to me? How will I use this writing task to improve? Why am I interested in this topic? How can I get interested in this topic?

7. **Product goals**: After looking at examples of this genre, what specific rhetorical strategies will I use in my own writing? How will I imitate examples of the genre I've studied? How will I add my own creativity, my own voice? How will I use strategies explicitly stated in the rubric for this assignment?

8. **Self-regulating goals**: Where am I going to write? When will I write, and for how long? How will I minimize distractions when writing in digital spaces? How will I reward myself for getting the writing done? Who will I talk to about my task? Who will I show drafts to? How and when will I use my instructor, peers, or the Writing Center as reviewers of my work?

Reviewing

(For after you've written a draft or completed a writing task.)

1. **Goals**: How did I do with the goals I set as a writer? Why didn't I achieve my goals? Which goals were most useful to me? Which didn't really help?

2. **Rhetorical decisions**: Why did I make the rhetorical decisions I did? What in my writing demonstrates my awareness of audience? To what extent have I achieved my purposes for writing? Why did I pick the rhetorical strategies I did? How did I use genre effectively or ineffectively?

3. **Quality**: Where in the writing do I feel most confident? Where am I weakest? What would I change if I had more time? If I had a rubric for this assignment, how would I rate my writing with the rubric? What am I most proud of? Where in the writing do I feel I'm most engaging, interesting, clever?

4. **Writing processes**: What writing process did I use to write this? How well did it work for me? What needs to change, moving forward? What

invention strategies did I use, and how well did they serve me? How useful to me were my peer reviewers or instructor feedback? How could I better prepare my reviewers in the future? How thoroughly did I revise this work based on the feedback I received? How carefully did I proofread and edit my draft when completed?

5. **What I learned**: What did I learn from this writing task? What was the hardest part? What's something new I'm taking away from it? What part of the process interested me the most? What is my *theory* of writing now? What did my instructor do to help me learn?

6. **How I'll apply what I learned**: How will I apply what I learned from this writing task to future writing tasks (in my major, for example, or in the workplace)? What in my planning, practicing, or revising needs to change next time I write? What new goals will I want to set?

I hope you're convinced now that being an effective writer means much more than just sitting down and writing the first thing that comes to mind the day before the writing is due. Mindful writers plan, practice, revise, and reflect. They relish the process. Reflective writing will help you grow mindful as a writer, develop self-efficacy, and take control of your own learning.

I'm so glad I decided to study the math portion of the GRE the second time around. Studying made me realize that if I put some time into it, I could figure it out enough to at least not embarrass myself. Now that I have kids struggling with math, I've learned how to help them write a different core narrative about themselves—one that depends on what Carol Dweck calls the "growth mindset." I learned that math ability, like writing ability, is not something DNA does or does not hand down to me. Maybe Jeremy was better than me at math, but that didn't mean I couldn't be a Math Person. I hope reflective writing helps you develop that core narrative about your writing identity so that you think of yourself as a *writer*.

Works Cited

Ambrose, Susan A. *How Learning Works: Seven Research-Based Principles for Smart Teaching*. San Francisco: Jossey-Bass, 2010. Print.

Bandura, Albert. "Self-Efficacy: Toward a Unifying Theory of Behavioral Change." *Psychological Review* 84 (1977): 191–215. Print.

Bolton, Gillie, ed. *Writing Cures: An Introductory Handbook of Writing in Counseling and Therapy*. London: Routledge, 2004. Print.

Dweck, Carol. *Mindset*. NY: Ballantine, 2006. Print.

Kost-Smith, Lauren E. et al. "Gender Differences in Physics I: The Impact of Self-Affirmation Intervention." *AIP Proceedings* 197 (2010). Web. 10 March 2015.

Pajares, Frank and Gio Valiante. "Self-Efficacy Beliefs and Motivation in Writing Development." *Handbook of Writing Research*. Ed. Charles A. MacArthur, Steve Graham, and Jill Fitzgerald. NY: Guilford, 2006. 158–170. Print.

Pennebaker, J. W. *Writing to Heal: A Guided Journal for Recovering from Trauma and Emotional Upheaval*. Oakland, CA: New Harbinger Publications, 1997. Print.

Wilson, Timothy D. *Redirect*. NY: Back Bay, 2011. Print.

Yancey, Kathleen Blake. *Reflection in the Writing Classroom*. Logan, UT: Utah State UP, 1998. Print.

PART 3

ARGUMENT

Rhetorical Decisions Matter

In chapter 2, I told you about a friend of mine who was called by the military to serve in Iraq before he completed his schooling to become an army chaplain. I sort of left the story hanging there, so let me finish it. My friend decided to write the required petition letter asking the Army to defer his tour of duty so he could finish his degree. He sat down at the computer, like you yourself have done many times, and, like a good soldier, he *strategized*. With each sentence, he made rhetorical decisions that he thought would best help him influence his audience (i.e., change their judgment about the timing of his tour of duty). Maybe he wondered if he should play the sympathy card: *My family will suffer if I don't finish this degree!* Or perhaps he thought of appealing to the Army's self-interest: *Let me wait, and I'll be a more experienced and credentialed chaplain.* He probably chose his words and evidence carefully, proofreading his finished letter with precision so he wouldn't look sloppy.

Whatever he did, it worked. The Army granted his petition, and he completed his Master of Divinity and became a full-fledged chaplain when he deployed to Iraq months later.

This anecdote illustrates a great truth about rhetoric: Rhetorical decisions matter. They make a difference in the world. Rhetorical strategies open doors, soften hearts, change attitudes, loosen up funds, provoke minds, secure justice or mercy, entertain the bored, inform the ignorant, convince the skeptical, energize the faithful. Or, they don't. It's up to you.

In this book we discuss a variety of rhetorical strategies you'll want to consider when an exigence calls you to action. While there are many situations in which deliberate rhetorical thought is not required (at lunch with a best friend, perhaps), most opportunities to speak and write are opportunities to choose strategies mindfully that help you achieve your goals and make the world better.

Yes, I just said that rhetorical strategies make the world better. I can't help myself. Too many people believe that rhetoric is a tool for Voldemort-like evil. When graduate student Shannon Soper and I studied English corpora (a *corpus* is a collection of texts; *corpora* is the plural), we noticed that at least 75% of the time, the word *rhetoric* means unethical speech that is weak, false, or inflammatory. I call this the "rhetoric-as-poison" perspective, and I don't really know how rhetoric changed in popular usage from a powerful tool for communicators to a weapon of mass deception. When politicians talk about an opponent's "rhetoric," it's not a compliment.

But now you know better. And now you can help me spread the word. For starters, every intelligent person should understand that they use rhetoric all the time, and not just when they're being sneaky. Earlier I said that rhetoric is like dance in some ways—it's a universal human activity you find in nearly every culture, and it can be used for any purpose, good or ill. A few classical rhetoricians even argued that when you study rhetoric, you necessarily study how to be a good person and use rhetorical strategies for good in the world. (The missing *Avenger* superhero is Captain Rhetorician.) The Greek rhetorician Isocrates (436–338 BCE), for instance, believed that by practicing rhetoric, we "cultivate intellectual and moral character" based on "the values of the good and useful citizen" (Walker 121). Whether or not that's *necessarily* the outcome of studying rhetoric, it's certainly empowering to think of ourselves as moral agents learning to use strategies that will promote virtue and happiness.

What is needed the most, said the Roman statesman Cato (234–149 BCE), is the good person skilled in speaking (*Vir bonus, dicendi peritus*). That's you: Captain Rhetorician, defender of truth and justice.

Anyway, the strategies we'll talk about in the next few chapters represent centuries of experience with rhetorical influence. I'm not just making them up or passing along fossilized rules that worked for some tunic-wearing Greek guy 2500 years ago. The Roman orator Cicero (106–43 BCE)—perhaps the most famous rhetorician of all time—explained in his dialogue *On the Ideal Orator* that strategies find their way into textbooks like this one because "certain people have observed and collected the practices that eloquent men [and women] followed of their own accord. Thus, eloquence is not the offspring of art, but art of eloquence" (Cicero 90). In other words, the strategies I present in this book are tried-and-true influence strategies that come from actual practice. They're *useful*, in all kinds of settings. You'll find these strategies celebrated across cultures and disciplines. Modern science supports them as well. (Check out Robert Cialdini's book *Influence*, for example.)

Can you think of a more important subject to study, or art to master?

Selecting Appropriate Strategies

So, which strategies do we use—and when, and why?

Repeat after me: It depends on the rhetorical situation (your audience, purpose, exigence, etc.). My man Aristotle (384–322 BCE) defined rhetoric as "an ability in each particular case, to see the available means of persuasion" (37). Your means of persuasion are dizzyingly vast; even a font type speaks to your audience. If you want rhetorical vertigo, visit Gideon Burton's website *The Forest of Rhetoric* (rhetoric.byu.edu) where you can choose from hundreds of cool rhetorical moves to master.

Your instructor can walk you through this forest of rhetoric some time. In this text, I'm going to share with you the four *Biggies*; when you enter any new rhetorical situation, you'll want to **pull out your ACES:**

Argument

Character

Emotions

Style

Okay, acronyms are corny, and mostly forgettable. But let's give this one a go anyway. We'll spend some time on all four of these strategies because they're so useful. Anytime you sit down to solve a writing task, you'll want to have these strategies at your command. And: ACES will help you understand how other people use rhetoric as well.

The first three—the ACE of ACES—correspond to what you may know as *logos, ethos,* and *pathos.* These Greek terms come to us from Aristotle's *On Rhetoric*, a series of lectures he gave at the Lyceum, his school in fourth-century BCE Athens. In *On Rhetoric*, Aristotle argues that we're most persuaded "when we suppose something to have been demonstrated" (33). And how do we demonstrate something to the satisfaction of others? By using artful strategies (*pisteis* in Greek, meaning something like "proofs"—the "means of persuasion"): Logos (could mean reason, logic, or a governing principle—here we're calling it argument), ethos (character), and pathos (emotion) are, for Aristotle, the fundamental strategies of persuasion, and you should learn how to use all three to your rhetorical advantage in writing and speaking.

The rest of this chapter is about *argument*, the first of our ACES. (I actually recommend not using the term logos because students often confuse it with logic—another term I don't recommend we use because of its quasi-mathematical connotations—or facts.) Then we'll spend one chapter on character and emotions, and two on style. In some ways these four rhetorical strategies are *generic*, meaning that they teach you broad principles you can apply in any setting. However, we must always remember that rhetorical situations create their own ecologies for persuasion. While Aristotle's pisteis can be deployed in some fashion in most situations, the way they're applied is situation-specific, contingent on exigence, kairos, rhetor, purpose, genre, and audience.

Argument

The word **argument** has negative connotations. Say the word out loud—what's your first impression? An uncomfortable disagreement, maybe. Fighting? Political adversaries on the streets with forehead veins pulsing? A domestic disturbance? If you write "argument" in Google Images, most of the pictures you'll see are of people getting in each other's faces, shouting at each other with their teeth clenched, spit flying, eyeballs almost popping out.

Well, that's one definition. We're going to focus on another, more useful definition.

The word itself comes from from the Latin word *arguo*, meaning "to prove or demonstrate"; related is the Latin *arguere*, which means something like "to make clear." Those words suggest that an argument is a kind of test in which language is used to clarify, prove, or assert something. An argument, then, can be a *process* through which this happens. Two people can *have an argument*: They can go back and forth trying to test out the strength of an idea. Think of it as an intellectual process.

In a female dorm room, for example.

Let's set the stage:

It's late on a Sunday night. Three roommates in for the night. Homework's completed. Television comedy streaming on a laptop open on a coffee table, and everyone's huddled under blankets on a couch.

Roommate 1: Last night my sister set me up on a blind date with this loser who just plays video games all day.

Roommate 2: Is he cute?

Roommate 1: What does it matter if he's cute? All he wants to do with his spare time is play Xbox!

Roommate 3: What's wrong with playing Xbox?

Roommate 2: Wait—you didn't answer me. Is he hot?

Roommate 1: I did answer you. Hotness doesn't matter if all he's interested in is playing Call of Duty on his Xbox with his roomies. I'm not interested in someone who can't talk about anything except one thing that I don't care about.

Roommate 3: Well, if all he wanted to do was play basketball, would you be interested then? Or do you want your dates to be, like, always going to art galleries or museums or something?

Roommate 2: If he was hot, you wouldn't care if he Xbox'd, so he's obviously not hot.

Roommate 1: Are you kidding me? He *is* hot—*really* hot actually—and *no*, I don't expect my dates to "like" go to art galleries all the time! I just want to date a guy with more than one interest and definitely more interests than video games! That's so one-dimensional!

A million arguments like this one happen all around us, all the time. We dismiss them as the flatulence of culture—the crackling social static, the dorm room back-and-forth, the sports bar jabber, the comment thread flame-outs, the playground throw-backs, the white noise of modern life. It's easy to dismiss if you think of it as meaningless chatter, but take a closer look at our script and you'll see some interesting intellectual gymnastics going on in this argument. Gerald Graff would call it "hidden intellectualism" (214)—it's an argument, and it takes critical thinking to have one.

An argument is an intellectual process, as we said. Having an argument is an act of critical thinking because critical thinking means taking propositions (i.e., statements that represent some kind of judgment) and testing whether or not we should accept them. American philosopher John Dewey (no, not the Dewey decimal guy) thought of critical thinking as "active, persistent, and careful consideration of any belief or supposed form of knowledge in the light of the grounds that support it, and the further conclusions to which it tends" (Dewey). Science grows from this kind of thinking. "Why does an apple accelerate as it falls from a tree?" wonders Isaac Newton. And he figures out why. "Why do I have a curfew?" asks my thirteen-year-old son Ben at the dinner table one night. "None of my friends have one!" My wife Amy's eyebrow goes up. "*None?*" she asks. "Not a single one of your many friends has a curfew?" See, she's testing a proposition through argument.

An argument is also a *thing*, a product. One of the most popular rhetorical strategies in the universe has a simple anatomy: make a point and support it with some kind of evidence. We call this an argument, too.

Let's walk through an example.

One time I was at the Monterey Bay Aquarium, in California, and saw this sign on a paper towel dispenser in the bathroom:

PAPER TOWELS = TREES

Mysterious! That's bizarre math. Paper towels equal trees? What do you think I was being told? I'm thinking the sign was a gentle reminder that paper towels come from a natural resource (trees, dude!) that human beings generally want to protect and conserve.

So the sign was giving me an argument: A point (*You should not use more paper towels than you need…*) with supporting evidence (*…because paper towels come from a natural resource*).

We'll call these two parts the **claim** (the point) and the **reason** (the support).

But there's a third part. Notice that the *strength* of the argument depends on an unspoken something that passes between me and the aquarium people as I stand there, hands dripping, reading the sign. They *assume* that I'm on board with the idea that we should conserve our natural resources to the point where I'm willing to use fewer paper towels when drying my hands in a public restroom. They don't need to say that because that part of the argument is built into the air, like electricity. They assume I accept the reason as valid evidence to support the "further conclusion to which it tends," in Dewey's words.

(Some folks want to separate reasons from evidence because they assume evidence means something like *fact*. Since facts can be presented as reasons for claims, I call *reasons* anything used as the supporting "stuff" of a claim.)

Now we have three parts to our argument anatomy: **claim, reason,** and **assumption.** We'll have more to say about assumptions later, and while they often go unspoken, as they do in the paper towels example, they are essential to our discussion because they're what make arguments *rhetorical*. An argument, of course, is audience-based. We provide reasons we hope an audience accepts. When I say to you, *Take my umbrella because it's raining outside*, I'm assuming you're the kind of person who doesn't like to get wet. I'm assuming you're like me in that respect, and I don't need to add, *and I assume you're like me and you don't like to get wet unless you want to*. And if I say to you, *I don't want to date guys whose only real interest is video games because they're so one-dimensional*, I'm assuming you accept the idea that being one-dimensional is a bad thing. (Is it? Always?)

So, an argument is an assertion—a claim—that is accompanied by an attempt to prove or support the claim—the reason (Arg = C + R). When a parent asks a teenager why she is coming home late and she says, "I lost track of time," she is providing an argument: I am late (the *claim*) because I lost track of time (the *reason*). From the parent's perspective, it's a lame argument (the assumption = losing track of time is a legitimate reason for being late), but it has the essential elements of our definition of argument: a claim supported by a reason to accept the claim.

To understand how arguments work as rhetorical strategy, we need to understand the relationship between claims, reasons, and assumptions.

I once overheard a female student talking on the phone about a romantic movie she had seen the night before called *The Vow*. It was clear by her tortured voice that she had been disappointed by the movie. She even said as much: "I was so looking forward to it, and it was just really disappointing!" Had she made an argument? Nope. Not yet, at least. All I had heard so far was a claim: *The Vow* is disappointing. We have a C, but no R.

Any time you hear a claim dangling out there, you can ask, *Why?* or *So what?* Global warming is a myth. *Why?* Global warming is real, and manmade. *So what?* You should clip your toenails. Textbooks are too expensive. Prostitution is wrong. Video games make you smart. Gluten-free diets. Apple products. Viral cat videos. College tuition. CIA torture memos. Texting while driving. Police and racism. *Why? Why? Why?* An argument just ain't an argument without a reason. To paraphrase the female vocalist Pink, just give me a reason—just a claim is not enough...to call something an argument.

So this student's claim that *The Vow* was a disappointing movie was *not* an argument—until she provided a reason. Which was this: "The ending was so bad! It totally didn't resolve anything and just kinda left you hanging." The *reason* completes the argument. It invites us—the audience—to accept or reject the claim and agree with the arguer. Is it a *good* reason?

What do you think?

There is power in argument. In fact, there is scientific evidence that arguing is a healthy trait we humans have developed to help us deal with the truckload of information dumped on us each day. We use arguments to justify who we are and what we do. We come up with claims and reasons to support our decisions and encourage others to see things our way. We analyze arguments that challenge our beliefs, values, or well-being. Recently in the journal *Behavioral and Brain Sciences*, Hugo Mercier and Dan Sperber argued that argument is central to the way we think. In fact, they *argue*—fittingly!—that the primary function of thinking itself is to produce and analyze arguments to defend our behavior. Apparently, argument comes as natural to us as sleeping.

One last note on the idea of argument before we move on. It has no doubt occurred to you that argument is central to rhetoric—the art of persuasion and social cooperation. It is also central, as rhetoric itself is, to democratic life. Democracy depends on the judgment of the citizens. It's a scary thought, I know, but we're all we've got. And we cannot exercise good judgment to make good decisions about life if we do not hear arguments—not only good ones, but bad ones as well—about what we should be doing and why we should be doing it. All the crucial political questions that almost flummox us and grind the gears of government to a halt—like *What should we do about the nation's uninsured? What if an enemy of state produces a nuclear weapon? How should the wealthy be taxed? How do we improve the schools? How do we get more people into college? How much should the Internet be regulated? What do we want from our media?*—need answers, and those answers take the form of arguments: claims, supported by reasons, backed by assumptions.

Finding Claims

In the course of your life, you will be asked to make arguments about this and that. Sometimes you'll have to make an argument in the spur of the moment without much preparation. One time while my wife and I were on a walk, she told me she wanted to replace the windows on the house, and she asked me what I thought about it. She might as well have asked me what I thought about carbon nanotubes or gluten-free diets or Sumerian architecture or anything else I had spent exactly zero minutes thinking about. Any argument I could make in that moment would be on the fly, without any analytical thought or research. We all have to make such arguments from time to time, and it's a bummer because sometimes we sound uninformed when we do.

In writing classes, you have the luxury of crafting your arguments in advance by going through a rigorous writing process involving *rhetorical invention*, which we talked about in chapter three.

How does one *invent* arguments? You've learned about rhetorical situations already. The kinds of arguments you make will depend on the rhetorical situation you find yourself in and the genre the situation demands. (And, yes, some rhetorical situations don't call for *arguments*. They might call for genres that inform—like a brochure on an illness at the doctor's office—or delight—like a good slasher movie. There's a textbook called *Everything's an Argument*. Do you think that's true?)

Once you feel like you understand your situation, you're ready to go looking for an argument that you hope will be suitable for your audience and purpose.

So let's assume you have a sense of your audience, and you understand your purpose and topic. One way to invent claims is to think about them as answers to questions—very big questions, in fact.

Questions like:

- What exists? And what kind of *stuff* is it made of?

- What is good?

- What should we do?

I'm willing to bet that almost every claim you hear is going to fall into one of these three categories, so they can be useful to know. Let's give them specific names and flesh them out a bit.

What exists? And what kind of *stuff* is it made of? Let's call this kind of claim a *substance* claim. Substance claims make claims about the nature of reality, about facts, about the status of things, about history and events, about definitions and essences. If I make the claim that humans cause climate change by burning fossil fuels, I'm making a substance claim. If I argue that political campaign contributions are "free speech," that's a substance claim, too (definitions are about substance or essence). If I claim that bicycle riders on campus pose a danger to other students, or that baseball is a religion, or that no cinnamon gum lasts longer than Big Red, or that it is impossible to balance the national budget without raising taxes, or that the public schools are in crisis, then I'm making a substance claim.

What is good? This kind of claim is a *value* claim. Value claims are statements about what is good or bad, right or wrong, ought or ought not, moral or immoral, effective or ineffective, best or worst, righteous or wicked, dumb or smart, cool or lame, ethical or otherwise. It's wrong to eat animals for any reason, says a value claim. And a value claim answers right back: Eating beef is a good old-fashioned American tradition! A value claim calls a movie—like *The Vow*—disappointing, or an action—like downloading copyrighted music outside legal channels—immoral. This candidate is better than that one. Vampires are not as cool as werewolves. It's justifiable to start a war if there's a credible threat. The cost of parking on campus is a scandal. Sexist remarks online are cowardly. Tax cuts for the wealthy are good for the economy. You get the point.

What should we do? My wife argues that we should replace the windows in the house. I argue that we shouldn't. At least we agree on what we disagree about, and what we disagree about is what we should do, which we call a *policy* claim. Policy claims are statements about things that should be done. Think of the way legislatures (ideally!) approach public problems. What should we do about rising health-care costs? Require everyone to have insurance, answers one group; another claims that we should reduce frivolous malpractice lawsuits. Should the university prohibit skateboards on campus? Should your instructor give everyone A's this semester?

In argument practice, reasons also can be categorized in these three ways. Someone, for example, might use what we call a substance claim as the reason to support a policy claim. An example: We should remove the emergency phones on campus because nearly every student now has a cell phone. Since arguments are made up of two assertions—we've been calling them claim and reason—the two parts can be categorized differently, and most likely are. You can support a policy claim with a policy reason (*We should replace the windows because we should conserve energy*), but it might be more effective to support a policy claim with a substance reason (*We should replace the windows because the cheap ones we now have lose 45% of the heat in the house, costing us over $100 in unnecessary heating bills*).

What's the unspoken assumption behind this argument about replacing windows? Remember, the arguer often doesn't speak the assumption because he or she assumes the audience accepts the assumption already. In this case, maybe the assumption is: *It's bad to lose 45% of the heat in the house.* We'll talk more about assumptions in a moment.

We've talked about three ways claims, reasons, and assumptions can be categorized. What's another way to invent an argument?

In *Teaching the Argument in Writing*, argument scholar Richard Fulkerson uses the acronym GASCAP to teach a structured method for inventing arguments. Now, let's pretend we want to write an argument on health issues for students. Let's say we want to look into the nutrition and dietary behavior of freshmen on college campuses. Here's an example of how the GASCAP principles can help you generate arguments. (You can apply this to your own topic.) As you read these examples, think about what makes this kind of argument strong and what might make it seem weak.

G is for *generalization*. If a sample group has X trait, then the bigger group has X trait. This kind of argument depends on whether the sample is really representative of the population. (If you go on a date with a loud, obnoxious male student, are you justified in thinking all male students are the same? Would that conclusion be justified after two, three, ten similar dates with different men?)

> *Example:* If students at State U. eat more empty calories during finals week than they do at any time in the semester, then we can assume college students nationally do the same. OR, to put it in our C + R structure: (C) College students eat more empty calories during finals

week than any other time in the semester, because (R) students at State U. do.

We're pattern-seekers. Scientists can't study every single stork or volcanic rock or television viewer, so they take samples. We can't judge the behavior of every single toddler; your nephew represents them all. We abstract from small samples to large populations. That's how we advance in knowledge. It's also how prejudices are formed (*I don't like this race or sex or religion or age because of the few I know*). So you can see how generalizing can make effective arguments, but my guess is you can also see its weakness.

A is for *analogy*. X and Y are alike enough that if X has Z traits, then Y likely has Z traits. Like generalization, this argument's strength rests on similarity—this time between two alike things or groups. For you poets out there, metaphor functions like this (see chapter eleven). If I compare thee to a summer's day, I'm arguing that summer's days have certain qualities that you, too, possess.

> *Example:* If students at the University of Wherever eat more empty calories during finals week, then we can assume that State U. students do the same.

Fulkerson explains that "an analogy is made stronger by a greater number of *relevant* similarities, and it is weakened by dissimilarities" (31). As I write this, the creators of the movie *Selma*, a critically acclaimed historical drama about the Civil Rights movement in Alabama in the 1960s, are being criticized for portraying President Lyndon B. Johnson as an enemy of the Selma campaign, which some historians say is not true. One editorialist compared *Selma* to another movie—*Zero Dark Thirty*—that depicts C.I.A. agents using testimony taken from torture to find and kill terrorist Osama bin Laden, which, some historians say, didn't happen. The argument goes like this: (C) The movie *Selma* should be criticized because (R) it's like *Zero Dark Thirty* in its historical inaccuracies. The strength of the argument, of course, depends on the similarities.

S is for *sign*. X means that Y is the case. If there's smoke, there's fire. If she doesn't call you back, she's just not interested. If a straight-A student starts blowing off class and assignments mid-semester, I may suspect that something has gone wrong in his or her personal life—but then again, I may be reading the signs incorrectly. Acts are signs of character. We believe that a person's acts reveal a coherent character hiding underneath. (We'll talk about that when we talk about ethos, in the next chapter.)

> *Example:* State U. freshmen tend to gain around seven pounds during their freshman year. (This may or may not be the case, by the way; I made it up.) The weight-gain is a sign that the students' diets change significantly once they move away from family and common routines.

C is for *causality*. X caused Y, or Y is a consequence of X. A tricky one sometimes. After a horrible school shooting in Columbine, Colorado, in 1999, journalists tried to argue that hard-rock music, video games, bullying, or parenting caused two young men to bring guns to school and murder their classmates. Was that really the case? Causal or consequential arguments appeal to us because they suggest sequences that seem to make sense. Our brains demand connections. Some of them are sound, some are not.

> *Example:* Students who play more video games than other students tend to be less healthy than other students. OR: (C) Students who play more video games than the average student are more unhealthy because (R) video games lead to a sedentary lifestyle.

Can you think of a reason why such arguments might not work? Sometimes it's hard to determine the actual *cause* of something. In the Columbine case, it was clear from investigations after the tragedy that the two shooters were bullied at school. Did the bullying push the two students over the edge? Is it accurate to say that no bullying = no shooting? But other students were bullied at Columbine High and didn't go on a murderous rampage.

A is for *authority*. If an expert on a given issue says X, then X is probably true. Well, who's an expert? Someone who knows quite a bit about a subject or who has spent a significant amount of time working in a particular field, OR someone who has intimate experience with the subject, OR someone who has some kind of credential related to the subject (like a PhD in microbiology), OR someone who is nationally recognized as an authority on a subject.

> *Example:* The *New England Journal of Medicine* reports that college students who play two or more hours of video games a day consume three times more soda than the national average. (Yeah, I made that up, too. But doesn't it sound authoritative?) So, the argument looks

like this: (C) College students do X, because (R) the *New England Journal of Medicine* says so. And we assume the *NJM* did some kind of scientific study to come to that conclusion.

Authorities are strong insofar as the audience accepts them as legitimate. How do audiences come to accept authorities as convincing? Well, think about it for a moment and you tell me. Another question: Is the authority *alone* in this perspective? Do other authorities agree or disagree? Is *this* authority—in this example, the *New England Journal of Medicine*—stronger or more convincing than another authority—let's say *Lancet*, the premiere medical journal of the United Kingdom—that may say something different?

P is for *principle*. X is true or just or right or moral. These kinds of arguments depend on what values are shared between the writer and the audience. Think about the various ways of thinking that create moral judgments: religion, politics, philosophy, culture, intuition. Things can get tricky in there. Psychology professor Jonathan Haidt has argued that moral judgments, though powerful, are sometimes difficult to defend because they come from deep within the strange mazes of our intuition. And yet, so many of our public arguments come from the moral or ethical realm.

> *Example:* (C) State U. should provide healthier options in the cafeteria (R) because colleges are responsible for the health of their students.

The principle in this argument is represented in the reason provided: Generally, we believe that universities are morally obligated to help their students stay healthy. The power of the argument rests on whether the audience accepts this principle or cultural value.

Anatomy of Arguments: A Closer Look

How do you know what makes an effective argument for your audience? Or: How do you know if an argument for which *you* are the audience should be convincing?

This is quite a vexing question. What do I mean by the word "effective"? One answer might be, "Whatever persuades your audience!" *Effective*, in other words, is *audience-specific*, based on what rhetorical theorist Gerard Hauser calls "local norms of reasonableness." An argument that might convince a convention of evangelicals in Texas might not convince readers of a physics blog. Each **discourse community** has a different way of creating knowledge and making arguments, and sometimes those ways are very specific, even exclusionary.

However, this answer, though probably true to the way rhetoric works much of the time, is in some ways unsatisfactory. For one thing, it seems to suggest that the point of rhetoric is to use whatever arguments will convince a specific audience, and no one else. If it works to scare people, whip up the mob, make wild and unsupportable claims, stereotype, lie, attack others, reinforce ignorant prejudices, or distort an opposing view, well...then it works! While it is true that very specific discourse communities will have their own way of arguing, in public discourse we are *ethically obligated* to pursue the public good through our arguments—in other words, to make arguments with good reasons that help to refine, rather than dull, public judgment. Team Rhetoric fights for truth and justice! Your challenge is to grow in rhetorical knowledge by devising reasonable, emotionally salient arguments that even people who disagree with you might accept as respectable.

In that spirit, then, we can say that there are ways we evaluate arguments that depend on general principles of reasoning—principles that, though general, work in specific situations as well. We can think of arguments as *strong* or *weak*, depending on whether they have certain virtues of good thinking—critical thinking.

If arguments were like mathematical equations, then the problem of persuasion would be solved: As long as the audience accepts the definition of the numbers and other math symbols, then the conclusion is inevitable. The same goes for logical *syllogisms*. A syllogism is a logical statement of two claims, called premises, and a conclusion. If the premises are true, then the conclusion is true. Here's an example:

- Premise #1: All humans will die.

- Premise #2: You are a human.

- Conclusion: Therefore, you will die.

Bad news, I know. Someone tell Alphaville that we're not gonna live forever or be forever young. If premises #1 and #2 are true—and I'm pretty sure they are—then the conclusion follows. In fact, it follows with a kind of *violence* because there's no way for you to reject it and remain a rational person. Face it: You're gonna die.

But everyday arguments don't really take the form of a syllogism, nor are they *logical* in the philosophical sense of that word. Rather, they are *rhetorical*. Take our movie critic. Her first premise (her claim) is: The Vow *is a bad movie*. Well, maybe! Unlike in the *All humans will die* example, we need to be *persuaded* with good reasons before we will accept that *The Vow* is a bad movie and get on the same page as our arguer. Master writers understand how this process works; they can analyze arguments by dissecting claims, reasons, and assumptions. They also invent arguments with these three parts of argument in mind.

Your goal as a writer of arguments is to write good ones. As you construct claims and reasons, you'll want to analyze them through "active, persistent, and careful consideration...in the light of the grounds that support" them, as Dewey put it. Let's go back to the PAPER TOWELS = TREES argument for a moment. How could we analyze the argument as we reconstructed it earlier? We can't just confront the claim because a claim by itself isn't an argument (remember?). So let's take a closer look at the other parts of the argument:

1. The first thing we could do is **question the reason.** Notice that the reason (*paper towels come from a natural resource*) to accept the claim (*You should not use more paper towels than you need...*) is a fact-based claim—a substance claim. The arguer is telling me, as my drippy hands reach for the dispenser, that to make paper towels for restrooms, someone has to go out and chop down a tree. Is that really true? Who knows! Maybe paper towels are made from recycled materials or cloth or wood pulp, or maybe very few trees are used in the process, or maybe trees are used to make paper towels but not "these towels"—the ones in the Monterrey Bay Aquarium, which are actually made out of shredded wheat. The point is that you can begin analyzing an argument by checking to see whether you'd call the reason a *fact* we can depend on. In this case, since I have nothing but the Monterrey Bay Aquarium authorities to rely on, I'm going to go ahead and assume they're right about where paper towels come from. (Do you agree?) Every reason or assumption has a certain level of adherence—meaning the level to which others agree with it. Facts have high levels of adherence; opinions might not.

    Granted, assessing the reason might be easier when you have a statement like "these paper towels are made from a natural resource" than when you have, as in our movie critic example, a statement like "the ending doesn't resolve things." Seems like a subjective statement to me. If *I* were to throw caution and good taste to the wind and go see *The Vow*, would *I* think that the ending didn't resolve things? When it comes to these kinds of judgments, sometimes we must depend on the *ethos* or authority of the speaker to help us determine whether or not to accept this reason. (More on ethos in a later chapter.) But in sum, your first task as a critical thinker is to analyze the reason and determine whether the reason is a fact—something you could look up and confirm—or some other kind of assertion.

2. The second, and more challenging, way to assess an argument is to **look at the *assumptions* that make the argument possible**. But assumptions are hard to "look" at, because usually they're not there. Assumptions are the (often) unspoken values, beliefs, or principles that arguers assume they share with their audience. In the case of the movie critic, the unspoken underlying assumption could look like this:

> *Assumption:* Movies that have endings that don't resolve things are bad.

You may have thought of other ways to express this assumption that go deeper into underlying assumptions. You could say that as movie audiences we expect a certain structure to our movie plots, and the structure gives us a kind of pleasure, which drives us back to the theaters. When a movie violates that structure contract—say, by concluding in a manner that leaves too many loose ends—it should be condemned. We've gone way beyond where I think the student movie critic was going, but these assumptions seem to underlie her argument. She means to express them without saying them because she assumes that her audience assumes them, too. And it's our job as the audience to analyze whether her assumptions are legitimate.

Analyzing assumptions is challenging, but sometimes it's the only way we can assess whether or not an argument is strong or weak. Let's go back to the paper towels argument:

> *Claim:* You should not use more paper towels than you need…

> *Reason:* …because paper towels come from a natural resource.

What does the speaker/writer/aquarium staff assume is true in this case? One way to express the unspoken assumption might be:

Assumption: Natural resources should be conserved or used sparingly.

With the assumption now on the table, can we say whether this is a good/bad, strong/weak argument?

It depends. It depends, of course, on the audience and whether the audience accepts the reasons, data, and assumptions. But in this case I'll take a chance and say that this assumption probably enjoys quite a bit of *adherence* in public discourse. Adherence in argument studies means *agreement*. Many people, I'd guess, agree that natural resources should be conserved or used sparingly. So maybe I want to conclude that since the assumption is strong—i.e., enjoys widespread adherence—then this argument is strong.

But not so fast. A rhetorical critic doesn't let assumptions off the hook that easily. We may go further and ask this assumption a "why" question: *Why should natural resources be conserved?* What if trees are so plentiful that they don't need to be conserved? Now we're getting into a third strategy for inventing and analyzing arguments.

3. Finally, you can rebut the claim by **coming up with a counter-claim**. We've looked at the reason and the assumption, and now we should test the argument by coming up with possible rebuttals. We've already done some of that work above by asking whether the paper towels in the dispenser actually come from trees. Think about rebuttals as "unless" statements that cast doubt on the argument:

You should not use more paper towels than you need because paper towels are made from a natural resource.

...*unless* they *aren't* made from a natural resource.

...*unless* we don't need to conserve trees because there are so many of them.

...*unless* conserving trees will be too expensive or have other negative consequences—on the economy, for example.

08

Argument as Strategy, as Critical Thinking

As a budding rhetorician, you should practice identifying claims, reasons, assumptions, and counter-claims in the arguments you write and the ones you hear each day. Philosopher Stephen Toulmin created a simple chart to teach the anatomy of argument, and it looks something like this (and you should already know what each letter stands for):

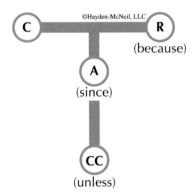

Toulmin here rediscovers Aristotle's understanding that argument (he called it *enthymeme*) is a human practice that follows ordinary patterns of thinking. It's just that in ordinary practice, we often don't think much about these patterns, nor do we stop to test the strength (through critical analysis) of arguments we or other people use.

Armed with this layout, you can invent convincing arguments when arguments are needed. When people talk about critical thinking, they're talking about learning how to apply C + R + A + CC thinking so you can understand, analyze, evaluate, create, and judge meaningful arguments in daily life. Of course, "daily life" arguments are quite complicated and tangly. We've talked as if CRA are easily discovered in the arguments you encounter. Sometimes you have to reconstruct CRA from what's been given you. You'll also notice that many written arguments look more like CCCRRRRRAAAAAA: multiple claims and sub-claims, backed by several reasons and assuming a dozen assumptions. Your job as rhetorical critic is to disentangle this mess o' argument as best as you can, using the critical thinking skills you've mastered, ever keeping your eye on whether the arguments are persuasive for intended audiences.

I believe that if we would all get better at this kind of thinking, our public discourse would improve, as would our judgments.

Works Cited

Aristotle. *On Rhetoric*. 2nd ed. Transl. George A. Kennedy. NY: Oxford, 2007. Print.

Dewey, John. *How We Think*. Project Gutenberg eBook. 14 September 2011. Web. 28 March 2015.

Fulkerson, Richard. *Teaching the Argument in Writing*. Urbana, IL: NCTE, 1996. Print.

Hauser, Gerard. *Introduction to Rhetorical Theory*. 2nd ed. Prospect Heights, IL: Waveland P, 2002. Print.

Mercier, Hugo and Dan Sperber. "Why do Humans Reason? Arguments for an Argumentative Theory." *Behavioral and Brain Sciences* 34.2 (2011): 57–74. Web. 8 May 2015.

Toulmin, Stephen. *The Uses of Argument*. Updated Ed. Cambridge: Cambridge UP, 2003. Print.

CHARACTER

In this chapter we'll cover the C of ACES: character as rhetorical strategy. You won't go far as a writer unless you understand how you can present a convincing *ethos* for your audience.

Ethos: Who We Are (to Audiences)

Something bizarre happened at the 2009 MTV Video Music Awards. When singer-songwriter Taylor Swift, then only nineteen years old, waltzed out to accept the VMA for Best Female Video (for the syrupy-sweet country pop song "You Belong with Me"), rapper Kanye West jumped onto the stage and snatched the microphone out of her hand in the middle of her acceptance speech. Apparently he had a speech of his own to give:

> "Yo, Taylor, I'm really happy for you and I'mma let you finish, but Beyoncé [another female vocalist up for the award] had one of the best videos of all time. One of the best videos of all time!"

Then West shrugged, handed the mic back to a stunned Swift, and walked off. Swift was so shocked she couldn't finish her speech.

Wikipedia tells me that retribution for Kanye was swift—pun intended. The audience booed him off the stage. In the weeks that followed the VMAs, other celebrities like Janet Jackson, 50 Cent, Pink, Kelly Clarkson, and Donald Trump publicly condemned Kanye's actions. Even President Barack Obama threw him under the bus when he told a reporter he thought Kanye had been a "jackass." Ouch. Kanye did his best to make amends. He wrote a blog post and a few tweets, went on Jay Leno and said how ashamed he was, even contacted Taylor Swift personally to apologize. The public was not impressed. *Forbes* magazine reports that Kanye's earnings dropped from $25 million to $12 million in the year following the event (Greenberg). Ticket sales for a music tour with Lady Gaga were so low he had to cancel.

Take a moment and think about what's going on here. What did Kanye do wrong?

It's hard to feel bad for Kanye West: Two critically acclaimed smash-hit albums later, he's back on top of the world. In some ways the vitriolic response of the public to his stunt with Taylor Swift seems like an overreaction—I mean, was what he did really *that* bad? Like, $13 million dollars bad?

Mr. West learned a difficult lesson: *our character influences attitudes.* Remember that the goal of writing is to influence the attitudes of others. In the last chapter, we talked about how you can influence attitudes by providing compelling reasons for the claims you make. You can also influence attitudes, in good or bad ways, by the way you present your Self—in writing, certainly, but also in public speaking and interpersonal communications, in the clothes you wear, in the way you treat other people, your likes and dislikes, what you know and don't know, who you associate with, your accent and word choices, your Facebook posts and photos, who you listen to, what games you play, your sense of humor. Like it or not, all these things lead your audiences to make judgments about you. If we're mindful about it, the person we present to other people can be a rhetorical strategy. We call it ethos.

Ethos is another funky Greek word, yes, but like kairos, it's a useful word. "Since rhetoric is concerned with making a judgment," says our Grandpappy Aristotle, "it is necessary not only to look to the argument [like we did in last chapter]…but also for the speaker to construct a view of himself [or herself] as a certain kind of person" (112). Aristotle used the word *ethos* to describe this act of construction—how the speaker, in the speech, presents a persuasive self to the audience. He also, and somewhat confusingly, thought of ethos as the character of the audience itself; he encouraged his eager students to study psychology to understand the way people behave and their likes and dislikes in order to appeal to their collective ethos in speaking. Maybe in making this argument, Aristotle was remembering what Socrates, the noble philosopher, said about rhetoric in Plato's dialogue, *Phaedrus*: "Oratory is the art of enchanting the soul, and therefore he who would be an orator has to learn the differences of human souls." Rhetorical power comes from understanding what makes a persuasive character for various audiences.

It may surprise you to hear that Aristotle believed that "character is almost, so to speak, the most authoritative form of persuasion" (39). Maybe he's right.

How Character Persuades

So: How does character persuade? If it's true that when you write you bare your soul, what kind of soul is the most convincing? And how do we use writing to establish our ethos?

Let's go back to chapter two for a moment to remind us of the big, universal determiner of any rhetorical strategy: the rhetorical situation. Whether or not you're successful using any of our ACES strategies depends on your exigence and purpose for writing and, of course, your audience. Genre matters, too—significantly. Think about cover letters for jobs. When you write a cover letter, you have to present yourself as a certain kind of person—professional, experienced, responsible, creative—and avoid looking like another kind—unskilled, entitled, conceited, clueless. Rhetorical situations are culturally contingent as well, meaning that the kind of character some cultures or discourse communities might find persuasive may not persuade other cultures or communities. For example, my acquaintances from Korea are far more respectful and deferent to people over forty than the Americans I know, especially the younger Americans I know.

Ethos, then, must be appropriate for the rhetorical situation. (You should have this kind of thinking seared into your brain by now: rhetorical strategy depends on rhetorical situation!) Sometimes we bring our ethos with us into a rhetorical situation, so that our character persuades before we even say anything. Let's call this *established ethos*.

When a five-star general steps up to the podium to address issues related to national defense, his character already is convincing us before he says a word. Or if an internationally renowned psychologist has something to say about bullying, we lean into her message more than we would if she were an accountant or just an angry parent (Aronson 77). Even good looks can convince: legal studies have shown that "attractive defendants are twice as likely to avoid jail as unattractive defendants," regardless of the gender of the defendant, judge, or jury (Cialdini 147).

Established ethos also works against folks: Past misdeeds, guilty associations, ignorant comments, obvious self-interest, or perceived prejudices can kill a message. Kanye West will wear the Taylor Swift incident around his neck for as long as cultural memory preserves it. When he was caught visiting prostitutes and forced to resign as governor of New York in 2008, politician Eliot Spitzer found audiences reluctant to accept his arguments about the economy, even though he knew quite a bit about how the economy works.

It may be that we're convinced so easily by established ethos (the decorations on a general's uniform, a doctor's lab coat, a distinguished title, the relative hotness of a defendant) because it saves us time and cognitive effort. In *Thinking, Fast and Slow*, Daniel Kahneman, a brilliant Princeton psychology professor and winner of the Nobel Prize, explains that we often make errors of judgment because our minds work in two speeds: fast and slow. Fast judgments come from our intuitions and take very little effort. Slow judgments require "effortful mental activities," like calculations, analysis, or careful attention (Kahneman 21). Both judgments are necessary for a good life, but slow judgments often correct the errors our fast judgments make. Prejudice, for example, is often a result of fast judgment ("I don't like Catholics—my aunt is Catholic, and she's a monster!"). Established ethos is powerful because our brains don't really want to listen carefully to someone's argument to find out if we should be convinced; we'd rather just see a white labcoat and say, "She's a doctor. She's right. I don't have to think now."

If you want to learn more about the potential pitfalls of established *ethos*, Google "Stanley Milgram."

On a less sinister note, established ethos is useful for us as writers. When you use sources to support an argument (in a research paper, for example), you want your audience to know if your sources have established, convincing characters. Look two paragraphs up. What did I tell you about Daniel Kahneman? Did I need to include that bit about him being a Princeton psych prof? See how I threw in his Nobel Prize, too? Did you find yourself leaning more willingly into his argument about fast and slow thinking because I established his ethos? Can you imagine being equally persuaded if I'd written, "My uncle Roger thinks our brains work in two speeds"? I doubt it.

What do we do when we have to write and we don't have some hoity-toity established ethos to slap down on our readers? Well, we need to *invent* an ethos, then, with our words. (Thanks to Sharon Crowley and Debra Hawhee for teaching me about this distinction between established and invented ethos.) Aristotle teaches us that persuasion through character "should result from the speech, not from a previous opinion" (39)—that's what we mean by invented ethos. While established ethos does, indeed, work wonders (in spite of what Aristotle may think), much of the time when we write, we write without commanding credentials, and we write to total strangers who often don't care who we are or what we've done. In those situations, we'll have to win them over with an invented ethos. We'll have to construct for them a convincing ethos through our words.

I must stress one last thing here. For Aristotle, ethos is an *argument*— it's an argument connecting claims and reasons by connecting character to actions. While we may say that "actions speak louder than words," it turns out that words are, in fact, actions, and word-acts invoke character. As audiences, we look for patterns in the characters of others. We read rhetorical action as evidence of character, and we expect rhetorical acts to be consistent with what we understand of someone's character. We get suspicious when people say or do things that seem "out of character" because inconsistency seems inauthentic. When politicians reverse course, we think they're just weather-vaning (i.e., turning any way the wind blows) their way to getting elected. However, a supporter might argue that reversing course is an *act* that represents *wisdom* or *intellectual engagement* or *pliability*. Rhetorical acts argue for character; they are the signs of character.

We've covered five principles of ethos I want you to remember:

1. Character convinces—in fact, it's one of the most important rhetorical strategies we have.

2. Character is argument—i.e., the relationship between acts and character is like the relationship between reasons and claims.

3. The convincing power of ethos depends on the rhetorical situation (kairos, exigence, rhetor, purpose, genre, audience) and the shared culture of writer and audience.

4. Character can be either already established (think white lab coat), or invented.

5. We can—and should!—invent convincing ethos in our writing.

Strategies for Inventing *Ethos* in Writing

Keep in mind that the word "invented" doesn't imply imaginary or phony ethos. It refers to the ethos you must construct in the act of writing. For the rest of the chapter, we'll cover three major strategies for inventing ethos in your writing: credibility, relationship with the audience, and other virtues.

Credibility

As I write this, *NBC Nightly News* anchor Brian Williams is under fire for lying about being, well, under fire. For years, Mr. Williams has claimed that while covering the war in Iraq in 2003, his helicopter was shot down by a rocket-propelled grenade and made a dramatic emergency landing. Earlier this week, several military veterans who witnessed the event came forward, after over a decade of silence, to say that Mr. Williams' story is bunk: the helicopter he was in was actually *behind* the one shot down, and it took no enemy fire. After the story broke all over the media, a news analyst said that Williams' lie "raises serious questions about his credibility in a business that values that quality above all else" (Mahler, Somaiya, and Steel). Maintaining credibility can be a tricky business.

When we believe someone is credible, we trust them; we find them believable. We find what they have to say convincing because they create a sense of *gravitas* with their words. Credible people speak with authority; they've either done their homework on a topic or they have personal experience that gives them an edge over others who don't. Their credible acts cue us to their credible characters, and we move in their direction. We know how this works with established ethos (i.e., we respect recognized authorities with credentials like academic degrees, or prestigious job titles, or relevant experience, or fame). But inventing a credible ethos in writing can be a challenge, especially when you're a first-year writing student trying to edge your way into conversations already controlled by published experts and commentators.

So how do you convey credibility in writing? There are three methods you'll want to learn:

1. **Do your homework.** The first method is to demonstrate, simply, that you know what you're talking about. You want to convince your audience that (a) you've done your homework on the issue—i.e., you're in command of the relevant facts, events, and players (like other credible sources—just make sure your audience understands why they're

credible); (b) you have kairotic awareness of what makes your topic timely, interesting, of the moment; (c) you know the lingo (the key terms or concepts, the "lexical field") of the discipline or subject you're writing in, and you're all about the details, the how-to, of academic writing; (d) you understand the conventions of the genre—in other words, you're an insider, someone who knows what you're supposed to do in situations like these; and, (e) you know how to use the English language really well, avoiding obvious errors that might slow down the reading experience and lead audiences to form unflattering judgments about you. (A quick note about (e): Mistakes are a fact of life, sure, but it's also a fact that they can tarnish your credibility. In one research study, business executives surveyed felt that errors convey the message that the writer is hasty, careless, uncaring, uninformed, or poorly educated [Beason]. While not all errors are equally egregious to audiences, and some aren't even noticed, they can still chip away at your ethos.)

In looking smart, do you risk looking *too* smart? Yes. No one likes a smarty-pants; Hermione Granger learned this over the course of the *Harry Potter* books. That's why you study the third strategy for inventing *ethos*—the virtues—which we'll discuss soon.

2. **Use personal experience.** When it's appropriate to the genre you're writing, use relevant personal experience to demonstrate that you've been there, done that. In *My Age of Anxiety*, writer Scott Stossel introduces us to the history and science of anxiety and panic disorder through his own experience. "I struggle with emetophobia," he writes, which is "a pathological fear of vomiting, but it's been a little while since I last vomited. More than a little while, actually: as I type this, it's been, to be precise, thirty-five years, two months, four days, twenty-two hours, and forty-nine minutes" (65). Stossel's personal struggles with anxiety give him a unique perspective that boosts his credibility, especially when he supplements his experience with significant research on anxiety.

But be careful. Personal experience sometimes can't be generalized (see chapter eight about *generalization*). Just because you take better notes on a laptop than a notepad doesn't mean everyone else does. There's another danger, too: Audiences can sniff out a fake (take note, Brian Williams!). If you're an Amazon reviewer, one of the best ways to sink your ethos with me is to admit you've never actually used the product you're reviewing. (Amazingly, this happens all the time.) Men get themselves into trouble by assuming they understand the experience of women; adults often are not fully empathetic to the pain and suffering of children. ("It's just a scrape—quit your whining!" "So your balloon popped—big deal, we'll get you another one!") Writers can project cultural insensitivity or a lack of empathy by assuming that their own experience is the right experience, or by dismissing the experience of others. To sum up: use personal experience, but be authentic and empathetic.

3. **Show balance.** One of the easiest ways to win people over is to project a fair and balanced *ethos*. Aristotle tells us that "we believe fair-minded people to a greater extent and more quickly than we do others, on all subjects in general and completely so in cases where there is not exact knowledge but room for doubt" (38). Social psychology backs this up: We trust people more when it looks like they're not pushing their own agenda. Self-interest is a turn-off when it's too obviously in play (Aronson 78–81). While it may be true that we all have biases, wearing them on our sleeves can destroy our credibility.

You build credibility by showing that, though you have an argument to make, you've looked at the issue from multiple sides and weighed evidence for and against your proposal. In a massive study of the most successful businesses, Jim Collins and his research team discovered that the most influential leaders were not afraid to confront the "brutal facts" or invite others to criticize their management practices (69). This approach projects not only fair-mindedness but confidence. When in our writing we give a full hearing to opinions that go counter to ours, we show we have nothing to hide. We tell readers we want them to judge for themselves whether or not we've made a convincing case. (This is an especially strong move for well-informed audiences; it's not as strong for audiences who have already made up their minds. See Aronson 94.) When we take seriously alternative viewpoints or weaknesses in our own perspective, we convey wisdom. We create credibility by acting, by doing, by speaking and writing.

Credibility convinces. Enact yours, and your audience will lean into your argument.

Relationship with the Audience

Back to T-Swift: What was Taylor Swift planning to say before Kanye West ripped the mic out of her hands? Later she told the press that she just wanted to thank the fans for voting for her video. She wanted her words to create a connection with her adoring audience—she wanted to bring the love. That's a great rhetorical move. Audiences lean in when they feel a writer has their interests and needs in mind. If writing is a social, other-directed activity, as I've argued, then we do it better when we form constructive relationships with readers.

In the literature about rhetoric, this ethos strategy is often called *goodwill*. As a writer, you want your audience to feel like you have their best interests in mind. You want to demonstrate that this whole writing thing is really all about them, not you. Maybe that's a stretch, but it's a stretch worth making.

So, how do you get perfect strangers to like you?

1. **Be kind.** One way to convince others is to be *kind* to them. Psychologist Jonathan Haidt argues that when it comes to reasoning, we're like a rider on an elephant's back—and the elephant is our intuitions, passions, and biases. "When discussions are hostile," he writes, "the odds of change are slight. The elephant leans away from the opponent, and the rider works frantically to rebut the opponent's charges. But if there is affection, admiration, or a desire to please the other person, then the elephant leans *toward* that person and the rider tries to find the truth in the other person's arguments" (68). He concludes that good reasons can, in fact, persuade, but "especially when reasons are embedded in a friendly conversation" (71). Show respect for adversaries. Assume that your readers are smart and willing to weigh the evidence. Demonstrate that you want what's best for the community or public. Avoid sounding smug, condescending, or holier-than-thou.

2. **Give awesome content.** Quality writing is a compliment to your reader. By writing a witty, smart, polished, well-argued paper, you've created a good experience for someone else. By sharing engaging links through social media, you give gifts; when you share lame-o stuff, you waste everyone's time. Imagine your writing instructor, slogging through a neck-high stack of papers, finally taking your paper from the stack and finding, to her joy, a masterpiece, a genuinely pleasurable reading experience, an experience created by your best thinking and writing, by stylistic and design pizzazz, by your persistent

acts to minimize static by avoiding errors and design problems. Quality builds ethos.

3. **Connect with your audience.** Yet another reason why you need to know your audience as well as you can. As Robert Cialdini explains, the social science research is clear: "We like people who are similar to us" (148). The rhetorical theorist Kenneth Burke called this principle *identification.* You persuade someone, reasoned Burke, if you show you talk their language and identify your interests and purposes with theirs (55). One way to do that is to suggest that your writing has implications for a shared issue; in other words, your writing is meant to chip away at problems in the community at large. Let me share a brief example from the world of psychology. When psychologist Timothy Wilson wrote a book on how interpretations of the world can influence our well-being, he wrote:

> Our interpretations are rooted in the narratives we construct about ourselves and the social world, and sometimes, like the pessimistic calculus student, we interpret things in unhealthy ways that have negative consequences. We could solve a lot of problems if we could get people to redirect their interpretations in healthier directions. (Wilson 10)

Notice that Wilson uses the first-person plural to connect with the audience: *our* interpretations, the narratives *we* construct, *we* interpret things. In essence, he suggests that his scholarship will help us solve these problems of interpretation and make us healthier. By writing in this way, Wilson builds a relationship with us by saying, in essence, "My concerns are your concerns, and my project your project, my culture your culture, my solutions *our* solutions."

If at the end of your text a reader has to ask, *What does this have to do with me?*, then you've missed a chance to build *ethos* by creating a relationship with your audience.

Other Virtues

We've covered *credibility* and *relationships* as rhetorical strategies. I conclude here by suggesting that there are other convincing character traits that can be conveyed in writing. Certain *virtues of character* endear us to other people and prepare our attitudes for adjustment.

I'm not competing with *Us Weekly* for celebrity coverage, but let's go back—for the last time, I promise—to Kanye's stunt at the Video Music Awards in 2009. He said, you'll remember, that Beyoncé's video "All the Single Ladies" was one of the best videos of all time. Clearly he felt that some injustice had been done when Taylor Swift won the VMA over Beyoncé. (He did the same thing, though off-stage to *E!* reporters, after the 2015 Grammy's when the musician Beck won Album of the Year over Beyoncé.) Later in the broadcast, though, Beyoncé herself, the reigning pop diva, asked Swift back to the stage. She gave Swift a big hug and invited her to finish her speech.

Now, how about *Beyoncé's* ethos? She could have been upset, like Kanye, about losing to Swift. Instead, she turned the awkward moment into a classy, gracious redress for a wronged sister musician. Her ethos capital soared to new heights, if that's even possible for someone as universally well-liked as Beyoncé. Her gracious acts reinforced our perception of her character.

Beyoncé gained rhetorical power by being gracious in that moment. You, too, can gain rhetorical power in your writing by demonstrating that you have certain virtues of character respected and admired by your audience. In *On Rhetoric*, Aristotle suggests that people who possess *arete*—virtue—are more persuasive than those who don't (112). Virtue here means *excellence* (not merely sexual purity), and it was a big deal to the Greeks. It's a big deal to us, too. We listen to people we admire, people who we think of as *good people*: funny people, courageous people, humble people, passionate people, just (as in *fair*) people, ethical people, self-reflective and self-sacrificing people (see Brooks), complimentary people, talented people, charitable people.

How do you project all that in writing? By performing rhetorical acts that reflect good character. Telling stories about yourself helps. Expressing appropriate emotional responses to situations can signal certain convincing qualities about yourself (see next chapter). Showing you have a sense of humor, or that you're a sensitive and just person, or that you're up on recent news stories or pop culture trends, or that you want what's best for the community—those moves present to readers a writer they can respect and trust, even like.

In her memoir *Bossypants*, comedian Tina Fey talks about her body— "wide German hips that look like somebody wrapped Pillsbury dough around a case of soda"—in such a self-effacing, humble, and hilarious way that we can't help but like her:

> I would not trade any of these features for anybody else's. I wouldn't trade the small thin-lipped mouth that makes me resemble my nephew. I wouldn't even trade the acne scar on my right cheek, because that recurring zit spent more time with me in college than any boy ever did. (25)

We admire people who don't take themselves too seriously, so long as their joking is appropriate to the situation and they don't come off as being full of themselves.

Though in person we can create convincing character with nonverbal vibes, writers can still invoke an ethos audiences can connect with. When that connection is made, your audience will lean more readily into your argument.

A Brief Word about Bias

Before we close the door on ethos, I want to say something about *bias*.

These be dark days for trust and expertise. A late-2016 Gallup poll showed that only 32% of Americans trust the media; a mere 14% of Republicans say they trust what they see on the news. Partisan politics casts a lean, mean shadow on every comment anyone says publicly, so that even facts are considered opinions and everyone accuses everyone else of bias.

Since, as we've seen in this chapter, the power of persuasion is tied up intimately with credibility, we need to think critically about who to trust and why.

The word *bias* has its roots in the shape of things—as in, when something slants or warps or skews or swerves in one direction and not another. To be biased is to "incline to one side," as the Oxford English Dictionary puts it. On the one hand, bias is inescapable since we show bias simply by living and making choices about the things we like and want. If you argue for something, you show bias. When someone covers a news event in one way and not another, that person shows a degree of bias simply by choosing.

On the other hand, we've come to understand bias as a kind of cognitive blindness that keeps us from seeing clearly and judging fairly. Racism, of course, is a bias, but so is "availability bias," which is when we overestimate the value or accuracy of something just because it's easier to call up from memory. Wikipedia lists over 100 such biases that have been discovered through research in psychology and behavioral economics.

When you accuse someone of bias, you're not complimenting them on their choices; it is a condemnation. The problem is that bias is nearly impossible to avoid. Judges and police officers aren't supposed to be biased, but we know they can be. (Judges, for example, are more likely to grant parole after eating lunch.) Parents shouldn't be, or school principals—and yet people can't help but have favorites. (I was my parents' favorite child, for sure.) Scientists should not let their personal interests influence the outcome of their research, and yet we know that when interest groups (like drug companies) fund research, the research all too often skews in that group's favor.

What are we to do in a world of bias, fellow rhetoricians? Many of my students tell me that they learned from grade school research projects to avoid all .com websites and always trust .org or .edu ones. That's too bad, because some of the most accurate reporting comes from the .com website for *The New Yorker*, where news stories are fact-checked far more rigorously than many .org or .edu websites. Other students rely on "peer-reviewed" journals—the kind you find in academic databases with names like *The Journal of Applied Animal Welfare Science* or *The Journal of Pipeline Systems Engineering and Practice*. (Real names!) And yes, journals like these include reliable findings from rigorous methods that have been vetted by other experts. But sometimes those sources won't help us find the right information because they are too specialized or too specific. (And beware of special interest sponsorship!)

This chapter, I hope, has shown you the path through the bias briar patch. Think of the following questions when you ponder the ethos of the sources you consult:

1. **Rhetor**: Who wrote this thing? What person or group or organization put its stamp on it? What do we know about the rhetor?

2. **Credibility**: What particular expertise does this person or group bring to this issue? What reliable, convincing evidence does this person/group use to support its positions? What kind of work and care goes into gathering and presenting information? How does the source use personal experience, observation, scientific evidence?

3. **Balance**: Is this source committed to the truth, wherever it can be found? How does this source acknowledge alternative perspectives? What side of the issues does this source fall on, and how do I know that? How is this source funded? What is its mission? How does this source commit itself to discovering the truth, no matter the consequences?

4. **Character**: How does this source treat its adversaries? How is this source performing a public service? How does this source represent other sources, opinions, or perspectives? Is this source committed to the truth and collective goodwill? Does this source "behave" respectably, nobly, even in rhetorical combat?

09

Works Cited

Aristotle. *On Rhetoric*. 2nd ed. Transl. George A. Kennedy. NY: Oxford, 2007. Print.

Aronson, Eliot. *The Social Animal*. NY: Worth, 1999. Print.

Beason, Larry. "Ethos and Error: How Business People React to Errors." *College Composition and Communication* 53.1 (2001): 33–64. Print.

Brooks, David. *The Road to Character*. NY: Random House, 2015. Print.

Burke, Kenneth. *A Rhetoric of Motives*. Berkeley: U of Cal P, 1969. Print.

Cialdini, Robert B. *Influence*. 5th ed. Boston: Pearson, 2009. Print.

Crowley, Sharon and Debra Hawhee. *Ancient Rhetorics for Contemporary Students*. 5th ed. Boston: Pearson, 2012. Print.

Fey, Tina. *Bossypants*. NY: Little, Brown, 2011. Print.

Greenberg, Zach O'Malley. "The Strange Symbiosis of Taylor Swift and Kanye West." 25 August 2014. Web. 3 Feb 2015.

Haidt, Jonathan. *The Righteous Mind*. NY: Vintage, 2013. Print.

Kahneman, Daniel. *Thinking, Fast and Slow*. NY: Farrar, Straus, Giroux. 2011. Print.

Mahler, Jonathan, Ravi Somaiya, and Emily Steel. "With an Apology, Brian Williams Digs Himself Deeper in Copter Tale." *New York Times*. 5 Feb 2015. Web. 6 Feb 2015.

Stossel, Scott. *My Age of Anxiety*. NY: Knopf, 2014. Print.

Wilson, Timothy D. *Redirect*. NY: Back Bay, 2011. Print.

10

EMOTION

Rhetoric sets up relationships. Knowing someone's ethos helps us know how much attention we should pay to them. Rhetoric orients us to each other, invites us to lean in, to bond, to identify with each other, to like and trust each other. Since emotions function like a glue for these bonds, then emotions are inherently rhetorical. So let's talk about them.

You may not have spent much time thinking about the relationship between schooling and poverty, but educator Jonathan Kozol has. Consider the following excerpt from his book *Savage Inequalities*, a book about the public school system in the United States. Kozol is in the middle of describing the rough conditions kids face in low-income areas of East St. Louis. I want you to make sure you're in a quiet place, leaning over the page, letting the full impact of the words work on you:

> As in New York City's poorest neighborhoods, dental problems also plague the children here. Although dental problems don't command the instant fears associated with low birth weight, fetal death or cholera, they do have the consequence of wearing down the stamina of children and defeating their ambitions. Bleeding gums, impacted teeth and rotting teeth are routine matters for the children I have interviewed in the South Bronx. Children get used to feeling constant pain. They go to sleep with it. They go to school with it. Sometimes their teachers are alarmed and try to get them to a clinic. But it's all so slow and heavily encumbered with red tape and waiting lists and missing, lost or canceled welfare cards, that dental care is often long delayed. Children live for months with pain that grown-ups would find unendurable. (Kozol 20–21)

Unless you have a heart of stone, you'll be moved by this account. Poor children with bleeding gums! Sitting in their little wooden chairs at school—in the kind of pain that would double over a grown-up! And we can't get them relief because of bureaucratic red tape! If you're like me, you feel empathy mixed with pity mixed with frustration. Kozol is inviting us to develop an attitude, and therefore a judgment, about the moral consequences of America's unequal education landscape.

I've said before that studying rhetoric increases your social intelligence— i.e., your ability to understand and intervene in situations in which working with others is necessary to get things done, situations for which writing can be a catalyst for change. We've talked about how you can increase your rhetorical power by using claims, reasons, and assumptions your audience will accept (*logos*, in Aristotle's language). We've talked about how establishing a convincing character in writing gives you rhetorical power (*ethos*). In this chapter, we'll talk about the E in ACES: emotion (*pathos*). Your quest to be a rhetorical superstar must include some understanding of how emotional appeals work, and why. Even mild emotions have "a highly significant influence on the way people form, maintain, and change their attitudes" in social situations (Forgas 149).

Emotions Are Rhetorical

What are emotions? You know, I know, everyone knows—things like anger, sadness, fear, joy, surprise, shame. But what, exactly, is the emotion itself? Is it the feeling that comes over us when our brain registers that our dog just got run over by a car? Is emotion the unstoppable tears streaming down our face, the impulsive quaking in our arms, the heavy downturn of our mouth and eyebrows? Or is emotion the conscious *attitude* we form as we think about poor Rover, our beloved pet, squashed like a pancake in the middle of the road? (Did I go too far there? Disgust, too, is an emotion.) Or to put the question more simply: Is emotion an involuntary physiological response to what happens to us, or is it a culturally formed judgment about what happens to us? Or maybe both?

Think of surprise. Have you ever jumped at something that happened in a movie, or had a practical joker startle you? Did you make a conscious decision to jump, to exhale or shout, to bring your arms up close to your body in a defensive gesture, to pop your eyes open, to race your heart? Nope—your body decided to do that on its own. The stimulus jumped out, and your brain—in neuroscience-speak, the "limbic system circuitry, the amygdala and anterior cingulate" (Damasio 133)—sent signals to your body at lightning speed and everything just did its thing without any help from conscious You. Evolution has equipped us with those reflexes for good reason: When the beast jumps out of the bushes, you don't want to have an internal dialogue about how you should respond.

Now think of someone you love whom you haven't seen in a long time. Imagine some crazy coincidence of seeing this person unexpectedly in a public place, across a crowded room. Imagine the face of that person turning to look at you—the wide eyes, the smile, the most happy surprise imaginable. You run across the room and embrace. What's the feeling now? Surely you don't feel the same feelings looking at the faces of the strangers in the room; the face of the person you love carries all the experiences and conscious decisions you've made over the years in your relationship. Unlike being startled, this time the stimulus leads to a *judgment*, whether obvious to you or not, about that person and what he or she means to you, *before* (somehow) your heart races and your mouth shoots upward and you feel like a million bucks. The emotion—joy—is the result of a social judgment.

The Oxford English Dictionary defines *emotion* as "natural instinctive affections of the mind (e.g. love, horror, pity) which come and go according to one's personality, experiences, and bodily state; a mental feeling." But let's channel the corny classic rock group Boston and say that emotion is *more than a feeling*. The philosopher Robert Solomon tells us that emotions are not "just" feelings; they represent "sophisticated and subtly structured perceptions of the world" (138, 141). Emotions are far more important than chemical responses in the bloodstream. They are "*strategies* for getting along in the world" and "means of motivating, guiding, influencing, and sometimes manipulating our own actions and attitudes as well as influencing and manipulating the actions and attitudes of others" (Solomon 3). In other words, emotions are *rhetorical phenomena*.

Aristotle's got Robert Solomon's back on this one. Here he is again, speaking across the centuries in his tunic and sandals:

> The emotions [*pathe*] are those things through which, by undergoing change, people come to differ in their judgments and which are accompanied by pain and pleasure, for example, anger, pity, fear, and other such things and their opposites. [...] I mean, for example, in speaking of anger, what is their *state of mind* when people are angry and against *whom* are they usually angry and for what sort of *reasons*. (Aristotle *Rhetoric* 113)

Remember that attitudes lead to judgments lead to behavior. As Aristotle says, we "come to differ" in our judgments because of the "state of mind" they put us in. Emotions lead to attitudes lead to judgments lead to behavior.

Is this a good thing? I mean, aren't emotions irrational? Don't emotions lead to sloppy thinking and manipulation and brain-dead citizens and propaganda and the rise of fiery demagogues who become tyrants and bestride a blood-soaked earth with the fury of hell in their crazed eyes?

Let's not get too carried away. Yes, over the centuries since the Enlightenment, Western thinkers have often championed what we call rational thought over emotions. Since emotions often begin with physiological reactions over which we have little control, and since emotions often seem to "hijack" the rest of our brain with alarming force (Goleman 14), it's reasonable to be suspicious of them. Some people believe that objective thinking *requires* that we become, somehow, dispassionate, devoid of any emotional experience, like Spock on *Star Trek* or maybe Sherlock Holmes the way Benedict Cumberbatch plays him.

Such thinking, we've come to discover, is impossible. Current neuroscience tells us that "emotions drive the brain" (Franks 59). In other words, the high-order functions of the brain (thinking, reasoning, analyzing, etc.) are connected to, and depend on, what happens in the lower brain regions (called subcortical) where emotions are generated (Damasio 128). Emotions are tied up in our thinking and decision-making; without them, we'd lack a profoundly important mechanism for acting in the world. So like it or not, emotions are central to our being in the world.

They're also a pain in the neck. They can be unruly, just as the rationalists feared. They can move quickly to hijack a moment and render us helpless victims. Fear keeps us from living, loving, risking, connecting. Anxiety clouds our judgment, rendering even the most harmless situation terrifying. Anger makes us say or do things we regret later. Shame leads us to doubt ourselves, devalue ourselves. Surprise leaves us speechless. Even happiness can be a trap: When we like or dislike something, we use that feeling as a lazy shorthand for making decisions, sometimes "with little deliberation or reasoning"—that's called the *affect heuristic* (Kahneman 12). When it comes to living with emotions, there be dragons, my friends.

That's where this chapter comes in. In this chapter, I want nothing more than to boost your EI—your emotional intelligence—so that you can motivate, guide, and influence the emotions of your audience. When Daniel Goleman wrote *Emotional Intelligence* in 1995, he believed EI constituted two general abilities: identifying emotions (in self and others) and influencing emotions (also in self and others) (43). Identifying emotions can be easy if we're looking at faces—even little babies know when someone's making an angry face at them. (What twisted goon makes an angry face at a little baby?) Goleman argues that emotions circulate more obviously in face-to-face interactions in which as much as "90 percent or more of an emotional message is nonverbal" (97). It takes mindful effort, and not a little imagination, to work with emotions in writing. Because of spatial and temporal distance, you'll find it hard to analyze a rhetorical situation to decide how an audience feels now and how it *should* feel after reading your writing. This looks like yet another job for Captain Rhetorician. (That's *you*.)

Robert Solomon concluded that "we can create better lives for ourselves only if we create better emotions as well" (215), especially if we are committed to being the Good Guys. Since we assume that good people respond with appropriate emotions because of a habitually moral way of life, emotional appeals are intimately tied up in ethos as well. Emotional appeals, then, work to create better lives. They're a necessary ingredient in any rhetorical strategy, since research demonstrates that arguments with emotional appeals are more effective than primarily or exclusively logical arguments (Aronson 85).

Let's talk first about how emotions are *appropriate* in rhetorical situations, and then we'll talk about some methods for making emotional appeals. I'll conclude with some dangers you'll want to consider as you analyze other rhetors' attempts at emotional appeals.

Appropriate Emotions

In the chapter on rhetorical situation, we talked about how kairos means using language at the opportune, fitting, appropriate rhetorical time. The ancient Greeks believed that speech should "address recurring topics and occasions properly," since "on certain occasions and before certain audiences only certain utterances are appropriate" (Poulakos 60). The Greeks called this virtue *to prepon*; in Latin, the word is translated as *decorum*. Effective emotional appeals invite audiences to feel appropriate (i.e., opportune, fitting, proper, suitable) emotions.

In his book on ethics, Aristotle teaches that we can experience emotion too much or too little, depending on the situation: "but to feel them at the right times, with reference to the right objects, towards the right people, with the right motive, and in the right way, is what is both intermediate and best, and this is characteristic of virtue" (*Nicomachean Ethics* 340). Keeping our emotions suited to the moment is a balancing act between too much and too little—we're looking for the Goldilocks dose of emotional response. Even anger, an emotion we usually associate with Hulk-like destruction, can be fitting if the person "is angry at the right things and with the right people, and, further, as he ought, when he ought, and as long as he ought" (389). How do we know when we're evoking the right kind or amount of emotion? It ain't easy, says Aristotle. (Gee—thanks, Aristotle!)

A brief political anecdote might teach us about this rhetorical principle. On April 20, 2010, an oil rig drilling in the Gulf of Mexico exploded, sank, and started gushing oil into the ocean. Before it could be capped, several months later, the rig had spilled around 5 million barrels of oil into the Gulf, the largest oceanic oil spill in history. In June of that year, a Washington Post–ABC News poll revealed that 75% of U.S. citizens believed the spill was a "major environmental disaster" ("Washington Post").

Now, imagine you're the President of the United States. How do you respond to this? What is the emotion most fitting for a disaster like this?

President Barack Obama first decided to play it cool. In May he called a press conference to update the public on plans to clean up the spill and actions taken against BP, the company responsible for it. In measured language, he explained what the U.S. government was doing to manage the crisis. Near the end of the speech, Obama noted that citizens were angry about the spill: "Every day I see this leak continue," he said, "I am angry and frustrated as well" ("Remarks").

For whatever reason, that anger and frustration seemed to many to be inappropriately muted. One journalist present at the press conference summarized this disconnect in these words:

> As I sat in the fourth row on Thursday, I was struck by the weirdly passive figure before me. He delivered lawyerly phrases and spoke of his anger about the oil spill but showed none in his voice or on his face. He was, presumably, there to show how aggressively he has handled the disaster, but he seemed cool, almost bloodless. (Milbank)

Even Obama's supporters felt that he had not been "angry enough" in a situation that seemed to call for righteous indignation (Hertzberg). To some of his audience, Obama's coolness made his arguments less convincing because the coolness suggested a detached character, a character out of touch with the needs of the moment. After mounting criticism, Obama tried to show a little more spit and vinegar, but by then it was too late—to some, the kairos for expressing anger had come and gone.

So: Where are we? We've learned the following principles:

1. Emotions are not just feelings—They're social *judgments* emerging from situations, habits, and social experience.

2. Emotions are not irrational—Emotional experience is necessary for rational thought, and emotional appeals are necessary for convincing audiences.

3. However, emotions *can be* dangerous—they can hijack rhetorical situations, if we let them.

4. Emotionally intelligent people can identify and influence emotions in themselves and others.

5. Emotions are signs of character—they reflect a habitual way of being in the world.

6. Like any appeal, emotional appeals should fit the rhetorical situation (purpose, audience, kairos, etc.).

Tattoo these principles on the fleshy tables of your heart, and you'll be a more effective rhetor.

Emotional Appeals

Now we get down to pragmatics—the "how-to" of emotional appeals. Like ethos, pathos concerns both the rhetor and the audience, both the emotions you *express* as a writer and the emotions you *evoke* in your readers.

Expressing Emotion in Writing

How do you tell someone how you're feeling in writing without saying something banal like, "I am sad about this"? We mock emoticons and emoji for being too cute or overused, but they are useful for conveying emotions to audiences who may otherwise have to guess at how you feel. Am I right or am I right? ☺

As the Obama oil-spill example revealed, people care how you ought to feel. They want to see, in writing, that your own emotional state is fitting for the moment, that your judgment is appropriately conditioned for the kairos at hand. (Sounds a lot like ethos; well, you've noticed already, no doubt, that rhetorical strategies bleed together.) In the last chapter, we talked about writing cover letters. Potential employers want to see that you're emotionally mature enough to have confidence in your relevant abilities ("I'm particularly confident in using JavaScript, Flash, and Python, and I'm excited to learn more programming languages in my career"). They want to see your passion for the content of the job ("Though I'm not yet a professional web designer, I've been creating web content eagerly since I was in grade school"). These moves are subtle, but they convey emotional content to readers.

Expressing emotion doesn't have to be as subtle. Consider this excerpt I took from a 2008 blog post by Michelle Malkin, a professional conservative blogger. She's writing about how young female celebrities often transition quickly from innocent child stars to sexualized, troubled young adults:

> First Britney. Then Lindsay. And now: Miley Cyrus. Do they ever learn?
>
> By "they," I don't mean the girls. I mean their parents. Where are they? What the hell are they thinking?
>
> I don't know how many times I've asked those questions over the years as a parade of young Hollywood starlets has burst onto the scene with wholesome charm, achieved dizzying fame and fortune, and then crashed back to Earth half-naked with corrupted souls and drug-glazed eyes.

Are parents without scruples more likely to sacrifice their daughters to the wolves of the entertainment industry? Or does show business sap all the common sense out of mothers and fathers who should know better? Either way, they are guilty of child abandonment. (Malkin)

How do you read this language? How does Malkin convey her own emotional state in this excerpt? Is it over the top, or appropriate to the situation she's responding to?

Political bloggers like Malkin seem to be in a perpetual state of outrage, which is one of the reasons why they're popular—we're drawn to passionate people, to the scrum of politics. We're used to the idea that some issues are worth getting mad as heck about—remember Aristotle's Goldilocks principle for fitting emotions. On the other hand, we may find the Perpetual Outrage Machine a drag. I find it hard to take comment threads seriously when every post spits venom at strangers. But that's beside the point. I wanted you to see in Malkin's post that the emotional state of the writer can be expressed in the words and phrases of the writer.

You might think certain genres don't lend themselves to emotional appeals. Lab reports, for example, or professional memos seem like bloodless documents. But consider, for a moment, how less conspicuous emotions (like optimism or frustration or satisfaction) could be woven into even the most straightforward of genres. When science writers end science reports by calling for more research, they are expressing curiosity, expectation, maybe even hope.

Evoking Emotion in Readers

Of course, bloggers like Michelle Malkin hope *her* outrage will become *your* outrage. (Maybe you're outraged at her outrage!) Ultimately, the reason we express appropriate emotions is to invite others to accept our judgment of the situation and match their emotions with ours. In a cover letter, you want to convey your own enthusiasm for the job so that the employer will feel "mirror enthusiasm" about hiring you. But you don't need necessarily to wear your emotions on your sleeve to evoke emotion in your audience.

Here are five tried-and-true strategies for evoking emotion in your audience:

1. **Give concrete details.** In *Made to Stick*, Chip and Dan Heath describe a study conducted by Carnegie Mellon University that tested how audiences respond to requests from charities. The researchers gave participants five bucks to complete a survey on technology, and then unexpectedly they asked participants whether they'd donate some of their money to a charity called Save the Children. For one group, the request letter gave statistics for the sad state of children in Africa, like "Food shortages in Malawi are affecting more than 3 million children" and "More than 11 million people in Ethiopia need immediate food assistance." Participants in this group gave on average $1.14 in response to these dramatic stats. However, another group's request letter introduced them to Rokia, a "desperately poor" seven-year-old girl from Mali, facing "the threat of severe hunger or even starvation." Participants who learned about Rokia contributed twice as much—$2.38 on average—as the group barraged with facts (Heath and Heath 166).

   Vivid examples have more persuasive power than a barrage of statistics; we have an "insensitivity to quantity," making it difficult to be touched by large, abstract numbers (Aronson 92–93; Greene 112). Tangible, concrete language creates images in the mind, which in turn act on our emotional imagination. It's hard to picture 11 million people starving in Mali; the magnitude, while certainly evocative, can't touch us as much as a single face: seven-year-old Rokia's face, for example. This bias for the concrete, for the viscerally evocative, can be problematic if it leads us into thinking that Rokia's face is somehow "more real" than relevant statistics (Kahneman 130). And yet the power of concrete imagery remains. Words and phrases that evoke sensory experiences in readers can lead them more effectively to emotional judgments. Think of Jonathan Kozol's poor children with bleeding gums and rotting teeth.

2. **Tell stories.** Why do we like stories? We're wired for them. For millennia, we've told stories to each other—stories about gods, devils, fairies, imps, spirit creators and tricksters, nature, great heroes and villains. We live in story while we sleep. As pattern-seekers, we use story to explain the unexplainable—from haunted houses to conspiracy theories. Nursery rhymes and fairy tales teach kids to beware the Big Bad Wolf. We tell stories in movies, TV shows, popular songs,

video blogs; we tell stories at camp, around the cooler, in the locker room, around the kitchen table. We even tell stories about ourselves—psychologists call them "core narratives" (Wilson 52)—and those stories influence how we feel, what we understand, and what we do with ourselves. "If you want a message to burrow into a human mind," writes Jonathan Gottschall, "work it into a story" (118).

Stories, of course, are *rhetorical*—we tell stories in particular situations for particular audiences and purposes. The emotional appeal of story is almost automatic; when we hear or watch a story unfold, our bodies respond as if we're part of the story (Gottschall 62–63). Some psychologists believe stories function like simulators of social life—the vicarious emotional experience teaches us something about how to live with other people, and how not to (Gottschall 58).

What goes into a story? In a way, a story is just a sequence of events: Yesterday I went to work until noon, then went to lunch with a friend, then came back to work and answered some emails, then went to a banquet with my wife, and then came home and read *Madeline and the Bad Hat* to my daughter. Call that a story if you want, but it's an incredibly boring story. Good stories, on the other hand, are almost always about *trouble*. It's the "universal grammar" of all stories (Gottschall 52). To tell a good story, put a person in some kind of predicament and then tell us what happens. Storytelling experts have diced the elements of a good story in all kinds of ways, but the four most useful elements are *character* (the protagonists in the tale), *scene* (the location of the action), *conflict* (trouble!), and *resolution* (how it all ends). Resolutions, which don't have to be happy and are often better not so, can be closed or open: closed endings answer all questions and curiosities and satisfy "all audience emotion"; open endings "leave a question or two unanswered and some emotion unfulfilled" (McKee 48).

When should you tell a story in writing? Let us repeat our rhetorical anthem: *It depends!* It depends on the situation, purpose, audience, and genre. Personal narratives are nothing but story, but even the stodgiest of technical grant proposals must tell the tale of how past attempts to solve a problem have failed and failed miserably. Research papers can begin with a story to hook readers emotionally; argumentative papers can use stories as evidence to accept arguments.

Where do you get stories? Four places: from your own life, from the lives of others (in your social circle, or in history or the news or biographies), from your imagination, or from existing fiction (novels, movies, folk tales, etc.). When I was young, my church pastor would tell the same story at Christmas every year: the story of George Bailey, banker of Bedford Falls, who learns from divine intervention to value his own life after trying to commit suicide. And every year, as he told the story, my pastor would sob—and the congregation would sob right with him—even though everyone knew he was just rehashing the plot from the Frank Capra movie *It's a Wonderful Life*.

3. **Tap shared values.** We talked about this strategy in reference to *ethos* and the relationship you build with your readers. One way to evoke emotion in your audience is to express support for something valued by the discourse community to which you and your readers belong. And conversely, you can evoke emotion by shouting "boo-hiss," so to speak, at the Bad Guys. This kind of rhetorical move was called *epideictic* in classical rhetoric: you praise the praiseworthy, or you blame the blameworthy (Aristotle *Rhetoric* 48). Value talk is central to public discourse, which often calls upon us to make moral judgments about how to get all the stuff to all the right people.

4. **Amplify with word choice.** You'll learn more about the term *diction* (meaning word choice) in the next chapter on style. For now, just think about how different words create different emotional buzzes in audiences. Think of the difference between the words *cheap* and *inexpensive*. If your friends told you that your dress looks *cheap*, would you take it as a compliment? But would you shy away from telling them it was a *bargain*?

Words have *denotations* (their standard dictionary definitions) and *connotations* (all the thoughts and feelings associated with a word in a context). The word *communism* may denote a political ideology, but in the United States the word evokes negative feelings beyond the word's definition. Some words evoke vague, but real, emotions because of the bundle of impressions they create in the minds of readers: words like *freedom*, *family*, *justice*, *love*, and *democracy*. Sometimes words used as metaphors can evoke powerful judgments. In 2005 *The Independent*, a center-left British newspaper, ran an online opinion article titled "The Rape of the Rainforest," about a Brazilian soybean farmer whose company worked to clear 10,000 square miles of Amazon rainforest in 2004 (McCarthy and Buncombe). How does the word *rape* work in the title? How are we meant to judge the Brazilian farmer's actions? Surely the word *rape* upgrades the act of cutting down trees to a violent crime.

Sometimes people use *euphemisms* to mute the emotional blow of something unpleasant. Employees are "let go" when their bosses fire them, and companies "downsize" when they fire a whole bunch of people; a man run over by a cement truck "passes away"; "pork" is the remnants of a pig that's been slaughtered, gutted, and sliced into pieces; your dog Rover is "put to sleep" when a vet injects him with massive amounts of pentobarbital; "having a drink" could mean slamming shots of Kentucky bourbon; a sexually promiscuous person has "been around the block"; an ugly person has a "sweet spirit"; thugs "talk some sense into him" by beating him senseless; a "slight delay" means she won't get on her plane for another three hours. All these euphemisms attempt to manage the emotions of the people hearing them. Certain words carry more emotional power than others.

5. **Call your audience to action.** Somewhere in your writing, you'll want to tell readers why what you've written matters. You'll suggest *implications* for your argument that answer the audience's burning question, "So what?" You want to convey to your readers that your ideas have consequences—and those consequences matter. You want them to feel a sense of urgency from the things you've said. One way to do that is to suggest that audiences take action. Even stodgy academic writers do this when—say, at the end of an article on the mating practices of the slipper limpet snail—they call for further research on the issue. Many genres invite this kind of move. At the very least, you can ask your readers to think differently about the issue you've addressed. Sometimes it's appropriate to suggest some kind of collective action ("As Group X, we need to do Y"). You may also find it appropriate to tell the government or some other organization to change its ways ("It's time for the state legislature to provide equal housing opportunities for everyone, regardless of sexual orientation"). Once you've invoked emotion, it's your rhetorical responsibility to help readers think about what to do with those emotions—in other words, how to act appropriately.

Decorum Is All

Undoubtedly it will have occurred to you—because you're wicked smart—that emotional appeals can be used to manipulate other people. You may feel that some of the strategies I've talked about sound like a recipe for bewitching people against their will. Am I asking you to play your audience like a two-bit piccolo? No.

Remember two things about pathos from our earlier discussion:

(1) You need some kind of emotional appeal, even when writing genres that seem formal or stuffy or official or otherwise all-too-rational; emotions, remember, drive the brain, and they help us form judgments, which is the whole purpose of rhetoric; and,

(2) emotional appeals, like all other appeals, should be *appropriate to the situation* you're writing in. They prepare your audience for appropriate action.

Yes—decorum, my friends, is all! When you're preparing to write, think about what kind of emotion is fitting for the situation. Overkill turns off your audience, especially if they don't share your opinion about the issue or see your emotional appeals as a fitting response or sign of good character. Emotional appeals can be subtle; at some low-burn level, comprehension itself (i.e., merely understanding something and feeling that knowledge work in you) delivers an emotional fix that invites us to judgment. But emotional appeals should be there each time you write, and they should be fitting.

I'll close with Daniel Goleman's words on emotional intelligence. Skill with emotional appeals allows writers "to shape an encounter, to mobilize and inspire others, to thrive in intimate relationships, to persuade and influence, to put others at ease" (113). That's powerful stuff.

Works Cited

Aristotle. *Nicomachean Ethics.* In *Introduction to Aristotle.* Ed. Richard McKeon. NY: Modern Library, 1947. 297–543. Print.

Aristotle. *On Rhetoric.* 2nd ed. Transl. George A. Kennedy. NY: Oxford, 2007. Print.

Aronson, Eliot. *The Social Animal.* Eleventh Edition. NY: Worth, 2012. Print.

Damasio, Antonio. *Descartes' Error: Emotion, Reason, and the Human Brain.* NY: Penguin, 1994. Print.

Forgas, Joseph P. "The Role of Affect in Attitudes and Attitude Change." *Attitudes and Attitude Change.* Ed. William D. Crano and Radmila Prislin. NY: Psychology P, 2008. 131–158. Print.

Franks, David. "The Neuroscience of Emotions." *Handbook of the Sociology of Emotions.* Ed. Jan E. Stets and Jonathan H. Turner. NY: Springer, 2006. 38–62. Print.

Goleman, Daniel. *Emotional Intelligence.* NY: Bantam, 2005. Print.

Gottschall, Jonathan. *The Storytelling Animal.* NY: Mariner, 2012. Print.

Greene, Joshua. *Moral Tribes.* NY: Penguin, 2013. Print.

Heath, Chip and Dan Heath. *Made to Stick.* NY: Random House, 2007. Print.

Hertzberg, Hendrik. "Spilled Oil." *The New Yorker.* 28 June 2010. Web. 16 Feb 2015.

Kahneman, Daniel. *Thinking, Fast and Slow.* NY: Farrar, Straus, and Giroux, 2011. Print.

Kozol, Jonathan. *Savage Inequalities.* NY: Harper Perennial, 1991. Print.

Malkin, Michelle. "The Seduction of Hannah Montana." 29 April 2008. Blog post. Web. 19 Feb 2015.

McCarthy, Michael and Andrew Buncombe. "The Rape of the Rainforest." *The Independent.* 20 May 2005. Web. 22 Feb 2015.

McKee, Robert. *Story.* NY: Harper, 1997. Print.

Milbank, Dana. "Obama's Oil Spill Response." *Washington Post*. 30 May 2010. Web. 16 Feb 2015.

Poulakos, John. *Sophistical Rhetoric in Classical Greece*. Columbia: U of South Carolina P, 1995. Print.

"Remarks by the President on the Gulf Oil Spill." The White House. 27 May 2010. Web. 18 Feb 2015.

Solomon, Robert C. *True to Our Feelings*. NY: Oxford, 2007. Print.

Washington Post—ABC News Poll. 3–6 June 2010. Web. 18 Feb 2015.

Wilson, Timothy D. *Redirect*. NY: Back Bay, 2015. Print.

11

PRINCIPLES OF STYLE

We've made it to the S in ACES (Go, Team Rhetoric!). We've covered

Argument
Character
Emotions,

and in the next two chapters we'll cover

Style.

Style—When You Do That Thing You Do

Every year, usually in the middle of Fall semester, my wife asks me about the new styles on campus. "What are students wearing these days?" she wonders. "What's trendy?"

And I answer, "I have no idea—I'm an absent-minded professor with more important things to worry about!"

But I'm lying. Like most everyone else, I'm not beneath noticing the trends hanging on the bodies of everyone on campus. Last year I noticed male students pegging (i.e., rolling up) their skinny jeans, which is something my friends and I did in sixth grade, back in 1986. One year, the galoshes came out—in all kinds of colors and styles—and replaced the sheepskin boots that passed for *Arctic chic* for a while. Popped collars come in and out. Having come of age in an era when hip-hop culture merged with Seattle grunge in an unholy alliance of baggy, sloppy, and flannel, I'm amused to see hipsters pulling off the sloppy but tightened-up lumberjack look. And this year the galoshes have been replaced by knee-high dressy leather boots, which soon will be replaced by herring-bone combat boots with SmartBoot® wearable technology built into the shoelaces. (I made up that last part.)

And I know that everything I just said will be woefully out of date in five minutes.

How do you define style? When you say someone is *stylish*, what does that mean? If I wear jeans, a faded green t-shirt, and my University of Arizona hat (Go Wildcats!), do I have *style*? When do you know something's *out of style*?

Style means a *manner* of doing something. Our dictionary definitions talk about style as a *particular way* of doing something, a manner or characteristic habit or practice. Style, then, is unavoidable. You have a style of walking, talking, dressing, dancing, playing sports, eating, or brushing your teeth—even if you're not trying to. When you walk, you choose, consciously or otherwise, how to put one foot in front of the other and how to swing your arms or hold your head. All those decisions add up to your style of walking. (Wanna go insane? Focus deliberately on the way you walk for an entire day.)

But I bet you know someone with a *distinguished* walk, a walk that really sticks out in your mind, because somehow, compared to other walks, it has its own special step, swing, or swagger. In this sense, then, style is more than manner: It's about distinct individual expression—it's about grace, purposeful self-expression, elegance, flamboyance, skill, spunk, a unique voice.

When I think about style as a quality of writing, I like to think of it in both these ways. Every time you write, you write with style. You can't help it. Each sentence you write reflects a series of rhetorical decisions, a sensibility, even if the writing seems straightforward and unadorned. Paul Butler defines style in this way as "the deployment of rhetorical resources, in written discourse, to create and express meaning" (Butler 3). That pretty much sums up all the writing we do. But writing with style also means writing with a distinct voice that conveys a distinct personality to the reader, a personality that seeks to make an impression, to make the reading experience pleasurable. Novelist Mary McCarthy defines style more in this second sense as voice: as "the irreducible and always recognizable and alive thing" (Yagoda 23). Sounds like ethos, doesn't it? Style is ethos.

This "always recognizable and alive thing" we call style is a big part of what keeps a reader reading your work, or not. With each sentence, you take shape in the brain of the reader, taking the cerebral stage as a character in a rhetorical drama. That character becomes recognizable and real to readers through style, and style makes the reading experience what it is.

In this chapter and the next, I want to help you improve how you write with style in both senses of the word—rhetorical choice *and* compelling voice. To make that happen, though, we need to get to work: There are things you need to *do* to improve your style, and there are concepts you need to *understand* to be a lifelong stylistic writer. We'll talk about both in this chapter. We'll save the nuts and bolts of style strategies for the next.

Your Stylistic Workout Regimen

If you want to master rhetorical choice and compelling voice, you'll have to hit the exercise equipment. Let me be your personal trainer for a moment. I suggest a regimen of seven exercises that will help you develop your writing style:

1. **Read good writing.** Good readers can become good writers in part because they internalize the language of writing. They see how the pros use prose. Your universe is full of amazing writers writing in every genre imaginable. Find some really great writing and read it. Try poetry. I'm not a natural poetry-lover, but I try to read at least one book of poetry each year from contemporary poets. Find an essay writer that makes you laugh (I like David Sedaris and Mary Roach). Look for a compelling ethos emerging from a blog or Twitter feed. Read online magazines and news outlets. Don't always settle for a quickie skim of the headlines; burrow into an article that takes more than five minutes to read. Read the National Book Award or Pulitzer Prize winners.

2. **Keep a journal.** You should have a special writing space where you can write whatever you want, capture cool quotes and sentences, wax bold and eloquent, make mistakes, and experiment with style. These writing spaces are often called *commonplace* books, described by one scholar as "blank bound volumes in which one writes down vivid images, great descriptions, striking turns of phrase, ideas, high points from one's life and reading" (Richardson 19). You don't need a pretentious moleskin notebook. You can use a note-taking app on your phone (if you have thumbs of fury) or an online notebook (blogs or Google Docs make good commonplace books); it's nice to be able to cut and paste. Become a sentence hunter: While you read, look for amazing sentences and jot them down. I have about 120 sentences in my collection, with writers ranging from Ray Bradbury to J.K. Rowling.

3. **Imitate cool sentences.** If you make sentence-hunting a habit, you can *imitate* some of your favorites so you can learn new strategies. Imitating sentences is old-school: kids in ancient Greece and Rome learned to speak and write with power by imitating the work of the masters (Clark). Imitation (the Greeks called it *mimesis*) has a bad reputation because everyone wants to be An Original these days. But originality is overrated—maybe even impossible, considering that creators influence each other all the time. As Kirby Ferguson points out,

everything is a remix. To imitate a sentence, try this method: (a) find a cool sentence you like—more complex sentences work better; (b) write down the sentence *exactly as you see it* in your journal; (c) study for a moment the way the writer has combined phrases and clauses or used punctuation; and then (d) write your own sentence using the same grammatical structure (same noun and verb phrases, same order and type of phrases and clauses). Try on the voice of another writer to get a sense of your stylistic range. Someone—it might have been Pablo Picasso—once said, "Good artists copy; great artists steal."

4. **Combine sentences**. Imagine two sentences: "I'm a writer" and "My mother is proud." How many different ways can we combine those two sentences to make meaning? Here are the first three I thought of: "My mother is proud that I'm a writer," "I'm a writer—my mother is proud," or "My mother, because I'm a writer, is proud." What choices did I make to combine these sentences? How does each new sentence convey a unique meaning different from the others? For years, research has shown that doing such exercises strengthens your ability to write compelling sentences (Dean 87; Strong 2). Your instructor can help you find sentence-combining exercises, and you can find more online.

5. **Learn some grammar terms**. Yep, I said it. You can't fully analyze a person's style, including your own, until you've figured out the way the English language works on the page. You don't need to go all out and memorize the hundreds of terms you find in a book on English grammar. In fact, packing your head with all that stuff might *hurt* you as a writer (Graham and Perin). At the very least, you probably should know something about *syntax*—how words, phrases, and clauses pile up in a sentence to make meaning—and *modification*—how words, phrases and clauses enhance the meaning of other words, phrases, and clauses. If you don't know how sentences work, you and your instructor won't be able to talk as freely and usefully about the sentences you write. We'll talk more about syntax and modification in the next chapter.

6. **Rewrite**. I learned to develop my style by rewriting the heck out of my own writing. And you can, too. Take a short paragraph of your own writing and see if you can rewrite the entire thing without looking at the earlier draft. Get in the habit of reworking sentences until

they *zing*—rewording, combining, rearranging, deleting, destroying, garnishing. Remember that "a difference of style is always a difference in meaning," even if the shift is subtle (Beardsley 7). You have options—use them. As you learn different sentence types and methods of modification, you'll have more moves to make as a writer. As you rewrite, you'll feel more freedom to play with language; novice writers often feel that when they write sentences, they carve them in stone. Without play, you can't develop your style.

7. **Compose out loud, revise out loud.** Sometimes when I'm in a conference with a student and we're stuck on a funky clunky sentence, I'll say, "Why don't you just tell me what you were trying to say here." Nine times out of ten, whatever they say, right there on the spot, is better than what they were trying to say in writing—and by "better" I mean clearer, more concise, more interesting, more voiced. In *Vernacular Eloquence*, Peter Elbow teaches writers that we have "a rich store of eloquent linguistic resources" from our everyday speech that often goes untapped in writing (7). As I've said before, speech is natural but writing requires explicit motor practice. Because writing is not natural, students often write in a stilted, stuffy, and formal way because they think that's what a teacher wants. We denigrate the way we speak as sloppy when in fact our speaking can be clearer, easier to process, more lively and diverse, and more emotionally engaging to audiences than our writing.

So Elbow suggests we use our natural speaking abilities at various stages in the writing process. For example, in the early stages we can try "unplanned speaking onto the page," by which he means talking through what we plan to write or using freewriting as a way to capture ideas that might otherwise be roadblocked by the fastidious editor in our brains (Elbow 139). He also recommends reading drafts aloud. Reading your drafts out loud is a revelation. I've rewritten many a sentence that looked fine on paper but sounded like a train wreck when I read it out loud. I find, too, that if I read out loud to my wife Amy, editor and friend now for fifteen years, I'm more attentive to the way I sound to someone else. When we read writing out loud, we develop empathy for our readers because we can *hear* how we sound in a reader's head.

Writers get better when they're mindful about getting better. Remember that Great Truth from Chapter One? Writers get better *at their style* when they *become mindful apprentices of style*. I'm inviting you to join me in becoming a Style Apprentice. We don't have uniforms or sashes or t-shirts or cookies or anything, but we do have rhetorical power!

Okay, we've talked about what you can *do* as a Style Apprentice. For the rest of the chapter, we'll talk about what you need to *know* about style.

The Virtues of Style

What makes a date a *good* date? When I was in my early twenties, a few of my family members and friends were foolhardy enough to set me up on blind dates. And after each one, I thought, "Does [fill in the blank with name of guilty family member] know *anything* about me?" It seemed that my date and I were about as compatible as a smartphone and bathwater. (I blame myself.) So maybe one cardinal virtue of a good date would be compatibility—that click-y "goes together nicely" feeling we get when we're with someone with whom we share a certain affinity.

What makes a writing style a good writing style?

According to the philosophers of antiquity, the Four Cardinal Virtues of the Soul are prudence, justice, temperance, and courage. The ancient rhetoricians had Four Cardinal Virtues of Good Style, too, and they still resonate today: Good writing is fitting, clean, clear, and compelling. As a writer, you should cultivate these four virtues as you write.

First: Good style—and here, surely, I'll shock the pants right off you—is **fitting.** Yes, my friends, style, like any other rhetorical decision, should be a welcomed guest to the rhetorical situation (see chapter six). You've seen this come up before in previous chapters. I don't want to oversimplify things, but in essence rhetorical choices are effective when they are appropriate, full-stop. In one of his dialogues, the Roman rhetorician Cicero has one of his characters say, "there is really no rule that I could give you at this point"—about style, he means—only that "we should see to it that [the style] is adapted to the problem at hand" (290).

Style is most effective when it's appropriate for the targeted audience. For example, I have had writing projects rejected by academic journals because the reviewers said my style was too casual for the venue. And I'm pretty sure if I'd written, as I did in the last paragraph, "here, surely, I'll shock the pants right off you" in a manuscript for a scholarly journal,

I would have been rejected in one hot minute. But I think of you as friends (really!), so I thought it would be okay (i.e., fitting) in this setting. Your genre will guide your stylistic decisions, as will your audience and purpose. This Cardinal Virtue reminds us that style is not necessarily something you find in a text; you find it in the *context*, in the interaction between writer and reader as mediated by the text. As two writing scholars have said, "style embodies or defines relationships between people" (Holcomb and Killingsworth 4). Style, then, is fitting when it's appropriate for the genre.

The reading experience creates an ethos that is either fitting or not-so-fitting for the work that needs to be done to respond to the situation's exigence. Your goal as a Style Apprentice is to imagine how your rhetorical choices influence a particular audience through the sound of words on the page or screen. Let the style fit the situation. You don't wear the wild Hawaiian-print shirt to the business interview (unless you're interviewing with a flakey tech start-up run by brilliant, iconoclastic college dropouts). Consider aspects like *level of formality, familiarity with the audience* (e.g., strangers often misread sarcasm), *idiomatic phrases, jargon or insider talk, allusions, contractions, slang, sexist language* (e.g., avoid the indefinite masculine), and what Holcomb and Killingsworth call "*the interplay of convention and deviation*" (39). This last consideration is important. Each situation has certain constraints and certain freedoms; it's important to know the difference.

I can't help but add one more thing about the concept of "fitting." I have many students who believe that the most fitting style for academic writing is a stuffy, formal, rhetorically-distant tone that approximates (at least the writer imagines it does) a scholar scholarizing. When we get to college, we have to write our way through it, and we often default to a formal tone—without warmth, full of jargon, and needlessly complicated. Though I've said that your style should fit the situation and genre, we have more latitude as writers than we think to write reader-friendly prose. I love how John Trimble says it in *Writing with Style*: "View your reader as a companionable friend" and "write like you're actually talking to that friend" (73). There's rhetorical space even in technical documents for a warm, simple, and direct style to be fitting.

Second, good style is **clean**. By *clean* I mean as free as possible from errors in grammar, spelling, punctuation, diction, mechanics, document design, and fact.

Look: I've said before that errors happen. We make them, no matter how careful we are. And William James is right:

> Our errors are surely not such awfully solemn things. In a world where we are so certain to incur them, in spite of all our caution, a certain lightness of heart seems healthier than this excessive nervousness on their behalf. (James 470)

In addition, language changes somewhat. It's flexible; it's our tool. There are varieties of English, from a variety of cultures, and we should celebrate that. We ourselves shift registers when speaking to different audiences; we present different selves in language, depending on rhetorical situation (Gee 87). Linguists think of grammar as a way to describe what we do with language, not as a system of rigid laws carved on the tablets of humanity. So you might as well criticize "the song of the humpback whale" or the spider's web as criticize the way we use language (Pinker 383). Some rules are solid and hardwired: the standard English subject-verb-object (SVO) formation tells me that writing *high grammar learned school you in* will cause serious problems for readers, even those readers who respect Yoda, the grammatically creative Jedi in *Star Wars*. Other rules are more like *conventions* of usage commonly accepted by People Who Seem to Know (like teachers). Sometimes those conventions make no sense. *Don't split infinitives*, they say. *Don't begin sentences with conjunctions like* and *or* but. And (ha!) these conventions get flouted by professional writers all the time.

But (double ha!) here's the thing: Errors, insofar as readers notice them, create static. Readers see them—not in any predictable fashion, sometimes, but they see them. Error, it's true, is mostly in the eye of the beholder, i.e., the reader, and if the reader doesn't see them, then they might as well not exist (Williams). However, we've already established in chapter seven that errors mar credibility; alas, they make us look dumb. One of the earliest and most charitable scholars of writing error, Mina Shaughnessy, writes that errors are "unintentional and unprofitable intrusions upon the consciousness of the reader." Often they "carry messages which writers can't afford to send" (12). Perhaps Cicero (first-century rhetorician) said it worst: "Nobody has ever admired an orator for speaking correct Latin; if he doesn't they actually make fun of him, and not only consider him no orator, but not even a human being" (238). It's mean to dehumanize people for their writing skills—and it reveals elitist thinking and ignorance of the dynamics of language. But, okay, Cicero may be right at least this far: Error has social consequences.

What I emphatically *don't* want to do is perpetuate the equally ugly idea that error-free writing is the end-all, be-all of learning to write. Many a student's writing spirit has been crushed in the claws of school teachers who treat learning to write as the art of not making mistakes. Forgive the soapboxing, but I feel that it's particularly cruel to mark up an elementary school child's writing with red ink for not getting the commas in the right place. If we fixate on error when learning to write, we become like a centipede overthinking where to put its feet while walking. (Thanks, Francis Christensen, for that metaphor.) When we write, we want to be treated like someone with ideas and thoughts and arguments and interesting things to say. Having our errors called out often feels like our ethos has been demolished because we have a slightly crooked tooth. Writing classes should be safe places to make mistakes and learn from them.

So: Where does that leave us on the whole *clean* issue? Remember, first, that you should attend to *surface-level issues* late in your drafting process, as we talked about in chapter three. In the drafting stage, you should just write with unfettered ecstasy and leave the problem of error to later reviewing, revising, editing, and polishing. But keep your audience in mind! Prepare your drafts so that peers or instructors will not get caught up in speed bumps that might be avoided with a quick proofread. As reluctantly as I might say it, you need to understand that your stylistic decisions constitute an *ethos*; with each sentence, you invite the reader into a reading experience. Glaring errors make both efforts rough rowing, especially when you're in the professional world. (I've seen hundreds of blog posts about how errors in business and social media writing can damage brands or reputations.) One last thought: many errors are actually *patterns* of error that show a kind of logical thinking about language (Shaughnessy). Look for patterns of error in your work when you're revising, and consult a handbook if you're not familiar with some of the more popular, and rhetorically important, conventions.

The third Cardinal Virtue is this: Good writing is **clear**. Clarity is one of those virtues that textbooks throw out there with great force, as if divine beings had commanded that we be clear in our writing. The word is also an abstraction—what does it mean? In the field of writing studies, it is somewhat controversial (Butler; Howard; Lanham). Some scholars feel that those who focus so enthusiastically on clarity as a cardinal virtue ignore not only the virtue of complexity and eloquence but the value of context. They make clarity sound Puritan; nobody wants to party with that boring stick-in-the-mud *Clarity*! Shakespeare is hard to read, and yet he is considered one of the five most important people in the last millennium.

Richard Lanham, one of clarity's skeptics, gives us a working definition: "clarity indicates a successful relationship between reader and writer" (57). Its first job "is to make us feel at home" (50). I like that metaphor: As readers we slip into a clear style like we slip into Grandma's comfy chair. That's what we want the reading experience to be like for our readers. We want our writing to be understood. We don't want to waste our readers' time or confuse them. In *Performing Prose*, Chris Holcomb and Jimmie Killingsworth help us understand that clarity is a "convention of readability" that exhibits five attributes: it's active (meaning, subjects and verbs are clear—more on this in the next chapter), it flows, it's organized for emphasis, it uses familiar language, and it's concise (41–48). We live in a saturated world. Your writing competes with a deluge of other activities people could be doing, like playing video games on their phones. When you write clearly, you set up the relationship quickly and smoothly, therefore advancing your purpose to influence attitudes.

I know this principle may sound abstract at this point. But there's a simple idea behind clarity: Most of the time, we want our readers to understand what we're saying without having to work too hard at it. There are exceptions, absolutely. Sometimes we want readers to lean over the page with scrunched eyebrows and struggle with us as we struggle with complex ideas. When we write stories or poems, we may be more interested in giving readers a profound (and confounding) experience than in delivering a simple message. In the busy flow of practical language, however, clarity is key. In 2010, the United States Government passed Public Law 111–274, titled the "Plain Writing Act of 2010," in order "to improve the effectiveness and accountability of Federal agencies to the public by promoting clear Government communication that the public can understand and use" ("Plain Writing"). The spirit of the law is instructive: When the stakes are high (imagine legal or medical writing), we are responsible to write in a language our readers understand.

Finally, good writing should be **compelling**. Let us, for a moment, consider the termite, as it appears in the language of Wikipedia (I've done some editing for length here):

11

Termites are eusocial insects in the cockroach order Blattodea. Like ants, termites live in colonies where labor is divided in castes. Termites feed mostly on dead plant material, mostly in the form of wood, leaf litter, soil, or animal dung. As pests, they can cause serious structural damage to buildings, crops, or forests. Termites are major detritivores, particularly in the subtropical and tropical regions. Their recycling of wood and other plant matter is of considerable ecological importance.

Ah, the language of science! This is, I'd say, a perfectly respectable paragraph. It's simple. It contains factual information (as far as I know—I'm no entomologist). You could say that it's *correct* and *clear*—two of our cardinal virtues. Maybe it's fitting for a crowd-sourced world encyclopedia used by strangers for quick factual information. But what happened to you as you read the paragraph? Did you feel yourself slipping into a familiar role as "reader of encyclopedic information"? Each sentence sounds about the same as the others. No ethos emerges from it except maybe an *ethos* interested in sharing somewhat disconnected facts about termites.

Now let's look at the way science writer Natalie Angier tackles termites:

Or consider termites, the primary groundskeepers of tropical rainforests. They gnaw through dead or rotting trees and return much of the woody wealth back to the forest floor. What is a termite but a set of jaws joined to a petri dish, its gut a dense microecosystem of many hundreds of strains of microbes. Bacteria allow termites to wrest sustenance from sawdust and, like Gepetto, give dead wood a voice. (Angier 185)

I'd argue that Angier's writing is more lively than Wikipedia's (no offense, I hope, to the hundreds of people who may have crowd-sourced that paragraph). In the first example, termites are "eusocial insects in the cockroach order"; for Angier, they're "groundskeepers," a term which personifies termites, making them sound like little squishy helpers taking care of business. Whereas the first example talks of "their recycling of wood," Angier uses her *W*'s and *F*'s in the sonorous "woody wealth back to the forest floor." She also plays with sound when she says "wrest sustenance from sawdust," an unusual and interesting phrase. She exaggerates the termite's anatomy, or underplays it: a "set of jaws joined to a petri dish." That's a fascinating image. Notice, too, the Pinocchio allusion at the end:

comparing termites to Gepetto, creator and father of the magical wooden boy, is both weird and wonderful. It surprises and delights. It's playful.

Both excerpts demonstrate rhetorical choices. The second one alone shows how writing can be that "always recognizable and alive thing"— a distinguished and unique voice meant to create a pleasurable reading experience. Writing can be, and most always should be, compelling in this sense. In the words of Aristotle, compelling prose makes "language unfamiliar"; as pattern-seekers, we pay attention to variations, surprises, delights (Aristotle 198). Classical rhetoricians often called this virtue *ornamentation*, but that word implies cosmetic frippery, making style seem like a fancy sweater on a ferret or something. Instead, I like the word *compelling* for the power it invokes. A reader admires a compelling prose style almost in spite of herself. It invites attention, interest, admiration, joy. It breaks the boring plane of row upon row of words and says, "Hey! I want you to *really enjoy* what I'm telling you!" Compelling prose is pathos, as well as ethos.

How do you make your writing compelling? I'll share a few ways in the next chapter, but here are a few strategies, for starters: metaphor, proverbs, schemes (clever language patterns, like repetition), humor, hyperbole, analogy, allusion, imagery, sentence variation, surprising use of words, irony, satire, sentence fragments, parallelism, rhythm, poetic patterns (like alliteration), questions, direct address, emphasis. Sometimes these strategies will just tumble out of you while writing. At other times, you can revise them into your drafts, always keeping in mind how your specific audience might respond to your stylistic invitation to dance. I'm not suggesting you choke your sentences with piled-up purply tricks that will weary the reader because they're too obviously playful. You still have to be fitting, clean, and clear. But you don't have to be *ordinary*. That's why we often encourage writers to avoid cliches—those tired phrases that are like beating a dead...well...that are overused.

May I be frank here? So much of what we read in our lives is boring. And I say that as someone with great respect for anyone who tries to get things done with writing. In spite of my best efforts to engage you, I'm sure from time to time I've bored you in this book. (If that's the case, please, for the love of Aristotle, don't tell me.) Learning to persevere through boredom is a life skill; at times we must work through boredom to find meaning and use in the texts we read. Smartphones have made boredom even more painful because we know we can reach in our pockets at any time and find instant delight in text messages, video games, social media feeds, or photos. But you, my friend, do not have to be boring when you write! Each time you write, you take the stage. You open a relationship. You tell another human being, "Come, sit down. I have something to tell you, and you're gonna like this." You create an experience rich with meaning, with possibility. You make *contact*. Even the most technical and seemingly boring genres have room for distinction.

Welcome to your style apprenticeship!

Appendix: A Brief Glossary of Style (for the Style Nerd in You)

Style is the manner in which a writer writes, the voice you hear on the page or screen, the sum total of decisions, conscious or not, writers make at the sentence level. Style also refers to the distinguished or unique use of language that makes writing an art.

Errors are perceived deviations from commonly accepted conventions of language, particularly in grammar, usage, diction, spelling, punctuation, or mechanics. (Of course, you can also make errors of fact or reasoning.) Some errors are more obvious than others; some people call some things "errors" because they don't like seeing those things. Perceived errors create intrusions in the minds of readers and, fairly or not, can send the message that the writer is uneducated or careless, even if the error isn't really an error.

Syntax is the order in which phrases and clauses appear in a sentence. English most often follows a subject-verb-object (SVO) order, but writers make stylistic decisions about how to build on simple SVO sentences with movable phrases and clauses as sentence openers, closers, and interruptors (see pp. 158–63).

Usage…see convention, below.

Grammar is often the catch-all term for all this stuff, even though it shouldn't be. In *Understanding English Grammar*, Kolln and Funk describe three different kinds of "grammars": (1) the language in your head: If you grew up in an English-speaking household, you've known for a long time how to speak English sentences without thinking much about it; (2) a linguist's description of how language works, mostly referring to syntax (including issues related to agreement, like the relationship between subjects and verbs or pronouns and antecedents) and morphology (the forms words can take—like past tense, prefixes, pluralizing, and stuff like that); and, (3) "linguistic etiquette"—all those do's and don'ts of English usage (Kolln and Funk 5). Grammar has come to mean any and all of those things.

Punctuation is what we use to link, separate, enclose, omit, emphasize, and finalize various parts of a sentence: You've got your commas, apostrophes, colons, semicolons, parentheses, hyphens, dashes, ellipses, periods, question marks, quotation marks, and exclamation marks. Some punctuation rules have rigid conventions (you can't omit the apostrophe in the contraction *can't*—unless (!) you're doing it for effect in creative writing), while others don't (using a comma after a short sentence opener is optional).

Mechanics is closely related to usage, but it's also related to design. You use mechanics to capitalize, put certain words in italics, use headings, write or use numbers, or cite and list sources in a specific style (like Turabian, MLA, or APA).

Spelling. You know what spelling is. We just want to make sure it doesn't get mixed up in grammar's strong gravity. With spell-checking programs, the amount of spelling errors in student writing has declined. But "wrong word" problems have increased (Lunsford and Lunsford).

Convention, synonymous with usage, is "an agreement among the members of a community to abide by a single way of doing things" (Pinker 190). Sometimes we call conventions rules of language. Some conventions are quite rigid: the past-tense for the verb *be* when following the word *we* is *were*. This isn't like a law of physics or anything—people in some parts of the U.S. use "we was" in speech and get along fine—but English readers expect it, and they notice if it's otherwise. Some conventions are about diction or word choice (like, When is it okay to use slang or jargon or idioms?), others about syntax (Can I put an adverb *like* boldly between the words *to* and *go*?), others spelling (catsup? ketchup?), others punctuation, others readability or genre. So, conventions are expectations for the way language should work, and expectations can change.

Conventions can be situational. In other words, you may have had a teacher tell you to avoid using the word "I" in an essay or starting sentences with conjunctions like *and* or *but*. But (he-he!) another teacher will be fine with it. Some people insist on certain rules that aren't really rules at all; linguist Steven Pinker calls the rule dictating the difference between *that* or *which* "phony" (Pinker 235). The main point is that when you write, you write in an environment of freedoms and constraints, and it's important to know what your audience expects from you as a writer. A good rhetor has control over the conventions.

Deviation is the freedom to break the perceived rules, to flout the conventions. Sentence fragments, for example. Like that last sentence, and this one. Sometimes you can get away with writing them. In academic writing, it is customary to front load a paper by placing a thesis at the end of the first paragraph; but what if I decide to delay it? Look at the following insult that might be written about me one day: A genius he *ain't*. That sentence violates our SVO structure and the common notion that ain't is improper. Well, in some situations it might add rhetorical flavor. Conventions and deviations are rhetorical. They depend to a large extent on an audience's expectations and a writer's purpose. Deviations can make your writing distinguished and unique, if you use them purposefully, mindfully.

Works Cited

Angier, Natalie. *The Canon*. Boston: Houghton Mifflin, 2007. Print.

Beardsley, Monroe C. "Style and Good Style." *Contemporary Essays on Style*. Ed. Glen A. Love and Michael Payne. Glenview, IL: Scott, Foresman, 1969. 3–15. Print.

Butler, Paul. *Out of Style*. Logan, UT: Utah State UP, 2008. Print.

Cicero. *On the Ideal Orator*. Trans. James M. May and Jakob Wisse. NY: Oxford UP, 2001. Print.

Clark, Donald Lemen. *Rhetoric in Greco-Roman Education*. NY: Columbia, 1957. Print.

Dean, Deborah. *What Works in Writing Instruction*. Urbana, IL: NCTE, 2010. Print.

Elbow, Peter. *Vernacular Eloquence*. NY: Oxford UP, 2012. Print.

Gee, James Paul. *Social Linguistics and Literacies*. London: Routledge, 2012. Print.

Graham, Steve and Dolores Perin. *Writing Next: Effective Strategies to Improve Writing in Adolescents in Middle and High School*. Report for the Carnegie Corporation of New York. 2007. Web. 2 March 2015.

Holcomb, Chris and M. Jimmie Killingsworth. *Performing Prose*. Carbondale and Edwardsville: Southern Illinois UP, 2010. Print.

Howard, Rebecca Moore. "Contextualist Stylistics." *Refiguring Prose Style*. Ed. T.R. Johnson and Tom Pace. Logan, UT: Utah State UP, 2005. 42–56. Print.

James, William. *Writings: 1878–1899*. NY: Library of America, 1984. Print.

Kolln, Martha and Robert Funk. *Understanding English Grammar*. 9th ed. Boston: Pearson, 2012. Print.

Lanham, Richard A. *Style: An Anti-Textbook*. Philadelphia: Paul Dry, 2007. Print.

Lunsford, Andrea A. and Karen J. Lunsford. "'Mistakes are a Fact of Life': A National Comparative Study." *CCC* 59.4 (June 2008): 781–806. Print.

Pinker, Steven. *The Language Instinct: How the Mind Creates Language.* NY: Harper, 1994. Print.

"Plain Writing Act of 2010." Public Law 111–274. U.S. Government Publishing Office. 13 Oct 2010. Web. 10 March 2015.

Richardson, Robert D. *First We Read, Then We Write.* Iowa City: U of Iowa P, 2009. Print.

Shaughnessy, Mina. *Errors and Expectations.* NY: Oxford, 1977. Print.

Strong, William. *Sentence Combining.* 3rd ed. NY: McGraw-Hill, 1994. Print.

Trimble, John R. *Writing with Style: Conversations on the Art of Writing.* 2nd ed. Upper Saddle River, NJ: Prentice Hall, 2000. Print.

Williams, Joseph M. "The Phenomenology of Error." *College Composition and Communication* 32.2 (1981): 145–168. Print.

Yagoda, Ben. *The Sound on the Page.* NY: Harper, 2004. Print.

12

ANATOMY OF STYLE

In the last chapter we covered the exercises of the style apprentice (that's you) and the Cardinal Virtues of Good Style. Now we get down to brass tacks. I hope what I've said so far helps you understand some theory behind style—why it's important, how you can get better at it, what makes it effective. In this final section, I invite you to master a vocabulary that will help you talk about specific surface-level strategies in writing. Without this vocabulary, we end up talking about style in the vague way we sometimes talk about love ("It's a feeling you feel when you're feeling a feeling you've never felt before"). This vocab will help you analyze stylistic strategies in other writers and use style more purposefully in your own writing.

Here I've been selective, and brief. The top shelf in my office is filled entirely with books on style. Handbooks are more thorough than this, websites more expansive (check out Gideon Burton's "The Forest of Rhetoric" website). In the interest of brevity, I don't cover emphasis, meta-discourse, rhythm, various grammatical and visual principles, and a slew of rhetorical terms from *anadiplosis* to *zeugma*. Your instructor will help you prioritize and build on what I'm giving you here, but the following seven principles work as a good enough start. (I'd invent a forgettable acronym, but amazingly there are no vowels to play with. How does DSMSFPD stick in your brain? Dissim seffped? Forget it.)

Seven Strategies of Style

11.1 Diction

In an article in *The Atlantic* about a terrorist group called ISIS (Islamic State in Iraq and Syria), Graeme (pronounced "graham," like the cracker) Wood explains how terrorists often speak so intelligently about their cause. Then he writes this sentence:

> If they had been froth-spewing maniacs, I might be able to predict that their movement would burn out as the psychopaths detonated themselves or became drone-splats, one by one. (Wood)

Zow! Ordinary? Hardly. Graeme Wood peppers his sentence with strategic words that catch our attention, creating both meaning and atmosphere. "Froth-spewing maniacs" combines imagery (someone spewing froth—ew) and moral judgment (we think of maniacs as unbalanced and dangerous). Psychopaths are, quite literally, the mentally diseased whose antisocial behavior is uninhibited and scary; in the context of terrorism, they *detonate themselves*. Finally, he creates the compound phrase "drone-splats" to describe the disturbing result of a military drone strike. It's almost too dismissive—the *splat* sounds gross, even ironically cutesy, which shocks us when we consider the controversial gravity of U.S. drone strikes in the Middle East.

Wood has made some stylistic choices here that we call *diction*. Many of you have heard the word before in English literature classes. It means word choice. It's weird, though, leaving it at that, since *all* the writing we do requires word choice; you can't get around it: you're always choosing words when you write. How else can you write? So how is diction a rhetorical strategy, and what do you need to know to use it effectively?

I have a few ideas, and undoubtedly your instructor will, too. Here are four biggies:

1. **Denotation and connotation**: Words have dictionary definitions. They also have cultural meanings beyond those definitions—meanings and associations evoked by the word but not necessarily synonymous with its dictionary definition. The dictionary definition is the *denotation*. The Oxford English Dictionary defines the word *government* as "the action of governing" or "the governing power in a State." But when we use the word *government* in writing, particularly in political writing, the word evokes certain attitudes and emotions beyond "the action of governing." For many people, like political conservatives, the word suggests overgrown bureaucracy, corruption, lies, strangling regulations (Lemann 108). Another example from politics: In the 1960s the word *liberal* had positive connotations; the politically minded scrambled to look and act liberal because it was popular to be a liberal. (Look up the word in a dictionary to find its denotation.) By the late 1970s, however, liberalism was associated with "spinelessness, malevolence, masochism, elitism, fantasy, anarchy, idealism, softness, irresponsibility, and sanctimoniousness" (Nunberg 43). Because the word has become so toxic, democrats like Hillary Clinton call themselves *progressives* to avoid negative connotations. Good writers are aware of the cultural connotations of the words they use.

   Likewise, we often use words or phrases to hide meaning. When we want to conceal the denotative meanings of unpleasant terms, we use *euphemisms* like "passed on" for *died* or "laid off" and "let go" for *fired* or "take a pit stop," "powder my nose," and "see a man about a horse" for…well, y'know. Writers use these terms to soften the blow of certain realities like sex, bodily functions, or war (e.g., "enhanced interrogation techniques" instead of *torture*). Sometimes we create euphemisms to deflect responsibility for terrible things. Euphemisms are rhetorically powerful, and sometimes irresponsible. We also use *cacophemisms* (don't you just love that word?) to do the opposite: make something sound more dreadful than it is. An estate tax becomes a *death tax* and end-of-life medical consultations get called *death panels*. Racial slurs and vulgar nicknames fall in this category, as do words that should be neutral but become derogatory because they're used to cast a negative judgment on something (like calling someone a *hipster* or a *jock* and not meaning it as a compliment).

2. **Lexical field**: Words create rhetorical relationships with audiences. When we write, we create what Jeanne Fahnestock calls a "lexical field," or a reading environment made up of words related to particular topics and ways of speaking (Fahnestock 62). If I were to thumb through a copy of the *Journal of Microelectromechanical Systems* (yes, there is such a journal), I wouldn't be able to make heads or tails of the articles because of all the specialized language related to the topic. I'm not a member of that discourse community, so the specialized words—jargon, we call it—wouldn't make sense to me as it would to engineers or scientists. We use certain words for certain topics to show that we're in the know on that topic. If you're talking about transgenderism, for example, you'll need to know what the term *cisgender* means.

We can also think of lexical fields in terms of formality and informality. When we want to sound more casual, we use allusions (to cultural artifacts, like movies), idioms—phrases not to be taken literally (like "she's just pulling your leg")—or slang or contractions; we create intimacy with our readers that way. (Should you use a casual lexical field in an email to a professor or a cover letter for a job application?) Some words just sound more fancy than others (and I could have said *ostentatious, rococo,* or *resplendent* instead of *fancy*). We use ten-cent words to sound intelligent; sometimes student writers will thesaurize their essays assuming that teachers will be dazzled. Businesses or governments might use the word "containerize" instead of *put in a box* or "consideration of deferred action" for *please don't throw me in jail* (see "WonderMark").

Consider this example of transgressive thesaurus use from Corbett and Connors' book *Style and Statement:*

> After the conflagration had been extinguished, the police obstructed the thoroughfare and forefended all inquisitive spectators from perambulating before the incinerated residue of the pyrogenic catastrophe. (9)

What the writer means to say is...

> After the fire had been put out, the police roped off the street and prevented all sightseers from strolling past the charred ruins. (9)

We're looking at two problems here: (1) the ten-cent words from the first example are just gilding the lily (ever heard that saying?), i.e., clothing simple concepts in too-fancy dress, and (2) the writer chooses clusters of words that could be replaced with one or two ("incinerated residue of the pyrogenic catastrophe" instead of "charred ruins"). The second practice leads to wordiness, a problem not of long sentences but of sentences with unnecessary fluff. Being *concise* is often a matter of picking the most fitting lexical field for the job, which reflects the virtue of clarity we talked about in the last chapter.

In sum, a lexical field is composed of all the words, key terms, and phrases you use in your writing. When you analyze diction, you're not analyzing a few scattered words: You're analyzing a constellation of words that create a persuasive atmosphere.

3. **Abstract and concrete**: Some words refer to concrete objects we experience with our senses. Other words evoke emotions or associations that you couldn't really sketch in a game of Pictionary. Take the word *freedom.* What does it mean? For Americans, the word could evoke anything from the end of slavery to ballpark hot dogs to "the how ya think about ya," as they sing in the musical *Shenandoah.* When we use abstract language, we assume that our audience shares our understanding of the word, when actually there's wiggle room. Abstractions aren't necessarily bad. Rhetorician Jeanne Fahnestock writes that "abstract language can be as rhetorically appropriate and effective as concrete language" if, for example, you want to express

grand ideas or shared values (66). When presidential candidates give speeches, they often use abstractions to invoke shared values that are hard to capture in words.

But abstract language can be too vague, too general, too unfitting for the situation. Write too generally, and your audience might think you don't know what you're talking about or that you're evading the truth. Vague words cause vague thinking. Specific, concrete language adds clarity, a sense that you're in control of the details. Why write the word *government* when you're really talking about the President or the Internal Revenue Service or some other specific government entity?

A particularly useful example of concrete language is *imagery*—another word a high-school literature teacher might have taught you. Imagery is vivid language that stirs our senses of sight, sound, smell, taste, touch. Check out Eric Schlosser's description of his visit to a meatpacking plant:

> A worker with a power saw slices cattle into halves as though they were two-by-fours, and then the halves swing by me into the cooler. It feels like a slaughterhouse now. Dozens of cattle, stripped of their skins, dangle on chains from their hind legs. [...] The kill floor is hot and humid. It stinks of manure. Cattle have a body temperature of about 101 degrees, and there are a lot of them in the room. Carcasses swing so fast along the rail that you have to keep an eye on them constantly, dodge them, watch your step, or one will slam you and throw you onto the bloody concrete floor. (Schlosser 170)

Schlosser uses this visceral imagery for both *pathos* and *logos* in his criticism of America's obsession with fast food. He hopes his descriptions of fast food nation will be both emotionally disturbing and logically convincing. He wants to evoke in you a specific sensory experience. Imagery can be powerful; concrete language evokes and provokes.

4. **Amplification**: Some words have more *zing* than others. I wrote "zing" in that last sentence when "rhetorical power" would have sufficed. But zing captures the meaning of amplification—the method of choosing words for their emotional power when less evocative alternatives are available. Surely *drone-splat* is more evocative than,

say, *victims of a drone strike*. I love finding examples of amplification because it helps me expand my own writing options. In Helen Macdonald's book on falconry, she writes this sentence:

> Maybe you've glanced out of the window and seen there, on the lawn, a bloody great hawk murdering a pigeon, or a blackbird, or a magpie, and it looks the hugest, most impressive piece of wildness you've ever seen, like someone's tipped a snow leopard into your kitchen and you find it eating the cat. (in Schulz 91)

A common hawk becomes a *bloody great hawk* and then, even more amplified, *the hugest most impressive piece of wildness you've ever seen*. Instead of catching a pigeon, it's *murdering* one, which makes the hawk's predator instincts sound evil. The snow leopard metaphor works to amplify the meaning as well: a ferocious beast in *your* kitchen, eating the cat. Not *a* cat, mind you—*the* cat, as in *your* cat.

Google the word *amplification* for additional examples and tricks. Ever heard of *hyperbole*, or overstatement? That's a form of amplification, too. When someone tells you there were, like, a zillion people waiting in line for the show, you know they're using amplification. The opposite of hyperbole is *litotes*, or understatement. If you called World War II a *skirmish* or *tiff*, you're using litotes for rhetorical effect. Amplification (and its opposite) serves our purposes by inviting readers into the play of language and meaning. In this sense, then, *irony* is a kind of amplification: You intensify meaning by inviting readers to understand that you mean something entirely different from what you're saying. Wink-wink.

5. **Concision**: There's also power in choosing words *not* to use. In the last chapter we talked about how clarity, as a cardinal virtue of style, helps readers understand what you say without exerting unnecessary brain power. Concision, or the art of brevity, is not only grace but charity.

As writers we're tempted to fill our sentences with fluff. Wordiness (called *prolixity*, for you members of the Style Nerd Army) may be a symptom of (a) the writer's attempt to sound sophisticated, or (b) the ease with which we fall into tired and flabby rhythms of language. We can do better.

In two ways. First, and most painless, we can delete unnecessary words or phrases without changing the meaning of our sentences. Consider this sentence:

> In my opinion, in Martin Luther King's speech that he gave to an audience large in size, he first and foremost expressed to his listeners his feelings and opinion that it was very important to see that the venerable Declaration of Independence, which was penned by Thomas Jefferson, did in fact apply to African Americans who, at that very moment, were actually being unethically denied their God-given rights of life, liberty, and the pursuit of happiness.

I've seen cousins of this sentence in student writing for fifteen years. Look at all the deadwood we can cut out without changing the meaning of the sentence or adding a single word:

> ~~In my opinion,~~ in Martin Luther King's speech ~~that he gave to an audience large in size,~~ he ~~first and foremost~~ expressed ~~to his listeners~~ his ~~feelings and~~ opinion ~~that it was very important to see~~ that ~~the venerable Declaration of Independence, which was penned by Thomas Jefferson, did in fact apply to~~ African Americans ~~who, at that very moment,~~ were ~~actually~~ being ~~unethically~~ denied their ~~God-given~~ rights ~~of life, liberty, and the pursuit of happiness~~.

From that sprawl, we get this:

> In Martin Luther King's speech, he expressed his opinion that African Americans were being denied their rights.

It's a boring sentence, but at least it's not cluttered. We've removed the slow wind-up ("In my opinion"), Captain Obvious (who else do you give a speech to but an *audience*?), the superlative flatulence ("that it was very important to see"), the redundant trivia ("penned by TJ"), the meaningless filler ("actually"), an unnecessary adverb ("unethically"), the highfalutin stuff ("God-given"), and Goes Without Saying ("life, etc."). In short, we've removed words that are meaningless, unnecessary, redundant, or repetitive. (Wait: Is using *repetitive* redundant? Wouldn't it be shorter to have written *We've removed meaningless etc. words*?) No other words were harmed in the process.

The second method for achieving concision is a little harder: changing words to reduce deadwood. Through this method, flabby phrases like "in the event that" or "in spite of the fact that" become *if* or *though*. Nominalizations, which are discussed in the next section, actually get transformed... Wait...let me try that opener again... Nominalizations, discussed in the next section, change into active subjects and verbs: "The government's management of public lands can be...." becomes *When the government manages public lands...* Relative clauses—the ones that start with *that* or *which*—disappear: "The Iron Man race, which is difficult but rewarding, is..." changes to *The difficult but rewarding Iron Man race is...*

Sometimes the problem is more drastic. The UK's "Plain English Campaign" tells us that when a customer wrote to an online retailer asking if they sold blank CDs, the company responded with this:

> We are currently in the process of consolidating our product range to ensure that the products that we stock are indicative of our brand aspirations. As part of our range consolidation we have also decided to revisit our supplier list and employ a more intelligent system for stock acquisition. As a result of the above, certain product lines are now unavailable through our website, whilst remaining available from more mainstream suppliers.

In other words, "No, we do not sell blank CDs."

Don't be afraid to take out a sword and murder your own words. They don't feel pain. But your readers will if you're wordy.

11.2 Syntax

(You may want to review online the eight parts of speech and some simple grammar terms before reading this next part.)

The Greek word *taxis* means arrangement or order. In writing, syntax refers to the order of words, phrases, and clauses in a sentence. Earlier I mentioned the SVO arrangement of English sentences:

Charlotte kicked the cat.

Charlotte must have had a bad day. In this sentence, *Charlotte* is the subject; *kicked* is the verb (and it's a *transitive* verb, meaning that it's a verb doing something to something else); and *the cat* is the direct object. That's a pretty simple sentence for us to consider. Turns out there are only about ten ways to write simple sentences like the one above, and they all have to do with how you add verby stuff (like Be verbs and linking verbs and transitive verbs, etc.) to subjects.

Here's the cool part about syntax: You can make all kinds of amazing stylistic decisions by building on simple sentences. You can build in the front, like this:

When she came home from school, Charlotte kicked the cat.

Virginia Tufte calls the new stuff an *opener* (155). By adding a sentence opener, I've added meaning and a little drama to why Charlotte kicked the cat.

You can also build at the end:

Charlotte kicked the cat, **sending it tumbling down the stairs.**

We'll call this a *closer*, for obvious reasons. Now we have a sequence of events that fills out the story of the sentence even more. (I wonder, though, if cats *tumble*. They find their feet pretty fast.)

And you can even build right in the middle of the simple sentence:

Charlotte, **a feisty girl in a bad mood**, kicked the cat.

This new stuff is an *interrupter*. It splits the subject and the verb. Check out how novelist Virginia Woolf splits subject (Life itself) and verb (was enough) in this lovely sentence:

Life itself, **every moment of it, every drop of it, here, this instant, now, in the sun, in Regent's Park**, was enough.

You can also split the verb and the object, but in this instance it sounds a little weird:

Charlotte kicked, **with great malice**, the cat.

If you're in a daring mood, you can use an opener, closer, and interrupter all in the same sentence:

When she came home from school, Charlotte, a feisty girl in a bad mood, kicked the cat, sending it tumbling down the stairs.

Not every sentence should look like this one, but I like what the syntax creates here. There's a rhythm. Our attention goes on an interesting journey with Charlotte and her feisty violence. (No animals were harmed in the drafting of this book.)

Another interesting choice for you: Sometimes we can move around these little add-ons—let's call them **modifiers**, because they enhance the meaning of the various parts of the simple sentence—to change the meaning we want to convey, like this:

> Charlotte kicked the cat **when she came home from school**. (Notice we don't use a comma here.)

I like the "when" stuff better as a sentence opener because the last part of the sentence gets the emphasis, and the kicking should be emphasized.

So the first thing I want you to understand about using syntax is that simple sentences grow into more complex, interesting sentences when we build on them in various ways.

You should know a few things about these growths called modifiers. First, modifiers can be words, phrases, or clauses. A phrase is a bundle of words that go together in a sentence:

- the big red car (this is a noun phrase)

- under the table (prepositional phrase)

- associate director of lab sciences and author of many articles (appositive phrase)

- his eyes bloodshot from crying (absolute phrase—all it's missing to become a clause is *were*)

- foaming at the mouth (participial phrase)

- would have been killed (verb phrase)

It's useful to understand how phrases work so you can use them to add variety, rhythm, and emphasis to sentences. When you vary your sentence lengths and syntax, you create what we often call *voice*, though I prefer *ethos*. We're not going to dive into all the different phrases and their uses here, but let me show you just a couple of incredibly useful phrase types you can use for rhetorical effect:

Participial phrases start with a verb ending in -ing or -ed, as in this lovely sentence from education writer Amanda Ripley:

> In other places, I saw kids bored out of their young minds, kids who looked up when a stranger like me walked into the room, **watching to see if I would, please God, create some sort of distraction to save them from another hour of nothingness.** (Ripley)

Appositive phrases are used to give more information (like authority) about a noun close by, like this:

> Natalie Angier, **Pulitzer Prize-winning journalist for the *New York Times*,** argues that we should learn about science solely because it's fun.

A *clause*, however, is more than a phrase—it has a subject and verb. So:

> foaming at the mouth

is a phrase, but

> My neighbor's German shepherd was foaming at the mouth

is a clause. Clauses can be complete sentences, but they don't have to be:

> *Since* my neighbor's German shepherd was foaming at the mouth...

That's a clause—an adverbial clause, actually, because it's giving us a reason or condition for an action—but we call it a *dependent* clause because it can't stand alone as a sentence. It needs to become an *independent clause* to mature into a sentence, like this:

> Since my neighbor's German shepherd was foaming at the mouth, **I decided not to pet it.**

Like phrases, clauses work in a variety of ways (e.g., as adverbials or, in the case of relative clauses, as adjectivals). A good writing handbook will help you sort through the different types and their operations.

We now have several shapes of sentences to consider (the x's represent the stuff we add—the modifiers—to the simple sentence or base clause):

_____. Here's our basic SVO "Charlotte kicked the cat" sentence.

_____, xxxxxxxxxxxxxx. The SVO as clause, with a closer on the end.

xxxxxxxxxxxxxxxxxxx, _____. With an opener.

_____, xxxxxxxxxxxxxx, _____. With an interrupter.

xxxxxxxxxx, _____, xxxxxxxxxxxx, _____, xxxxxxxxxxx. With the whole funky parade.

If you've ever heard of simple, compound (two independent clauses fixed together with a coordinating conjunction), complex (a dependent clause attached to an independent clause either as an opener or closer), or compound-complex sentences (dependent clause and at least two independent clauses), then you already know something about syntax, which, you now know, is all about building sentences by putting words, phrases, and clauses together in a variety of ways, like my kids build a variety of wooden trains by coupling engines and cars together in different orders. (How would you map out that sentence I just wrote?)

So, who cares? What's the point of this syntax talk? When you know how to use syntax, you add variety and rhythm to your sentences. You build meaning, sending your readers on little jogs of thought. Often I find myself playing with syntax after I've completed a draft. I'll combine two shortish sentences by turning one into an adverbial dependent clause, or, if all the sentences in a paragraph sound about the same, I'll shake things up by adding a subject-verb interruptor (like an appositive) to a sentence. Sometimes I'll change a sentence so that the most important point falls at the end, because the end gets the emphasis.

If you're a committed sentence-hunter, you'll find delightful sentences everywhere you look, in all varieties, like spring flowers, each a one-of-a-kind. Here's one Anne Fadiman wrote in her book *The Spirit Catches You and You Fall Down*, about a three-year-old Hmong girl named Lia whose seizures kept her hospitalized for much of her early life in Merced, California:

One night, while Lia Lee was in the emergency room at MCMC for the umpteenth time and a translator was present, Dan Murphy, who happened to be on call, brought up the subject of her anticonvulsant medications. (Fadiman 53)

The base clause in this sentence is *Dan Murphy brought up the subject*. Everything else in the sentence is syntactic jewelry, demonstrating Fadiman's options as a stylist. (Can you write your own sentence in imitation of her syntax?)

Passive and Active Syntax

Since syntax depends so much on the verbs you use, we should talk briefly about the difference between *passive* and *active voice*, terms you may have heard in previous writing classes. The idea behind passive sentences is simple: A passive sentence hides the actor that "does" the verb, like this:

Oxycodone was given to the patient.

Who gave oxycodone to the patient? Nobody knows. Could have been anyone.

Passive constructions like the one above have a bad reputation. You may hear a writing teacher say, "Don't write in passive voice," making that rule sound like the eleventh commandment. I've also seen writing instructors teach students to eliminate every *to be* verb in their writing, even though many *Be* patterns are not passive:

Brian is a writing teacher.

Brian is down in the basement playing *BioShock 2*.

Brian is impatient but handsome.

Brian is just waiting, with John Mayer, for the world to change.

I suppose if all you've got in your repertoire are *Be* sentences, you're in trouble. But these sentences ain't passive. And sometimes it makes rhetorical sense to use passive syntax. Take the oxycodone example. What if we don't care who gave the patient the oxycodone? In some instances, the actor is not as important as the receiver of the action. What if the sentence read like this:

Oxycodone was given to the patient, and the patient had a dangerous allergic reaction.

The focus, then, is on the patient's reaction to the medicine and not the giver of the medicine. This sentence would be particularly useful if we were trying to avoid pinning blame on the giver of the oxycodone (Don't sue us, dear patient!), or if we don't know who gave it. (Mom hears a crash, comes running, sees shards of broken flower vase on the carpet, looks at you and your sister, asks, with exasperation, "How did this happen?", and you say, "The ball was kicked into it.") You may also find that passive syntax gives your sentence a particular rhythm that works well. The sentence

Oxycodone was given to the patient by the doctor.

is still passive, even though now we have an actor (the doctor), but maybe I like this construction better, for whatever reason (see Tufte 78).

So why avoid passive syntax? Several style textbooks encourage us to get actors and actions together as often as possible (Lanham *Revising Prose*; Williams and Colomb). Remember that we're hardwired to appreciate a good story, and sentences tell stories about actors acting (e.g., Charlotte kicking cats); that's how we're programmed to understand sentences. Try to tease out actor and action in this sentence:

The utilization of offshore banking leads to reductions in taxation collection at the federal level.

We're in luck: I just Googled this sentence and no one, in the Googleverse, has ever written this pile of tripe. What this sentence wants to say is

When American corporations bank offshore, the federal government can't collect as much tax revenue from them.

And of course this upsets the Citizens for Tax Justice. But what's more upsetting is that the first banking sentence buries actors and actions: In the first part, the actor (American corporations) doesn't even make an appearance, and the verb (potentially, *bank* or *use*) is obscured by what we call a *nominalization*—that's a nouny thing that could be a verb, like "utilization of" instead of *use*. (Did you notice that I just used passive voice to obscure myself as the writer of the bad sentence? The verb "is obscured.") The writer and teacher Joseph Williams made himself famous fighting the battle against these kinds of sentences. Let's join him.

So: When you write active sentences, you do several things. You…

1. bring actors (if at all possible, humans) and actions together in clear S-V format;

2. avoid what Richard Lanham calls "blah blah *is that*" openers, like "The fact of the matter is that…" (12);

3. avoid preposition pile-ups, like "The policy **of** the mayor **from** the beginning **of** her second term **of** office **in** the city **of** Detroit **for** education policy was…." Lanham calls this stuff *lard* (4); and "You," thus: lard (4); and you…

4. avoid nominalizing away perfectly good verbs: They use *present* (not presentation of), *avoid* (avoidance of), *fund* (funding of), *abandon* (abandonment of) (Williams and Colomb 32).

As you can see, there's lots to say about syntax. We've scratched the surface. The books I've cited in this section and, of course, ever and always, your writing teacher will take you further on the path to writing with rhythm, voice, variety, and emphasis by using syntax effectively.

11.3 Metaphors

Rhetoricians in the past define a *trope* as a rhetorical strategy that changes the ordinary, taken-for-granted meaning of words. So technically, irony or hyperbole are tropes (Lanham *Handlist*). I'm going to focus on the kind of tropes that make comparisons—you know them as metaphors, similes, analogies, personifications, synecdoches, parables, etc. Since all these comparisons are, in essence, metaphors, I'm going to talk about metaphor as the general rhetorical strategy.

I've said before that humans are pattern-seekers. We like to see similarities, make connections, find old experiences that explain new ones, use comparisons to make sense of things. Metaphors make these connections for us by spinning meaning in new ways. The Greek word *metaphor* means, quite literally, to carry over or across—meaning, in this case, to carry across meaning or essence from one thing to another. James Geary talks about metaphor, as Aristotle did, as a kind of weird math problem that looks like this:

$$X = Y.$$

The unexpected, almost illogical nature of this equation is part of the fun. So when the blues artist Sonny Boy Williamson bellows out, "Bet you my bottom dollar, I'm not fattenin' no more frogs for snakes," he's saying

> dating a woman who will end up with another guy = fattening frogs for snakes.

You already know how this works. You've been hearing and making metaphors all your life. As Geary writes, "Metaphorical thinking is the way we make sense of the world, and every individual metaphor is a specific instance of this imaginative process at work" (10). It's a mistake to confine metaphors to literary texts: "What we do every day is very much a matter of metaphor" (Lakoff and Johnson 3). They tumble out of our mouths when we talk (*tumble out* is one), even if we're not aware of them ("I've been *down* this week," "Things are looking *up* for me," "I *see* what you're saying," "She's a *bright* kid"). Yesterday I saw the following headlines in two major national newspapers, all of them dropping metaphors:

"Chaos in Yemen **Stymies** Terror Flight"

"**Torrent** of Cash Exits the Eurozone"

"CEO Tries to Put Brand **Back on Track** After Being **Lapped** by Rivals"

"Glenn Allison Still **Splits** Bowling World with Perfect 900"

"The **Soaring** Dollar is **Crunching** Profits"

"U.S. Private Equity Firms Find a **Chilly** Reception in Australia"

"A Story of Rape Keeps **Unraveling**"

"Netanyahu's Likely **Next Steps**"

"Science Museums Urged to **Cut Ties** with Kochs"

I had to look up the word *stymie* because I didn't know if it was a legitimate trope. Turns out *stymie* is a Scots term for when one golf ball blocks the path of another on the green. Maybe that's not well known, but I feel cooler now that I know the origin. The second headline is clearer: Money is leaving the Eurozone like a violent rush of water, like rainwater flushing down a slot canyon or something. Metaphors fill our everyday talk.

Metaphors work rhetorically by both delighting and convincing. Romeo tells us "Juliet is the sun" to amplify her beauty, to convince anyone listening that (a) Juliet is way hot, and (b) Juliet's hotness comes at you like the sun comes out of the east, killing the darkness and the "envious moon." Do we buy this hyperbole? Doesn't matter: it's cool. Metaphors excite, delight, engage, and confuse. They swerve from ordinary meaning. "The mind is a plastic snow dome," writes James Geary, "most beautiful, most interesting, and most itself when, as Elvis put it, it's all shook up" (16). Metaphors shake up your writing.

They also convince us by working on our attitudes and judgments. As Geary writes, readers should know that:

> Metaphorical choices don't just reflect opinions and actions; they help shape them. So becoming aware of which metaphors are at work— and why—provides an essential reality check in political debate. Bringing metaphorical meanings to the surface enables us to evaluate them, and to decide for ourselves the extent of their influence. (Geary 135)

A good rhetorical critic like yourself will pay careful attention to the way writers use metaphors to make comparisons. Ask yourself: Do I really believe in this case that X = Y? In political discourse, illegal immigrants are often compared to pollution, contaminants, infection, disease, flood (Cisneros). What do these metaphors do as arguments? What connections do they ask us to make? What values or assumptions are at play, and do we agree with them?

As a writer, you should make your writing memorably sticky by lacing it with metaphors. You have several options. You've heard, I'm sure, that *similes* use the word "like" to make the comparison direct and obvious. Direct metaphors tell readers directly that X is Y. Here's how journalist Matt Tiabbi described a particularly powerful investment bank in an article for *Rolling Stone*:

> The world's most powerful investment bank is a great vampire squid wrapped around the face of humanity, relentlessly jamming its blood funnel into anything that smells like money. (Taibbi)

Other metaphors are implied, like the "Cut Ties" headline mentioned earlier. For example, *synecdoche*, an implied metaphor, takes a part of something as the whole, like when we call American soldiers "boots on the ground."

Metaphors can be developed beyond phrases or sentences—allegories or analogies are *extended* metaphors.

Here's a brief example of how an extended metaphor—an analogy—works in writing. When I was in graduate school, a campus political group held an "affirmative action bake sale," an extended metaphor in action, in which prices for cookies dropped for minority students. The group wanted other students to see what they thought of as the unfairness of affirmative action, which is a policy by which some institutions change admission or hiring policies to provide equal access to racial minorities. In the student newspaper the next day, a student wrote the following analogy in rebuttal:

> From the beginning, the white males generally have horded all the recipes as intellectual property; owned all the ingredients, the cookie sheets, the ovens, cooling racks and the cookie jars; controlled the flow of cookies to eager hands while eating the majority of each batch themselves.... In essence, white males in general have created the crisis of democracy that affirmative action seeks to address—the wide divide between those who own the means of making cookies and those who don't.

We have here an exciting Battle of Metaphors! The campus political group compares cookies to all the goods and services distributed to racial minorities; the prices, for them, illustrate the unfairness they see in affirmative action. We don't reduce the price of baked goods for racial minorities, they're arguing, so why should they receive preferential treatment in the college admissions process? The student writer, on the other hand, compares the historically situated power of white males to the entire baking apparatus, arguing by analogy that historical inequality makes affirmative action necessary. Whether or not you agree with these metaphorical arguments, you can see how extended metaphors create strong affinities between two things, creating a new way of thinking about them.

A final thought about writing and reading metaphors: Beware of bad metaphors that, upon closer examination, don't really make sense. Because I wrote a letter once to U.S. Senator Orrin Hatch, I get the "Hatch Dispatch," his periodic newsletter describing his adventures as the third-oldest senator in Congress. In one of the newsletters, he compared government spending to a runaway train:

The runaway spending train enveloping Washington, D. C., is threatening to decimate the future of our children and for all Americans for generations to come.

Trains still run away from time to time, so the metaphor has power: Ain't nobody but Superman (or actor Denzel Washington) stopping one. But do trains *envelop*—wrap up, cover, surround, like fog might? Or *decimate* the future—kill, destroy, or remove? Runaway trains can kill, but I'm not sure how the future can be killed or removed, so the *decimating train* idea doesn't really work for me.

Other bad metaphors are more obviously bad because they mix metaphors and thereby cloud the comparison. Here's one from a comment thread on a local newspaper:

Where there's smoke, there's fire...could this be just the tip of the iceberg???

Metaphors, like all rhetorical strategies, should be *fitting*. And they should make sense.

11.4 Schemes

Classical rhetoricians separated *schemes* from metaphors and other plays with words. A scheme is a rhetorical strategy that plays with the arrangement of words through repetition or balance or some other variation from the norm. Schemes are patterns, often across a series of sentences, and you can find types and subtypes online in the *Forest of Rhetoric*. I'll talk about two.

Check out this excerpt from the book *America*, written by comedians from *The Daily Show with Jon Stewart*:

Though the president is very powerful, he cannot make laws. The president can suggest laws. The president can call individual congressmen and threaten, beg, and cajole them to make laws. The president can use the bully pulpit and appeal directly to the people to ask Congress to make laws. The president can promise that if these congressmen pass the laws the president likes he will make them a delicious sandwich. The president can hold his breath and pound his fists and threaten to run away. But the president cannot make laws.

We call this particular scheme *anaphora*—the writers repeat the same word or phrase ("the president") at the beginning of successive sentences.

Also notice that the writers repeat the phrase "make laws" at the *end* of sentences—that's called *epistrophe*. Abraham Lincoln used it at the end of the Gettysburg Address ("government of the people, by the people, for the people…"), and Wikipedia tells me rapper Nicki Minaj uses it in one of her songs. And if you can find another sentence on Earth that pairs up Lincoln with Nicki Minaj, I'll give you a quarter.

This kind of repetition sets up patterns of expectation with readers. It also lets them know that you're a *writer writing* and having a blast doing it. Just for kicks, let's look at another delicious example from David Foster Wallace's essay "A Supposedly Fun Thing I'll Never Do Again":

> I have seen sucrose beaches and water a very bright blue. I have seen an all-red leisure suit with flared lapels. I have smelled what suntan lotion smells like spread over 21000 pounds of hot flesh. I have been addressed as "Mon" in three different nations. I have watched 500 upscale Americans dance the Electric Slide. I have seen sunsets that looked computer-enhanced and a tropical moon that looked more like a sort of obscenely large and dangling lemon than like the good old stony U.S. moon I'm used to. I have (very briefly) joined a Conga Line.

Another scheme is *balance*. Balance shares pattern-passion with repetition, but it's more flexible:

> I am honestly curious about saliva, but I am also curious about obsession and its role in scientific inquiry. (Mary Roach, *Gulp*, 102)

> My feeling is that if more guys would join mellow, purposeless, and semi-dysfunctional organizations such as the Lawn Rangers, then there would be a lot fewer guys getting involved in aggressive, venal, destructive, and frequently criminal organizations such as the U.S. Congress. (Dave Barry, *Dave Barry's Complete Guide to Guys*, 103)

In these two examples, the writers balance grammatical constructions by using pairs like "I am…but I am also…" and "If…then…" That's an interesting trick. Look, particularly, at how humor writer Dave Barry balances multiple parts of his two clauses:

> more guys would join…a lot fewer guys getting involved in…

> mellow, purposeless, and semi-dysfunctional…aggressive, venal, destructive, and frequently criminal

organizations such as the Lawn Rangers...organizations such as the U.S. Congress

You can create balance with either/or, neither/nor, not only/but also, from/to, when/then, if/then. Richard Lanham lists thirty-four different ways to create balance. One simple way is to contrast something unfavorable with something favorable, like, "While it may be true that X, it is also true that Y." Here's the delightful science writer Mary Roach, balancing between two ideas—one appealing, and one not so appealing:

> Yes, men and women eat meals. But they also ingest nutrients. They grind and sculpt them into a moistened bolus that is delivered, via a stadium wave of sequential contractions, into a self-kneading sack of hydrochloric acid and then dumped into a tubular leach field, where it is converted into the most powerful taboo in human history. Lunch is an opening act. (Roach 15)

Notice how she sandwiches (a metaphor!) the gross realities of digestion between the two more palatable (zing!) ideas of meals and lunch. That's balance for you.

11.5 Flow

A text is *coherent* when we feel it has shape, focus, direction, that it all hangs together to make a whole greater than the sum of the parts. A text is *cohesive* when we see how one part connects to another, when, in the words of Jeanne Fahnestock, "the meaning of a text unfolds easily from sentence to sentence, with little conscious effort on the listener's or reader's part" (345). The phenomenon of flow, a word often too vague to be useful, is something the reader experiences; it's also something the writer can create in four different ways. And since you work with cohesion most effectively at the paragraph level, I've given you paragraph examples from professional writers for each of the four methods.

1. **Repeat pronouns**. Pronouns have antecedents. Naturally, they lead us back to previous material. Using them (see what I did there?) helps us avoid repetition, too.

   > We've seen that in all of this activity, we no longer experience <u>interruptions</u> as disruptions. We experience **them** as connections. We seek **them** out, and when **they're** not there, we create **them**. <u>Interruptions</u> enable us to avoid difficult feelings and awkward moments. **They** become a convenience. And over time we have

trained our brains to crave **them**. Of course, all of this makes it hard to settle down into conversation. (Sherry Turkle, *Reclaiming Conversation*, about social media use)

2. **Create topic or theme chains**. You've likely heard of topic sentences. They state the main point of a paragraph. Sometimes the first sentence is the topic sentence, sometimes not. But the other sentences in the paragraph can prop up the topic by repeating key terms or ideas in a chain of cohesion. In the following example, I've **bolded** one chain and <u>underlined</u> another.

> The **1918 pandemic** has been remembered as the "**Spanish flu**" because the Spanish press was the only Western media to adequately cover its <u>massive toll</u>. Despite the name, **Spanish flu** <u>struck the entire world</u>—that's what made it a *pan*demic instead of simply an *epi*demic. It was not the first **influenza pandemic**, nor the most recent, but it was by far the <u>most deadly</u>. Whereas AIDS took roughly twenty-four years to kill 24 million people, the **Spanish flu** <u>killed as many in twenty-four weeks</u>. (Jonathan Safran Foer, *Eating Animals*)

3. **Use transitions**. Transitional language helps readers know how to process the info you're giving them. They can help you:

> *compare*: also, likewise, similarly
>
> *contrast*: however, nevertheless, conversely
>
> *imply cause and effect*: as a result, consequently, therefore
>
> *form logical relationships*: since, therefore, for this reason
>
> *set a sequence of events*: next, and then, first/second/third
>
> *provide examples*: for example, for instance, for one thing
>
> *give more*: furthermore, additionally, moreover

Here's an example of a writer using transitions effectively:

> **So far in *Outliers***, we've seen that extraordinary achievement is less about talent than it is about opportunity. **In this chapter**, I want to try to dig deeper into why that's the case by looking at the outlier in its purest and most distilled form—the genius. **For years**, we've taken our cues from people like Terman when

it comes to understanding the significance of high intelligence. **But**, as we shall see, Terman made an error. (Malcolm Gladwell, *Outliers*)

4. **Use the known-new pattern**. This one's pretty cool, but tricky. The first two verses in the Hebrew Bible show the way: "In the beginning, God created the heaven and the earth. Now the earth was unformed and void...." You see how the first sentence ends with a new idea that is then picked up first thing in the next sentence, in a kind of ABBC style. Known information first, then new. See if you can detect the pattern in this paragraph.

> Time with people teaches children how to be in a relationship, beginning with the ability to have a conversation. And this brings me back to the anxieties of the Holbrooke teachers. As the Holbrooke middle schoolers began to spend more time texting, they lost practice in face-to-face talk. That means lost practice in the empathic arts—learning to make eye contact, to listen, and to attend to others. Conversation is on the path toward the experience of intimacy, community, and communion. Reclaiming conversation is a step toward reclaiming our most fundamental human values. (Sherry Turkle, *Reclaiming Conversation*)

Notice the ABBCCD pattern here? Let's see if we can mark these patterns in the sentences:

> <u>Time with people teaches children how to be in a relationship, beginning with the ability to have a conversation.</u>

> <u>And this</u> brings me back to the anxieties of **the Holbrooke teachers**.

> **As the Holbrooke middle schoolers** began to spend more time texting, they *lost practice in face-to-face talk*.

> *That means lost practice* in the empathic arts—<u>*learning to make eye contact, to listen, and to attend to others*</u>.

> <u>*Conversation is on the path toward the experience of intimacy, community, and communion*</u>.

> <u>*Reclaiming conversation*</u> is a step toward **<u>reclaiming our most fundamental human values</u>**.

So, flow. Hope this was helpful. You won't use all these tricks for every paragraph, but you'll want to create cohesion somehow. Check out a handbook, online or otherwise, for more tips for creating cohesion through paragraph types (like descriptions, compare/contrast, narrative, or analysis).

11.6 Punctuation

Since I haven't written this book as a handbook, I won't go over all the specific rules of punctuation here. If you're after the rules, I would recommend finding a good handbook or a Web source you trust. I'm more interested in the effects of punctuation. Punctuation is a deviling thing, and you'll spend a good part of your writing life figuring out how to use it well. Here I want to say, simply, that stylistic punctuation uses punctuation to create rhythm, interrupt flow, or separate ideas for emphasis. Punctuation helps you create syntax in a variety of ways. And instead of lecturing you about it, I'm going to let you come up with principles yourselves as you look at the examples from my collection of sentences:

The Comma

Commas separate out the various parts of sentences so everything doesn't just slam together. Commas make sentences breathe, but you shouldn't put them in every time you think you should take a breath. Commas space phrases and clauses, they separate items in lists, they tell you what's modifying what, they work to emphasize asides or editorial comments or amplifications. Commas help build associations in the minds of readers.

> The ethos of the Koran, the value system it endorses, was, in essence, the vanishing code of nomadic Arabs, the matriarchal, more caring society that did not leave orphans out in the cold, orphans like Muhammad, whose success as a merchant, he believed, should have earned him a place in the city's ruling body, and who was denied such preferment because he didn't have a powerful family to fight for him. (Salman Rushdie, *Joseph Anton: A Memoir*)

> The universe passed through its unimaginable first moment, first year, first billion years, wresting itself from whatever state of nonexistence, inflating, contorting, resolving into space and matter, bursting into light. (Marilynne Robinson, *Absence of Mind*)

The Dash

Dashes, first off, are not hyphens. Hyphens are shorter; they connect words and parts of words, and often you can just do without them. Dashes, though, are rhetorical heroes. They add drama to a sentence—both graphically and syntactically. You can use dashes much like commas to separate phrases and clauses upon which you want special emphasis. Just make sure you have a clear rhetorical purpose for being dashing.

> Decomposition like this happens to any long-lived and successful style, surely; so the writer's—or critic's, or reader's—task is then to search for the irreducible, the superfluous, the margin of gratuity, the element in a style—in any style—which cannot be easily reproduced or reduced. (James Wood, *How Fiction Works*)

As Smith's memoir demonstrates, childhood—those first, fresh experiences of the world, unclouded by reason and practicality, when you are the center of existence and anything might happen—should be regarded less as a springboard to striving adulthood than as a well of rich individual perception and experience to which you can return for sustenance throughout life, whether you rise in the world or not. (Christina Schwarz, "Leave Those Kids Alone," *The Atlantic*)

The Semicolon

Most of the time, semicolons work like periods in that they separate two independent clauses that could stand alone as sentences just fine. But maybe you want to suggest a more intimate connection, a more casual transition from one sentence to the next. Then drop in a semicolon. You also use semicolons to separate out more complicated parts of sentences with multiple commas in lists, as Bill Wyman does in the example below.

> The one that killed him—a hospital-grade potion called propofol—was used to put to sleep a man who apparently couldn't find sleep otherwise, and it's easy to see why he would need help, his mind full of songs, ideas, melodies, dance moves; of his fantasies and his lies; of the memories of his silly, grasping, toxic family; of the kids who were, or were not, his kids; of the other families whose lives he had touched and made better and the ones he'd beguiled and corrupted; of the giant global scream of an audience that he could no longer face. (Bill Wyman, "The Pale King," an article on Michael Jackson)

The Colon

Colons trumpet what's to come. They announce lists or examples or quotations or summaries. They draw attention to relationships more dramatically than periods.

> In fact a swimming pool requires, once it has been filled and the filter has begun its process of cleaning and recirculating the water, virtually no water, but the symbolic content of swimming pools has always been interesting: a pool is misapprehended as a trapping of affluence, real or pretended, and of a kind of hedonistic attention to the body. (Joan Didion, *The White Album*)

Combinations

> Historical fundamentalism is marked by the belief that a particular and quite narrowly defined past—"the founding"—is ageless and sacred and to be worshipped; that certain historical texts—"the founding documents"—are to be read in the same spirit with which religious fundamentalists read, for instance, the Ten Commandments; that the Founding Fathers were divinely inspired; that the academic study of history (whose standards of evidence and methods of analysis are based on skepticism) is a conspiracy and, furthermore, blasphemy; and that political arguments grounded in appeals to the founding documents, as sacred texts, and to the Founding Fathers, as prophets, are therefore incontrovertible. (Jill Lepore, *The Whites of Their Eyes*)

11.7 Design

We're in the home stretch! (Where does that metaphor come from?) All that's left is a final word about style from the perspective of *design*.

When I visited my daughter Lydia's kindergarten class, she showed me how she could write the sentence, "I like my dad" on a sheet of lined paper. *Awwww!* She leaned over the page, struggling to get each word right, her tongue poking out of her pursed mouth. When she was done, I gushed about her writing skills—it's a miracle, as I've said—and then started packing up to leave.

Lydia grabbed my arm and said, "Wait! I have to draw you!"

Then, underneath the words she'd written with great care, she drew a picture of me—a cute little weird-looking daddy, with black-framed glasses and the kind of legs you'd find on a gorilla.

It dawned on me, then, that for Lydia, writing is only half the message. All her work up till then had been a combination of words and images, sentences and drawings—her syntactic compositions dancing, on the page, with her crayoned compositions. All the books we read out loud to her and her other siblings almost always used this multimodal dance to communicate. That multimodality may very well be trained out of Lydia as she gets older and teachers expect her to read books without pictures and write essays without drawings (Kress and van Leeuwen).

I've written this book without many visuals or colors because I've wanted to keep it cheap. (You can thank me by joining Team Rhetoric for life.) But the Web has blasted away any thought that we live in a strictly *alphabetic* world—a world governed only in words on pages. I don't need to tell you this or describe the multimodal symphony we experience online, because you live it. What I do need to say, though, is that *style* as we've talked about it so far, as something you do in sentences, is insufficiently narrow. New media, social media, and digital composing challenge us to think of style as the *artful* and *rhetorical* combination of various modes like words, images, color, data, feeds, and video.

Style, in this atmosphere, is more about *design* than anything else: How your multimodal message appears to audiences and how you can manipulate its elements to influence attitudes. But design has always been with us. When you make decisions about how a standard essay appears on the page (font, spacing, margins, citation style, headings), you're making design decisions that enhance or detract from the reading experience. A savvy rhetor will understand how to use these principles effectively to create compelling messages that engage audiences on multiple levels of communication. (Find online the brilliant and Pulitzer Prize-winning *New York Times* story "Snow Fall" by John Branch to get a sense of this potential.)

Effective design engages four aspects of communication simultaneously: rhetorical principles, visual principles, modes, and design tools. Entire books are written about these subjects, so I'll leave it to you and your instructor to decide what's important here. I've listed some possible principles in these four domains in Table 1.

Last Thoughts on Style

In *The Sense of Style*, cognitive scientist Steven Pinker argues that style is important for three reasons: It helps us communicate clearly and efficiently, it "earns trust," and it "adds beauty to the world" (9). All three of these benefits are rhetorical benefits. If you can learn to write with style, you'll influence attitudes, and therefore judgments and behavior. Remember that the exercises I suggest in chapter ten have been *proven* to help writers improve their style. I commend them to you, especially when you've written a draft of something and you're wondering how to take it to the next level.

Table 1. Domains of Design

Rhetorical Principles	Visual Principles		Modes and Design Tools	
rhetorical situation	simplicity	contrast	text	font
audience	repetition	alignment	color	shapes
purpose	proximity	empty space	table	chart
argument	order	flow	graph	diagram
character	framing	texture	video	image
emotions	balance	scale	animation	program
genre	texture	hierarchy	background	template
story	layers	transparency	bullets	transitions
style	grid	pattern	line	word process
arrangement	motion	emphasis	cameras	editing
flow	sequence	surprise	social media	design software
implications (so what?)	unity	point	mobile tech	
			(etc., etc.)	

12

Works Cited

Cisneros, J. David. "Contaminated Communities." *Rhetoric and Public Affairs* 11.4 (2008): 569–602. Print.

Corbett, Edward P.J. and Robert J. Connors. *Style and Statement*. NY: Oxford UP, 1999. Print.

Fadiman, Anne. *The Spirit Catches You and You Fall Down*. NY: Farrar, Straus and Giroux, 1997. Print.

Fahnestock, Jeanne. *Rhetorical Style*. Oxford: Oxford UP, 2011. Print.

Geary, James. *I Is an Other*. NY: HarperCollins, 2011. Print.

Hacker, Diana and Nancy Sommers. *Rules for Writers*. 7th ed. Boston: Bedford/St. Martin's. 2012. Print.

Kress, Gunther and Theo van Leeuwen. *Reading Images: The Grammar of Visual Design*. 2nd ed. London: Routledge, 2007. Print.

Lakoff, George and Mark Johnson. *Metaphors We Live By*. Chicago: U of Chicago P, 1980. Print.

Lanham, Richard. *A Handlist of Rhetorical Terms*. 2nd ed. Berkeley: U of Cal P, 1991. Print.

— — —. *Revising Prose*. 5th ed. NY: Pearson, 2007. Print.

Lemann, Nicholas. "The Word Lab." *The New Yorker*. October 16 & 23 (2000): 100–112. Print.

Nunberg, Geoffrey. *Talking Right*. NY: Public Affairs, 2006. Print.

Pinker, Steven. *The Sense of Style*. NY: Viking, 2014. Print.

Ripley, Amanda. Excerpt from *The Smartest Kids in the World*. NPR Books. n.d. Web. 8 March 2015.

Roach, Mary. *Gulp*. NY: Norton, 2013. Print.

Schlosser, Eric. *Fast Food Nation*. NY: Perennial, 2002. Print.

Schulz, Kathryn. "Rapt." *The New Yorker*. 9 March 2015. 90–95. Print.

Taibbi, Matt. "The Great American Bubble Machine." *Rolling Stone.* 5 April 2010. Web. 25 March 2015.

Tufte, Virginia. *Artful Sentences: Syntax as Style.* Cheshire, CT: Graphics Press, 2006. Print.

Williams, Joseph M. and Gregory G. Colomb. *Style: Lessons in Clarity and Grace.* 10th ed. Boston: Longman, 2010. Print.

Wood, Graeme. "What ISIS Really Wants." *The Atlantic.* March 2015. Web. 7 March 2015.

13

ON USING RHETORIC FOR GOOD

So, we've come to the end of our journey into rhetorical theory and mindful writing. You've learned about GRAPE, mindful reading and writing process, and ACES. These strategies will help you write and act in the world with convincing power.

How are you going to use all that power? Have you thought about that?

All the rhetoric stuff we've talked about has an ancient Western pedigree. Philosophers and scholars have been debating and refining these principles for over 2500 years. At the same time, many of these scholars have been freaked out by the power of rhetoric. Some of them have seen the power of words as a bewitching force, like a spell an evil sorcerer might conjure. Similarly, others (Plato, for example) were concerned that rhetors would use the ACES principles without understanding fundamental moral issues like, How should a person live with other people in harmony? Still others thought about rhetoric as an amoral tool that can be used for good and bad, depending on the purpose of the rhetor.

Where do you stand?

The Roman rhetorician Quintilian (35–100 C.E.) believed that in the truest sense of rhetoric, wisdom and eloquence were inseparable. In other words, the true rhetor is a good person first and a good speaker second. Good speaking in fact *required* the speaker to know that goodness meant more than artful language; it meant artful language in the service of a moral good. What else could "good" possibly mean?

Maybe Quintilian is right; maybe not. Seems to me that rhetoric, like computer programming skills, can be used for both good and evil. Our ACES can be used for all kinds of mischief, as well as good. It's up to Team Rhetoric to learn how to write and speak not only powerfully but ethically. Ethics, by the way, is the study of moral behavior; *moral* refers to how as beings responsible for our own behavior we categorize certain behaviors as good or evil, right or wrong. If you don't like the good/ evil dichotomy, you can think of morality as our ability to overcome our own selfish interests and live in cooperative harmony with the people around us.

211

While I'm not an ethics professor, by any stretch, I want to end *Mindful Writing* with what I think is the ultimate act of mindful communication: thinking about how we might use rhetoric to become better people. I say "ultimate" because in my mind learning to be a better person through our writing is a greater good than learning how to influence the judgment of other people, even though that can be good, too.

Rhetorical influence can be *instrumental*, meaning that it focuses our attention too much on what works rather than what's right. Sometimes we might use rhetoric merely to get what we want, and who cares what it does to other people? Rhetorical strategies bestow power; power gets us what we want. No wonder the word "rhetoric" has a bad reputation.

However, since we cannot just cast aside our need to persuade, to influence attitudes and judgments, to get people's attention, to draw them to our side, to help them become sympathetic to our cause, even to get things we need from them (like scholarships, or a parking ticket waived, or a bill passed)—because we can't set all that aside, then maybe we can talk about how we can balance that instrumental need to convince others with our moral responsibility to do no harm.

I'm assuming, of course, that it *is* our responsibility to use rhetoric in a morally responsible way. I don't know what religious, spiritual, or moral beliefs you have, but I'm convinced that we do have moral rhetorical responsibilities that can be said to transcend our rhetorical situations. Doesn't that *feel* right? In spite of rampant disagreement on the whole right/wrong thing, there is a significant amount of agreement about moral principles across cultures. In what follows, I won't refer to any specific creed or moral philosopher's teachings. I'm just going to share a few thoughts from my own experience, thinking, observing, and studying about how we can use rhetoric ethically. I invite you to think them over to see if you agree.

Defense Against the Dark Arts

Call me Remus Lupin.

I bet you know who that is. He's one of several professors at Hogwarts who teach The Defence Against the Dark Arts to wizards like Harry Potter. There are many ways we can use rhetoric for dark purposes. Scholar Wayne Booth called the rhetorical dark arts "rhetrickery." Just as in Potterworld, it's important for you to understand rhetrickery not only so you can avoid using it but also so you can defend yourselves against it. Here are just a handful of the cheap tricks deployed by naughty rhetors in their writing and speaking.

Ad hominem. In Latin, ad hominem means "to the person." An ad hominem rhetorical strategy is an attack on the character of a person, even when their character is irrelevant to the issue at hand. Name-calling, labeling, bringing up irrelevant mistakes in a person's past, dismissing someone's words because of their race, age, gender, religion, sexual orientation, or nationality—these are all ad hominem attacks. When someone labels someone else an idiot, a racist, a sociopath, an elitist, or any other word freighted with negative moral connotations, you're in ad hominem territory. Ad hominem attackers can't seem to (or refuse to) engage with an adversary on the level of ideas; they have to go after them personally. Ad hominem attacks are so much easier than taking the time to listen to someone else's point of view to understand it. Calling someone reprehensible is easier than imagining (imagine!) that they are doing their best to operate within a system of values and moral principles, just like you.

Misrepresentation. We know that outright lying is bad, but there are more subtle ways to be naughty by misrepresenting the truth. When rhetors intentionally misquote a source or twist someone's words around to get an advantage or take a quote out of context by ignoring the rest of the text, they're practicing the Dark Arts. Sometimes we misrepresent the truth by overlooking or ignoring or smugly dismissing what has been said. Sometimes we misrepresent by inventing a fake opposition to the point we're trying to make, so we can look clever. That's called a "strawperson" argument. An example: If you're writing a paper on student health, and you write, without doing any research, "Some college administrators argue that student health is irrelevant to the purposes of the university. But I argue..."

We can also misrepresent an argument by using *false equivalence.* That's when we present two sides of an argument as equally legitimate, even though clearly one side has more evidence to support it. If 50,000 or more scientists believe that the earth is round but a few mavericks believe it's flat—and astonishingly, this is not a hypothetical scenario—and if in your writing you present both sides as equally legitimate, you're using false equivalence to misrepresent the state of the issue.

Common enemy, or us/them. Most of us are mixtures of good and bad. We can be jerks; and we can do good things. When dealing with other people, it's useful to keep in mind their fundamental fallibility, and ours. Sometimes when we pursue our separate interests in the public square, we form groups (like political parties) to push our agendas. That's natural and necessary; finding common cause in opposition to other perspectives can clarify the struggle. However, it is quite common now to reflexively label groups outside our own as enemies of our tribe. This attitude is captured well in an old Bedouin proverb: "I against my brothers. I and my brothers against my cousins. I and my brothers and my cousins against the world."

Common-enemy talk is an amplification meant to make *difference*—whether it be race, religion, nationality, political group, whatever—a crisis, a thing to be feared, a threat from a group to be vanquished. Us/them talk erases the common humanity that binds us together across tribes. By "tribes," I'm talking about our tendency, well-documented by cognitive moral philosophers, to prefer members of our own group—even if that group is as arbitrary as fans of a sports team—and harbor feelings of suspicion, even repulsion, for members of other groups. Us/them thinking can make us favor our chosen tribe over others with blind loyalty, even though other perspectives may help us grow in wisdom. By "blind" loyalty, I mean that common enemy thinking blinds us to the good in other groups and the weaknesses of our own.

Emotional reasoning. In Chapter 10 I argued that emotional appeals are necessary to influence the judgment of audiences. I still stand by that. I've noticed lately, though, that rhetors all too often use anger and outrage almost as an end in itself. Anger can be a good emotion: It can focus our minds on injustice and clarify our relationship to important cultural norms. There are things worth being angry about. But is *everything* worth being angry about? And is it possible that some rhetors are inciting us to anger without explaining why we should be angry or what good our anger will do us?

Psychologists label emotional reasoning a "cognitive distortion." We are led to believe that the way we feel reflects the way things are. If we feel jealous, that means that our significant other is cheating on us. If we feel anxious, then there must be danger. If we feel angry, then we're victims of injustice. Sometimes rhetors stir up emotions in audiences without providing evidence that those emotions are appropriate for the situation at hand. In that case, they're only interested in getting us to think with the way we feel, and they're up to Voldemort business. There is some evidence that emotionally-charged rhetoric can lodge in our long-term memory and color our understanding of a topic for years. Beware emotion for emotion's sake.

Trolling. I'm not talking about the cute dolls with the shock of pink hair. I'm talking about those rhetors who write inflammatory things on the Internet (or anywhere) for the sole purpose of stirring up controversy. Debate is real. Debate is useful. Disagreement can sharpen our judgments, make us wiser. But trolling is looking for a fight, not a discussion. It's amplification to the Nth degree, just to burn it all down. A troll wants to make people angry. A troll may not even believe what he/she is saying. Trolls live for provoking angry responses for the fun of it. Their words are intentionally intemperate and incendiary. Oddly, they *want* to be hated and condemned and rebuked and retweeted by their enemies. They are not interested in dialogue; they just want to poke the fire.

Threats. This strategy also has a Latin phrase: "argumentum ad baculum"—the appeal to the club. Do I need to explain this one? Here's an example: In 2013 Anita Sarkeesian, a video game scholar, posted a series of videos on YouTube describing how women in video games are represented as sexy and helpless, in desperate need of rescue. She then received a barrage of messages threatening to assault and kill her. She even had to cancel a trip to a university because someone threatened to shoot up the school if she came. Another kind of threat is *doxxing*, which is the public posting of someone's address or phone number as a way to scare that person and invite others to menace them. Please, folks, can we decide, right here and forever, to go *nowhere near* using rhetoric to threaten?

Core Principles of Rhetorical Goodness

I conclude this chapter with a few core principles that I believe reflect an ethical stance to writing and speaking with others. I know there may be exceptions to all these rules (moral reasoning can be the trickiest kind of reasoning), but I contend that they're great rules of thumb for most rhetorical exchanges. Find ways to practice these principles, or look for others who do.

Use rhetorical strategies you'd want others to use with you. My kids are fond of saying the words "always" and "never," as in, "Dad, you never let me play Nintendo after dinner!" Never? Really? So I tell them: "Always and never are rarely true, kids. Try to use words to accurately reflect the way things are." And then days later, I say to one of them: "You always overreact when Charlotte takes your stuff!" And they say, "Always? Really??" And then I realize I'm being a hypocrite. A good rule of thumb here is to try to use rhetorical strategies in the way you'd want others to use them when you are the audience. Think about the kind of argument, or ethos, or emotional appeal that you'd want someone to express when trying to convince you. Imagine as you write that your words are being written by a political adversary who is writing to *you*, trying to change *your* judgment with those strategies. I think this principle is the fullest manifestation of the idea of goodwill I mentioned in the chapter on character. If someone were speaking to us, wouldn't we want to be respected? Listened to? Understood? Spoken to civilly, without malice, even in a disagreement?

Listen. Seek first to understand before you try to be understood. Recently I read Ta-Nehisi Coates' powerful book *Between the World and Me*. It is a masterwork of poetic anger. Coates, an African American, writes to his teenage son about what it means to be a black male in a country with deep historical racism. Early in my reading, even though I was enjoying the book, I felt this urge to push back, to take up my pen and write my counterarguments in the margins. For once, though, I suppressed that feeling and I just let myself *listen* to Coates' argument.

To be frank, it was a relief. I realized that as a reader I didn't always have to stand in judgment of what I read, devising, almost on impulse, how I'd situate myself in relation to someone else's point of view. Maybe my first, and sometimes only, job is to listen and make sure I understand what someone else is saying. I don't even have to "listen" by taking apart the argument's claims, reasons, and assumptions. I can restate what I hear—which is a great method to use when we're engaged in cross-cultural rhetoric—as carefully as I can, being as true as I can to the text, or beyond that, as true to the *person-rhetor* before me in the text. Listening requires patience; we listen not to respond, not to find our own rhetorical jumping-off point, but to understand—period. Listening validates the experience and rhetorical efforts of others. When we listen to others respectfully, they are more likely to listen to us.

One useful listening activity is to *summarize* or *restate* what you hear from other rhetors (like sources you're consulting for a research paper). It is also a useful, and humane, exercise to listen by trying to understand more fully the value system in which our adversary is operating. This kind of listening is an example of what I'd call moral curiosity. When we find opinions different from our own, instead of saying "Woah, they are dead wrong!"—granted, feeling that way is so *tasty* sometimes—we can say, "I wonder what value system he/she is operating under. What does he/she assume about the world? What are the assumptions, understandings, experience, goals? I'll need to listen more carefully." Moral curiosity can help diffuse tense situations. Still, it's hard to suppress that impulse to judge.

Be clear. We talked about clarity in the style chapters. When it comes to engaging with others, writing with clarity is an ethical decision. For one, you're making it easier for the reader to read you and enjoy what you have to say. For another, you are not hiding bad ideas behind fancy-pants jargony words. Clear words and phrases invite the reader to draw close to your message; jargon, obscurity, confusion, and clumsiness tend to alienate audiences.

Be humble. You ain't special. And neither am I. We're just mixed up folks trying to get the story straight. So why do we flex our rhetorical powers in other people's faces? I don't know about you, but sometimes I speak more assertively than I have a right to. Once I wrote an opinion editorial about a local school issue, and I wrote it with an embarrassing amount of ego. I knew I was right and that my adversaries were wrong. When I saw my intemperate words on the published page, I felt like a real horse's rear end. Yes, in many cases we have to assert when we write. We have to argue. However, we can adopt a humble ethos that will be both persuasive and ethical—especially if we think of ethical behavior as the struggle to overcome our own selfishness in order to live harmoniously with others. In academic writing, it is good practice to *hedge*. That means that when we write without the benefit of certainty, which is almost always the case, we use words that suggest we are making a modest, almost cautious proposal and that we might be wrong: *seems, tends to, looks as if, suggests, might be, possible that, often, sometimes, usually.* You acknowledge when you do not know all the facts. When you debate in writing with others, you make sure you are debating *their ideas* and not themselves, and that you do so with respect and humility.

You give credit to others for their contributions. You ensure that the words and ideas of others are attributed to them, not you.

Find common ground. Abortion is one of those issues that drive people to rhetorical warfare. The stakes are high. Intelligent, well-intended people disagree on the laws. Things get intense out there. I once heard of two women in a community in Missouri who found themselves on opposing sides of the issue. In the midst of their war of words, one of them invited the other to get coffee and talk over their differences (imagine!). One believed that life began at conception and that abortion was murder. The other believed that a woman's body was her own and that abortion promoted gender equality. They weren't going to budge on those two stances. To their amazement, they discovered they could agree on one thing: We should reduce the frequency of unwanted pregnancies. To find common ground, we begin by imagining what our audience, especially audiences with which we might disagree, would find acceptable. What values do we have in common? And on the other hand, when we are reading or listening to others, how can we prepare ourselves to (imagine!) agree with their perspective, to accept their assumptions, if we can? Why not make our minds available for change?

It seems to me that our tribalism makes it difficult, if not impossible, for us to accept the valid arguments of our adversaries. How embarrassing, we think, if we agree with our enemies! Yet there is power in being willing to be persuaded by arguments we haven't considered. It can be equally powerful if we fashion our arguments on common ground so that those who disagree with us will at least see the merits of our position and take a step towards us, as we step towards them.

Commit yourself to the truth. Okay, the word "truth" can be complicated. How do we find information we can trust, perspectives that represent, as closely as possible, the way things are? There are so many competing interests trying to make over the world. Still, truth is a necessary concept. And, seriously, it's not *too* complicated. Truth is the term we use to describe statements that genuinely reflect the way things are, the facts, the little thing we call reality as we know it. We engage in rigorous exploration of the world around us to find out what it is and how it works. We confirm with each other, using all kinds of investigative tactics from science to journalism to experience, that the way we observe the world is the same as the way others observe it. Facts have rhetorical power.

We live at a time when politicians talk about "alternative facts" and "multiple truths." Maybe we can't know, for absolutely positively certain, that this or that is the case, but we can do our best to find out what is *most likely true* based on our collective experience, observations, investigations, and tests. I'm less concerned about whether we can be absolutely positively sure about reality than I am about the unfortunate trend of denying even the possibility of truth.

Some rhetors make arguments without caring one bit about whether what they're saying reflects the facts as we know them. Others deliberately leave out inconvenient facts that would otherwise weaken their positions. Sometimes our moral outrage keeps us from looking into an issue carefully enough to come to a wise judgment about them. Recently there was a viral video of a cultural standoff between two groups at the Lincoln Memorial in Washington, D.C. (For my interests, the details are unimportant.) As the short video made the rounds, people took to social media to cast judgments on the people in the video. However, within 48 hours, more video emerged complicating those first impressions; even famous media rhetors had to do a little back-pedaling from their original uninformed stance in light of new data. Though our efforts will be imperfect, we must commit ourselves to understanding the truth, insofar as we can know it. We must be patient, and keep searching. We should be willing to acknowledge truth where we find it, even if that truth comes from sources we disagree with.

Back to the abortion issue for a moment. One time I had a student named James who wanted to write a research paper on abortion. Of course I didn't want him to. He'd already made up his mind that it was horrible and that women who had abortions were worse off for it. He pleaded with me to let him write about it. I finally relented but told him he had to do two things, or I wouldn't let him do it: (1) ask a question he genuinely didn't know the answer to, and (2) take his argument wherever the scientific evidence led him. He agreed and got to work. His question was, How does abortion influence the mental health of the woman? What he discovered surprised him. While he still opposed abortion, he had to concede, after committing to the truth, that there was compelling research showing little evidence that women who terminated pregnancies suffered significant emotional trauma. His honest exploration improved his critical thinking and, I'd like to imagine, his moral reasoning on a topic he felt strongly about.

We so often suffer from confirmation bias or myside bias. That's when we search only for the evidence that supports the judgment we've already come to, and ignore the rest. Our preexisting beliefs blind us to any evidence that might help us understand the issue better. I hope we can spend our lifetimes pursuing the truth and making little adjustments to our judgments as a result of our curiosity.

Seek justice. This one is perhaps more controversial than the others, but I can't help mentioning it. We live in a world in which power is unevenly distributed—rhetorical power, for example. There are many powerful people with wealth and influence; there are so many, many more with little. We can use our language to explore these power relationships and seek a more balanced world. We can study rhetorical situations to find out how genres create power dynamics that privilege some people and not others. We can see how some rhetors have access to rhetorical resources—education, publishing venues, media audiences—and some don't. We can listen to alternative voices that provide new perspectives. We can lend our voices to moral struggles about which we feel passionately.

Recently while teaching a first-year writing course I invited the students to write about a topic related to college student health. They came up with some fascinating projects on mental health, diet, exercise, sleep, electronic use, debt, and other topics. One writer, however, decided to write about how deaf students were often underserved because professors like me don't know how to better accommodate their abilities. It was a remarkable project, and it taught me how I could more effectively teach diverse students who experience the world a little differently than other students. The student writer saw a power imbalance and sought, through research and rhetoric, to respond to it.

***

Well, my friends, we're done. That's it. No more. I hope each of you has good experiences writing and speaking. I hope each new rhetorical situation will expand your abilities to use language not only to influence judgments but also to improve the way we all live together.

INDEX